Alison Jacobs

KETO SLOW COOKER COOKBOOK:

500 easy and delicious ketogenic recipes for your slow cooker.
Enjoy your healthy low-carb meals without stress.

TABLE OF CONTENTS

INTRODUCTION 10

CHAPTER 1: KETO DIET & SLOW COOKER BASICS 12

CHAPTER 2: KETOGENIC DIET TIPS & TRICKS 16

CHAPTER 3: SLOW COOKER TIPS & TRICKS.......... 20

CHAPTER 4: BREAKFAST...................... 22

CHERRY TOMATOES THYME ASPARAGUS FRITTFMOATA.22

HEALTHY LOW CARB WALNUT ZUCCHINI BREAD 23

SAVORY CREAMY BREAKFAST CASSEROLE.................23

LOW-CARB HASH BROWN BREAKFAST CASSEROLE 24

ONION BROCCOLI CREAM CHEESE QUICHE.................24

DELICIOUS THYME SAUSAGE SQUASH.......................25

MEXICAN STYLE BREAKFAST CASSEROLE 26

ALMOND LEMON BLUEBERRY MUFFINS.....................26

HEALTHY VEGGIE OMELET 27

ARUGULA CHEESE HERB FRITTATA.......................27

YUMMY CAULIFLOWER CRUST BREAKFAST PIZZA.........28

PARMESAN ZUCCHINI PAPRIKA & RICOTTA FRITTATA 28

SCRAMBLED EGGS WITH SMOKED SALMON 29

GARLIC-PARMESAN ASPARAGUS CROCK POT.............30

PERSIAN OMELET CROCK POT.......................30

BROCCOLI AND CHEESE STUFFED SQUASH 31

GARLIC BUTTER KETO SPINACH 32

KETO CROCK POT TASTY ONIONS 32

CROCK POT BENEDICT CASSEROLE 32

CRUSTLESS CROCK POT SPINACH QUICHE 33

BROCCOLI GRATIN WITH PARMESAN AND SWISS CHEESE 34

CROCK POT CREAM CHEESE FRENCH TOAST 35

KETO CROCK POT TURKEY STUFFED PEPPERS.................35

CROCK POT KETO ENGLISH MUFFIN 36

CAULIFLOWER CASSEROLE WITH TOMATO AND GOAT CHEESE 36

GREEK EGGS BREAKFAST CASSEROLE.......................37

CROCK POT TURKISH BREAKFAST EGGS 38

CHEESY GARLIC BRUSSELS SPROUTS.......................38

BLUEBERRY PANCAKE.......................39

SAUSAGE AND PEPPERS 40

BREAKFAST SAUSAGE CASSEROLE 40

STUFFED BREAKFAST PEPPERS 41

CHEESE AND SAUSAGE BREAKFAST.......................42

MUSHROOMS, CAULIFLOWER, AND ZUCCHINI TOAST....42

PESTO SCRAMBLED EGGS...........................43

KALE AND CHEESE OMELET 44

EGG CASSEROLE WITH ITALIAN CHEESES, SUN-DRIED TOMATOES, AND HERBS 44

KALE, MUSHROOMS, AND CARAMELIZED ONIONS.......45

EGG AND CHEESE CASSEROLE WITH CHAYOTE SQUASH ..45

SAUSAGE AND KALE STRATA.......................46

EGG CAKE RECIPE WITH PEPPERS, KALE, AND CHEDDAR 46

FETA CHEESE AND KALE BREAKFAST CASSEROLE 47

CAULIFLOWER AND HAM CASSEROLE 47

SAUSAGE-STUFFED EGGPLANTS 48

ZUCCHINI SAUSAGE BREAKFAST "BAKE" 48

CHEDDAR JALAPENO BREAKFAST SAUSAGES 49

CHOCOLATE PEANUT BUTTER BREAKFAST BARS 49

CHAPTER 5: VEGAN & VEGETARIAN 50

HOMEMADE VEGETABLE STOCK 50

CREAM OF ZUCCHINI SOUP 50

TOMATO SOUP 51

VEGETABLE KORMA 51

ZOODLES WITH CAULIFLOWER-TOMATO SAUCE 52

SPAGHETTI SQUASH CARBONARA 52

SUMMERY BELL PEPPER + EGGPLANT SALAD 53

STUFFED EGGPLANT.......................53

BACON CHEDDAR BROCCOLI SALAD 54

CRACKED-OUT KETO SLAW 55

ZUCCHINI PASTA 55

TWICE BAKED SPAGHETTI SQUASH 55

MUSHROOM RISOTTO.......................56

VEGAN BIBIMBAP.......................56

AVOCADO PESTO KELP NOODLES 57

VEGAN CREAM OF MUSHROOM SOUP 57

CREAMY CURRY SAUCE NOODLE BOWL.................58

SPINACH ARTICHOKE CASSEROLE.......................58

ASPARAGUS WITH LEMON.......................59

VEGGIE-NOODLE SOUP 60

ZUCCHINI AND YELLOW SQUASH 60

GLUTEN-FREE ZUCCHINI BREAD 60

EGGPLANT PARMESAN 61

ZUCCHINI LASAGNA 61

CAULIFLOWER BOLOGNESE ON ZUCCHINI NOODLES 62

GARLIC RANCH MUSHROOMS 62

EASY CREAMED SPINACH 62

GARLIC TOMATO, ZUCCHINI, AND YELLOW SQUASH......63

PARMESAN ZUCCHINI AND TOMATO GRATIN.............. 63
SLOW-COOKED SUMMER VEGETABLES..................... 64
CHEESY CAULIFLOWER GARLIC BREAD...................... 64
CHEESY CAULIFLOWER GRATIN 65
CREAMY RICOTTA SPAGHETTI SQUASH 65
CREAMY KETO MASH 66
KETO ZUPA TOSCANA SOUP 66
KETO SPINACH-FETA QUICHE 67
CHEESY ZUCCHINI-ASPARAGUS FRITTATA 68
SLOW-COOKED YELLOW SQUASH ZUCCHINI 68
CABBAGE, KIELBASA, AND ONION SOUP 69
PARMESAN MUSHROOMS 69
MASHED GARLIC CAULIFLOWER.............................. 70
BROCCOLI CHEDDAR SOUP 70
ELBOWS CASSEROLE 71
CHEESY BEER DIP SALSA...................................... 71
BRUSSELS SPROUT DIP 72
BRAISED CABBAGE 72

CHAPTER 6: APPETIZERS & SNACKS..................... 74

ASPARAGUS BACON BOUQUET 74
CREAMY ASIAGO SPINACH DIP 74
MADRAS CURRY CHICKEN BITES 75
SPICED JICAMA WEDGES WITH CILANTRO CHUTNEY 76
TERIYAKI CHICKEN WINGS 76
PORTABELLA PIZZA BITES...................................... 77
CANDIED WALNUTS 77
FLAVORFUL PECANS 78
HERB FLAVORED ALMONDS 79
ULTRA-SPICY ALMONDS.. 79
TASTIER NUTS COMBO.. 80
ZESTY CHICKEN WINGS 80
BUFFALO CHICKEN MEATBALLS............................... 81
FOOLPROOF BEEF MEATBALLS................................ 81
SUPER-TASTY PORK MEATBALLS.............................. 82
INSPIRING SAUSAGE SLIDERS 83
POTLUCK PARTY PEPPERS 83
PERFECT EGGPLANT TAPENADE 84
SWISS STYLE CHEESE FONDUE 84
TEX-MEX CHEESE DIP... 85
2-INGREDIENT CHEESE DIP 85
GARLIC PARMESAN CHICKEN WINGS 86
CANDIED PECANS.. 86
COCOA NUTS 87
THAI CURRY NUTS 87
PUMPKIN SPICED NUTS 88
TURKEY MEATBALLS 88

BOK CHOY BROWNIES 89
LEMON CUSTARD.. 90
BUFFALO CHICKEN DIP... 90

CHAPTER 7: LUNCH 92

AMAZING SOUR CREAM CHICKEN 92
MOUTH-WATERING MINCED PORK ZUCCHINI LASAGNA 92
FANTASTIC LEMON THYME CHICKEN 93
BEAUTIFUL BBQ RIBS 93
DELIGHTFUL BALSAMIC OREGANO CHICKEN 94
SCRUMPTIOUS BAY LEAF PORK ROAST SHOULDER........ 94
TANTALIZING CHICKEN BREAST WITH ARTICHOKE
STUFFING 95
GORGEOUS COCONUT TURMERIC PORK CURRY 95
TANTALIZING PORK CHOPS WITH CUMIN BUTTER AND
GARLIC 96
CROCKPOT BEEF ROAST 97
CHIPOTLE BARBECUE CHICKEN............................... 97
SPICY SHREDDED CHICKEN LETTUCE WRAPS............... 98
BACON CHEESEBURGER CASSEROLE.......................... 98
CROCKPOT RANCH CHICKEN.................................. 99
COCONUT CILANTRO SHRIMP CURRY 99
CROCKPOT BUTTER MASALA CHICKEN 100
KASHMIRI LAMB CURRY 100
CHICKEN WITH BACON GRAVY.............................. 101
GARLIC BUTTER CHICKEN WITH CREAM CHEESE 102
CHEESY ADOBO CHICKEN 102
KETOGENIC CHICKEN TIKKA MASALA 102
BALSAMIC CHICKEN THIGHS 103
CHICKEN LO MEIN 104
ETHIOPIAN DORO WATT CHICKEN.......................... 104
MEXICAN CHICKEN SOUP 105
APRICOT PULLED PORK 106
CHICKEN KALE SOUP 106
CREAMY ITALIAN CHICKEN 106
MISSISSIPPI ROAST... 107
TACO SOUP 107
CHICKEN AND VEGETABLES 108
CHICKEN GYROS 108
CHILI COLORADO 109
BEEF CHIMICHANGAS 109
PIZZA CASSEROLE.. 110
CHEESY CAULIFLOWER BREAD 110

CHAPTER 8: DINNER 112

MOIST AND SPICY PULLED CHICKEN BREAST............. 112
WHOLE ROASTED CHICKEN................................... 112

POT ROAST BEEF BRISKET 113
SERIOUSLY DELICIOUS LAMB ROAST 113
LAMB PROVENÇAL 114
GREEK STYLE LAMB SHANKS 114
HOMEMADE MEATBALLS AND SPAGHETTI SQUASH 115
BEEF AND CABBAGE ROAST 116
SIMPLE CHICKEN CHILI 116
BEEF SHOULDER IN BBQ SAUCE 117
DRESSED PORK LEG ROAST 117
RABBIT & MUSHROOM STEW 118
ITALIAN SPICY SAUSAGE & BELL PEPPERS 119
CHICKEN IN SALSA VERDE 119
SALMON POACHED IN WHITE WINE AND LEMON 120
EASY MEATBALL CROCK POT 120
BEEF & BROCCOLI 121
NEW MEXICO CARNE ADOVADA 121
BEEF CHUCK POT ROAST 122
CROCKPOT TURKEY BREAST 122
COFFEE- BRAISED BRISKET 123
CROCKPOT CREAMY SALSA CHICKEN 124
SLOW COOKER PORK LOIN 124
FLEMISH BEEF STEW 125
AMAZING SPICED BEEF EYE CROCKPOT 125
GARLIC LEMON SAUCE-LESS RIBS 126
GARLIC DILL CHICKEN THIGHS 127
OREGANO ITALIAN SAUSAGE MEATBALLS 127
TOMATOES MEXICAN CHICKEN 128
SLOW COOKER SHREDDED PORK 128
CHILI GROUND BEEF WITH PUMPKIN 128
BEST SLOW COOKER PIZZA 129
CUMIN CHILI STEAK 130
SPICY TURKEY STEW 130
SPICY BACON, SAUSAGES & RED CABBAGE 131
CUMIN THYME PORK SLOW COOKING 131
TURMERIC CHILI BEEF CURRY 132

CHAPTER 9: DESSERTS 134

TASTY APPLE AND CRANBERRY DESSERT 134
CARAMEL PECAN PUDDING 134
MOUTH-WATERING CHOCOLATE CAKE 135
FABULOUS PEANUT VANILLA CHOCOLATE BUTTER CAKE
.... 135
POPPY SEED BUTTER CAKE 136
WONDERFUL RASPBERRY ALMOND CAKE 137
SCRUMPTIOUS CHOCOLATE COCOA CAKE 137
LEMON CAKE 138
RASPBERRY & COCONUT CAKE 139

CHOCOLATE CHEESECAKE 139
CRÈME BRULE 140
PEANUT BUTTER & CHOCOLATE CAKE 140
BERRY & COCONUT CAKE 141
COCOA PUDDING CAKE 142
KETO COCONUT HOT CHOCOLATE 142
AMBROSIA 143
DARK CHOCOLATE AND PEPPERMINT POTS 143
CREAMY VANILLA CUSTARD 144
COCONUT, CHOCOLATE, AND ALMOND TRUFFLE BAKE 144
PEANUT BUTTER, CHOCOLATE, AND PECAN CUPCAKES 145
VANILLA AND STRAWBERRY CHEESECAKE 146
COFFEE CREAMS WITH TOASTED SEED CRUMBLE TOPPING
.... 146
LEMON CHEESECAKE 147
MACADAMIA FUDGE TRUFFLES 148
CHOCOLATE COVERED BACON CUPCAKES 148
CHOCOLATE, BERRY, AND MACADAMIA LAYERED JARS 149
SALTY-SWEET ALMOND BUTTER AND CHOCOLATE SAUCE
.... 149
COCONUT SQUARES WITH BLUEBERRY GLAZE 150
CHOCOLATE AND BLACKBERRY CHEESECAKE SAUCE 150
HOT FUDGE CAKE 151
FUDGY SECRET BROWNIES 152
BLACK AND BLUE COBBLER 152
BAKED CUSTARD 153
MAPLE POT DE CRÈME 153
SLOW-COOKER PUMPKIN PIE PUDDING 154
CHOCO-PEANUT CAKE 155
CROCKPOT APPLE PUDDING CAKE 155
CROCKPOT BROWNIE COOKIES 156
CROCKPOT CHOCOLATE CARAMEL MONKEY BREAD 157
SLOW COOKER COFFEE CAKE 157
SLOW COOKER APPLE PEAR CRISP 158
KEY LIME DUMP CAKE RECIPE 159
CROCKPOT CHERRY DUMP CAKE RECIPE 159
CROCKPOT PUMPKIN SPICE CAKE RECIPE 160
CROCKPOT BLUEBERRY DUMP CAKE RECIPE 160
CROCKPOT STRAWBERRY DUMP CAKE RECIPE 161
CROCKPOT BAKED APPLES RECIPE 161
SUGAR-FREE CHOCOLATE MOLTEN LAVA CAKE 162
BLUEBERRY LEMON CUSTARD CAKE 162
SLOW-COOKED PUMPKIN CUSTARD 163
ALMOND FLOUR MOCHA FUDGE CAKE 164
SLOW COOKER BREAD PUDDING 164
TIRAMISU BREAD PUDDING 165
CROCK POT SUGAR-FREE DAIRY-FREE FUDGE 165

Poppy Seed-Lemon Bread 166
Nutmeg-Infused Pumpkin Bread 166

CHAPTER 10: SOUPS & STEWS 168

Creamy Harvest Pumpkin Bisque 168
Zesty White Chicken Chili 168
Tuscan Zucchini Stew 169
Melt-In-Your-Mouth Beef Stew 170
Mexican Chorizo Enchilada Soup 171
Hearty Chicken Soup with Veggie Noodles 171
Superb Chicken, Bacon, Garlic Thyme Soup 172
Delightful Chicken-Chorizo Spicy Soup 173
Delectable Spearmint Liver and Lamb Heart Soup
.... 173
Lovely Lentil Sausage Soup 174
Tasty Corned Beef and Heavy Cream Soup 175
Delicious Beef Meatball and Sour Cream Soup . 175
Veggie Soup with Minty Balls 176
Chicken Cordon Bleu Soup 177
Ginger Pumpkin Soup 177
Toscana Soup 178
Rabbit Stew 178
Beef Stew 179
Chicken & Kale Soup 180
Chicken Chili Soup 180
Creamy Smoked Salmon Soup 181
Lamb and Rosemary Stew 181
Lamb and Eggplant Stew 181
Bacon and Cauliflower Soup 182
Vegetable Stew 182
Pot Roast Soup 183
Chicken with Kale Leaves Soup 184
Southern Paleo Crock Pot Chili...................... 184
Dairy-Free Chili Chicken Soup 185
Low Carbohydrate Crock Pot Soup.................. 186
Slow Cooker Cheeseburger Soup 186
Chicken Thigh & Breast Low Carb Soup 187
Beef & Pumpkin Stew................................... 188
Pepper Jalapeno Low Carb Soup 188
Lean Beef & Mixed Veggies Soup................... 189
Chicken & Tortilla Soup 189
Chicken Chile Verde 190
Cauliflower & Ham Potato Stew...................... 191
Minestrone Ground Beef Soup 191
Scrumptious Crab Meat Douse 192
Crock Pot Bay Carrot Garlic Beef Sauce.......... 192
Delicious Kernel Corn Taco Soup.................... 193

Sumptuous Ham and Lentil Consommé 193
Beef Barley Vegetable Soup 194
Delicious Chicken Soup with Lemongrass 195
Crock Pot Pork Stew with Tapioca 195
Delicious Bacon Cheese Potato Soup 196
Tasty Tomato Soup with Parmesan and Basil.... 196
Luscious Carrot Beef Stew with Potatoes 197
Delicious Lasagna Consommé 198
Sumptuous Cheese Broccoli Potato Bouillabaisse
.... 198

CHAPTER 11: MEATS 200

Balsamic Beef Pot Roast................................200
Beef Bourguignon with Carrot Noodles 201
Beef Brisket... 201
Beef Curry... 202
Beef Dijon... 203
Beef Ribs.. 203
Beef Stroganoff.. 204
Cabbage & Corned Beef 205
Chipotle Barbacoa – Mexican Barbecue 205
Corned Beef Cabbage Rolls........................... 206
Cube Steak.. 207
Eggplant & Ground Beef Casserole 207
Italian Meatballs & Zoodles 208
London Broil 209
Machaca - Mexican Pot Roast 209
Parmesan Garlic Nut Chicken Wings 210
Tikka Masala Chicken 211
Hot Spicy Chicken..212
Savory Duck Breast 212
Lemon Scented Chicken.................................213
Autumn Sweet Chicken 213
Coconut & Basil Chicken 214
BBQ Dip Hot Chicken Wings...........................215
Cheesy Chicken Pot 215
Beijing Chicken Soup 216
Lamb Curry 216
Lamb and Green Beans...................................217
Lamb Shoulder 218
Cinnamon Lamb 218
Lamb Stew 219
Lamb with Onions and Thyme..........................219
Lamb with Edamame Beans and Tomatoes.........220
Mustard Lamb...220
Sweet and Spicy Lamb 220
Chinese Style Lamb Shoulder 221

ORIENTAL BRAISED PORK.....................................221
PORK ADOBO 222
COUNTRY-STYLE PORK RIBS 222
ITALIAN MEATLOAF 223
SHREDDED TACO PORK......................................224
CROCK POT FAJITAS 224
SAUSAGE-STUFFED PEPPERS...............................225
PAPRIKA PORK TENDERLOIN 225
PORK CARNITAS 226
LEMONGRASS COCONUT PULLED PORK 226
PORK LOIN ROAST WITH ONION GRAVY 227
LIME PORK CHOPS..227
CARNE ASADA 228
LEMONGRASS AND COCONUT CHICKEN DRUMSTICKS . 228
BEST JERK CHICKEN 229
MEXICAN CROCK POT FAJITA CHICKEN 230
SLOW-COOKER ROASTED CHICKEN WITH LEMON PARSLEY BUTTER 230
GREEK CHICKEN 231
SESAME- ORANGE CHICKEN 231
CHINESE 5-SPICE PORK RIBS 232
PORK STEW WITH OYSTER MUSHROOMS.................232
CHILI PULLED PORK 233
PORK CHILI VERDE..234
BEEF, BACON & CABBAGE STEW 234
SWEET PEPPER BEEF TONGUE.............................235
EASY SLOW COOKER BEEF CHILI..........................236
COCONUT & BROCCOLI CHICKEN CURRY.................236
SPICED OXTAIL STEW 237
KALUA PORK 238
TASTY CUBAN MOJO PORK 238
GREEN CHILI PORK 239
THAI CURRIED PORK 239
RANCH PORK CHOPS...240
DELICIOUS COCONUT PORK.................................240
SPICY ADOBO PULLED PORK 241
TASTY LAMB SHOULDERS 241
THYME LAMB CHOPS 242
GARLIC HERBED LAMB CHOPS 242
TASTY PORK TACOS 243
ONION PORK CHOPS...243
CREAMY PORK CHOPS.......................................244
DELICIOUS BALSAMIC LAMB CHOPS 244
BARBACOA LAMB...246
LAMB WITH MINT & GREEN BEANS.......................246
SUCCULENT LAMB..247
TARRAGON LAMB & BEANS 248

BBQ BEEF BURRITOS 248
CHEESEBURGER & BACON PIE 249
ITALIAN MEATLOAF 250
BEEF BOURGUIGNON WITH CARROT NOODLES..........250
BEEF RIBS 251
BRAISED OXTAILS 252
BRISKET & ONIONS 252
ITALIAN RAGU 253

CHAPTER 12: FISH & SEAFOOD 254
BUTTERFLY TILAPIA...254
TUNA AND OLIVE-ORANGE TAPENADE 254
HEART AND TUNA STUFFED MUSHROOM 255
ETOUFFEE 256
POACHED SALMON 257
TUSCAN FISH SOUP 257
CHILI SHRIMPS..258
FENNEL SCENTED FISH STEW 258
CHINESE OYSTER SOUP 259
HEARTY WHITE FISH STEW 259
CATFISH CREOLE 260
MEXICAN CORN AND SHRIMP SOUP.......................260
COD WITH FENNEL AND TOMATOES.......................261
MAHI-MAHI TACO WRAPS 262
SHRIMP SCAMPI...263
SHRIMP TACOS 263
FISH CURRY..264
SALMON WITH CREAMY LEMON SAUCE 264
SALMON WITH LEMON-CAPER SAUCE 265
SPICY BARBECUE SHRIMP..................................266
LEMON DILL HALIBUT 267
COCONUT CILANTRO CURRY SHRIMP 267
SHRIMP IN MARINARA SAUCE..............................268
GARLIC SHRIMP 268
LEMON PEPPER TILAPIA.....................................269
CLAM CHOWDER..269
SOY-GINGER STEAMED POMPANO 270
VIETNAMESE BRAISED CATFISH 270
POACHED SALMON IN COURT-BOUILLON RECIPE........271
BRAISED SQUID WITH TOMATOES AND FENNEL 271
SEAFOOD STIR-FRY SOUP 272
SHRIMP FAJITA SOUP..272
FISH AND TOMATOES 273
HOT CRAB DIP 273
COD AND ZOODLES STEW 274
SLOW-COOKED TILAPIA......................................274
SALMON LEMON AND DILL...................................274

CREAMY CRAB ZUCCHINI CASSEROLE 275
LOBSTER BISQUE 275
SPICY SHRIMP FRA DIAVOLO 275
SHRIMP SCAMPI WITH SPAGHETTI SQUASH 276
TUNA AND WHITE BEANS 277
CROCKPOT SWORDFISH STEAKS 277
SWEET AND SOUR SHRIMP 278
LAZY MAN'S SEAFOOD STEW 278
HALIBUT VINAIGRETTE 279
CROCKPOT CRAB LEGS 279
ASIAN-INSPIRED GINGER TUNA STEAKS 279
RUSTIC BUTTERED MUSSELS 280
BOILED LOBSTER TAILS 280
CREAMY SHRIMP CHOWDER 281

CHAPTER 13: SIDE DISHES 282

CHINESE BROCCOLI 282
SLOW COOKER SPAGHETTI SQUASH 283
MUSHROOM STEW 283
CABBAGE STEAKS 284
MASHED CAULIFLOWER 284
BACON-WRAPPED CAULIFLOWER 285
CAULIFLOWER CASSEROLE 285
CAULIFLOWER RICE 286
CURRY CAULIFLOWER 286
GARLIC CAULIFLOWER STEAKS 287
ZUCCHINI GRATIN 287
EGGPLANT GRATIN 288
MOROCCAN EGGPLANT MASH 288
SAUTÉED BELL PEPPERS 289
FRESH GREEN BEANS 289
CROCKPOT CAULIFLOWER SIDE DISH 290
SLOW COOK CROCK POT ZUCCHINI TOMATO CASSEROLE 290
CHICKEN CAULIFLOWER – SIDE DISH 291
SLOW COOK CROCKPOT BROCCOLI 292
BALSAMIC-GLAZED BRUSSELS SPROUTS 292
ITALIAN MUSHROOMS – CROCKPOT SIDE DISH 293
KETO SLOW COOKER PEPPER JACK CAULIFLOWER SIDE DISH 293
GREENS MIX 294

MAYO SALAD 294
SEASONED CARROTS 295
QUINOA BRUSSELS SPROUT SALAD 295
SAUCY BEANS 296
CUCUMBER QUINOA SALAD 297
ZUCCHINI SPAGHETTI 297
BBQ SMOKIES 298
MARINATED MUSHROOMS 298
COWBOY MEXICAN DIP 298
GLAZED SPICED CARROTS 299
GARLIC GREEN BEANS WITH GORGONZOLA 299
PARTY SAUSAGES 300
COLLARD GREENS 300
GARLIC CHILI SPROUTS 301
CRISPY SWEET AND SOUR BRUSSELS SPROUTS 301
BAKED VEGETABLES IN THE CROCK-POT 302
CRISPY VEGGIES 302
OVEN ROASTED BRUSSELS SPROUTS IN THE CROCK-POT 303
CHILI LIME ACORN SQUASH 303

CHAPTER 14: BROTH, STOCK & SAUCES 304

BACON JAM 304
ROASTED GARLIC 305
GOLDEN CARAMELIZED ONIONS 305
GHEE 305
SPINACH-CHEESE SPREAD 306
HOT CRAB SAUCE 306
ENCHILADA SAUCE 307
CREAMY ALFREDO SAUCE 307
QUESO SAUCE 308
CLASSIC BOLOGNESE SAUCE 308
SIMPLE MARINARA SAUCE 309
CHICKEN BONE BROTH 309
HERBED VEGETABLE BROTH 310
BEEF BONE BROTH 310
CAROLINA BARBECUE SAUCE 311

CONCLUSION 312

Introduction

When it comes to dieting, some cooking methods are more suitable than others, e.g., grilling against frying. However, since Keto cooking is mostly about fats and then protein, you ideally want to try a convenient method that lets you preserve your meals' nutritional goodness and, of course, the necessary fats. And this where slow cooking can come to the rescue. In particular, slow cooking has the following advantages when being on Keto, and you better try this out:

It helps you control what goes inside and specifically the number of sugars and carbs. Since you will be the one choosing the ingredients to add, there will be no more guessing or having to read food labels to add low or zero sugar and carb ingredients like the ones listed earlier. It is perhaps the main benefit of using a slow cooker when on Keto. We have made this easier for you in this guide by outlining the basic nutritional info for each recipe, so you know exactly what goes inside.

It maintains all the fats inside. By now, you have already realized that fats should be your main priority when on Keto. The issue with other cooking methods is that they dissolve and sometimes burn and evaporate the fat, e.g., grilling, which gets rid of the extra fat we need for Keto and makes the fat oxidize, which isn't healthy at all. On the contrary, slow cooking is one of the very few cooking methods that help preserve the ingredients' original fat without oxidation, provided that you don't overcook your meals.

It lets you prepare low carb yet fully nutritious liquids and sauces. A Slow Cooker can be used to make excellent chicken, beef, fish, and veggie stock, which are nutrient-dense yet contain little to none carbs - and yes, this is what we are looking for when on Keto. You can use any of these stocks afterward as your base to cook healthy and delicious keto meats or veggie meals without having to add carb-heavy sauces on top to add flavor. Slow Cookers work best with a bit of liquid; this kind of stocks and sauces can become your staples.

Provided you use your slow cooker properly - and we'll attempt to outline all the basic steps and some tips and tricks, there is no reason you shouldn't use your slow cooker when being on Keto.

It will be tough to find people who are not in love with home-cooked food. But with the hectic work schedule of these days, it is extremely hard for a working person to find some time for elaborate cooking. It does not mean working people prefer eating out or depending completely on packaged foods. They, too, want to enjoy the richness of homemade foods, but it is their work schedules that stop them from cherishing their desire.

Culinary innovations have always brought boons for the people who are obsessed with cooking. The slow cooker is one such cooking medium that has been able to solve the trouble of the people who remain busy all day and desire to have homemade foods at the end of the day. It is nothing but a specialized electric cooker that has been designed to cook slowly. Precisely, it is the electronic slow cooker. There are several benefits of cooking with a slow cooker like it is extremely economical, the cooked foods are healthy, and it is super easy to cook on the slow cooker. The separate cooking settings enable us to cook different ingredients with specific precision. Most importantly, it is very easy to cook the Ketogenic recipes in the slow cooker. As the pot cooks slowly, it is easy for working people to dump the ingredients while leaving for work, and when they return home, they can enjoy the bliss of warm homemade dishes.

CHAPTER 1:

Keto Diet & Slow Cooker Basics

In the simplest of terms, a ketogenic diet is a very low-carb, high-fat diet. It isn't a new diet, either. It was created in the 1920s as a treatment for children who had epilepsy. It is still used today, but there has been more investigation to see if it is a breakthrough treatment for several other diseases and neurological disorders. So, this isn't just some weight loss trend.

The main goal is to place the body into ketosis. The body burns carbs as energy. But if the amount of carbs in the body is restricted, the body will start breaking down the fat stored within the body, and this will create what is known as ketones. These ketones are then used as fuel.

Move from the 1920s, researchers started to find that the keto diet provided benefits other than the control of epilepsy. Many wellness professionals, the world over, are embracing the word ketogenic. Many people have started using this diet to control and prevent diabetes and to lose weight.

Many studies have found that the ketogenic diet and other low-carb diets are perfect for losing weight. They tend to work better than a low-fat or reduced-calorie diet. The ketogenic diet is sometimes easier to follow because ketones can work as an appetite suppressant without consuming many carbohydrates; you aren't faced with sugar crashes or cravings for carbs. You eat plenty of fat to keep you feeling full.

What Are the Benefits?

Below are some of the benefits of ketones:

Weight Loss – The body has to burn fat to make ketones. When this happens, natural ketosis is going to cause weight loss. Some studies suggest ketones can help you lose weight while also curbing your appetite.

Diabetes Control – Many low-carb diets, like the keto diet, have been found to do a great job at lowering blood sugar levels and insulin resistance. Some studies have found that BHB ketone can reduce inflammation, which is another way to control diabetes.

Longevity – If you want to stay healthy and live a long life, occasionally fasting can help you do that. Studies have found that restricting carbs can help to lengthen your life expectancy.

Preventing Cancer – Glucose can increase cancer cells. When you don't let them have their favorite food, it can reduce cancer cells and help prevent and treat cancer. Many who are at risk of developing cancer or being treated for cancer will follow a ketogenic diet.

Resilience – Ketone bodies can provide your body with powerful and constant energy. They can also help to preserve your performance and resilience better than glucose ever could.

Brainpower – The ketogenic diet was initially meant to be an epilepsy treatment, but it has been found as a great way to protect the neurons in the brain. It can improve focus, mental energy, and create a sharper mind.

Slow Cooker Basics

Having a slow cooker is an effortless, fast, and most flexible cooking method at any home. It didn't require you any cooking skills; it saves your time as the slow cooker does all the working time for you, truly safe and can even be used in any places like a hotel room or even student dorm as they possess a kettle like-shape, making it more portable than a stove. So, in the following guides, we will be talking some of the helpful basic ways to guarantee that you get the best out of your slow cooker.

What is it?

The slow cooker appeared in 1970 and was marketed as a bean cooker. But as it was modified, people started to use it to heat food and keep it warm for prolonged periods. And look how far we've come; people are cooking delicious healthy meals in it. It is a perfect small kitchen appliance that consists of a glass lid, porcelain, or a ceramic pot (it is inside of the heating unit) and, of course, a heating element. The modern Slow Cooker could be of an oval or round shape and various sizes, from small to large. All the Slow Cookers have two settings: LOW (it corresponds to the temperature of 200°F mostly) and HIGH (up to 300°F). The WARM selection that is among the majority of the Slow cookers' options nowadays allows keeping the prepared dishes warm for a long time. Some of the Slow Cooker models have a timer that will enable you to control cooking time if you are busy.

The Cooking Utensils Needed

First of all, you will need a Slow Cooker. Even though most models make a range of good varieties, you need to make sure you chose the slow cooker that meets your requirement.

You need to have a chopping board and at least three knives: a paring knife, a chef's knife, and a cleaver. Combining these knives will make it easy to prepare your foods, from herbs to full fleshed chickens.

You will also need a few bowls. These are important if you are going to be doing any mixing, preparing your ingredients in advance, or if you will need to take out some food from the cock-pot to make room for more ingredients.

You will also need a blender for smooth soups, a pestle and mortar if you want to crush your fresh herbs and spices, and a whisk for mixing eggs and sauces. Although these are not necessities, they will make the cooking process much more manageable if present. But in cases where you will be doing some batch cooking, consider investing in some good quality, resilient Tupperware. That way, you will make a great batch of food in advance and refrigerate them for future use.

If you intend to cook shorter recipes while you are out and about, you will either need a Slow Cooker or a Crockpot with a timer, or a plug adapter with a timer built into it. In as much as the Slow Cooker are safe, it is inadvisable to leave your food on high pressure for eight to ten hours, as not only will it be an irresponsible act, but will most certainly ruin your food. In other words, timers are essential when cooking in absentia.

Required Cooking Skills

Cooking with a Slow Cooker requires absolutely no advanced cooking skills, as long as you can peel and chop vegetables, mix herbs in oil, put things into a pot, turn a dial, then you are most certainly fit to cook with a Slow Cooker.

The Cooking Precautions

Even though Slow Cooker cooking is incredibly safe, it is recommended that you should always be careful:

- Do not place the slow cooker close to the pot or its wires as this could cause a hazard.

- Do not leave the house if your slow cooker is on without setting a safe timer.

- Do not leave the slow cooker exposed within reach of children or animals.

- Do not leave the slow cooker on with nothing inside it.

- Do not place the slow cooker on an unstable surface.

- Do not leave foods in it when cooked and cooled, as this can be dangerous to your health. Always move the cooked foods to a refrigerator or freezer for storage.

- And always make sure to follow these safety guidelines.

- Always make sure your slow cooker is clean.

- Always make sure your slow cooker is turned off when not in use.

- Always put your crockpot somewhere safe and steady when not in use.

- Always follow the manufacturer's directions during usage, cleaning, and storage processes.

What Are the Benefits of Using the Slow Cooker?

What is the most difficult thing for you in the kitchen? You waste too much time in the kitchen when you might go to the cinema with friends? Do you spend too much money on products, and your ideas on what to prepare today are running out? The solution to all your problem? It is the Slow Cooker!

Firstly, it is possible to prepare meals when you are not at home. During those hectic family mornings, throw all the ingredients together following the recipe, switch the machine on, and go work.

Secondly, you don't like washing the dishes? Just clean the Slow Cooker and the plates after delicious meals. That's all! Using the Slow Cooker means having fewer dishes to wash.

Thirdly, the Slow Cooker cooks' delicious meals and saves your money!

These meals taste even better than usual, and also you can keep the leftovers in the refrigerator to eat afterward. How perfect are the spice flavors if you eat the dishes right after cooking! You might taste the cayenne pepper, cumin, ginger, and other favorite spices of yours. Buy simple products and follow the cookbook. It is easy!

The fourth benefit, the Slow Cooker, is the best way to keep your meal tender and always warm.

Fifth, the Slow Cooker reduces calories and fat. No oil (just olive or avocado oil), no frying is necessary.

Six is the step by step preparation.

Step by step preparation facilitates everyday cooking, especially for those who are not great fans of this process. In most recipes, all the ingredients are added at one time to the Slow Cooker.

Seven, it is energy saving. It requires less electricity than the regular oven.

The flexibility of the Slow Cooker is benefit number eight. You can take it on a trip, put it on the kitchen table or somewhere else. It doesn't need that much space.

And finally, benefit number nine is in the large quantities of prepared meals. Most of these recipes make large quantities of the end products, so you may feed an entire family and even freeze for tomorrow to make easy and quick lunches or suppers.

So, are you already looking for some recipes to get started? Check the great Keto Slow Cooker cookbook, and you'll find the best and most delicious dishes here! Cooking Keto recipes in the Slow Cooker will help you fit cooking into your daily schedule and stay healthy. After a long working day, you'll be back home, and a delicious meal will be there waiting for you.

CHAPTER 2:

Ketogenic Diet Tips & Tricks

The ketogenic diet isn't strict. It is an easy way of life, even for people who are always on the run, have little income, are unable to quickly cook, or have disabilities which impede mobility. In this guide, we will introduce you just to some simple tips & tricks to help make the ketogenic diet even simpler. With this advice, you will be on the road to real success in no time:

Limit Carbohydrates

When you enter the ketogenic diet, such a large part of what impacts how quickly you enter ketosis is how much glycogen you have stored in your liver & muscles. Glycogen, which is a stored version of glucose, can be kept up to 2 thousand calories worth within these parts of the whole body. Depending on how much glycogen you have accumulated from your pre-ketogenic diet, how active you are, and how low you're eating carbohydrates on the ketogenic diet will affect how quickly you enter ketosis.

Suppose you're hoping to enter ketosis as soon as possible, and therefore get over the keto flu quicker. In that situation, the great way is to limit your carbohydrate intake on the ketogenic diet as much as possible. While 25 net carbohydrates are the standard recommended daily amount on the ketogenic diet, you could limit it to 10 or 15 net carbohydrates to help your glycogen stores deplete faster.

Live Actively

When you first begin the ketogenic diet, and your body is attempting to adapt from being fueled off of carbohydrates and switching to using fat and ketones; instead, your athletic ability and endurance may decrease slightly. Thankfully, this only lasts an average of 3 to 4 weeks, and then you can expect your exercise performance to improve quickly. Studies have shown that ketosis can enhance your athletic ability, especially when it comes just to aerobic and endurance activities. If you are not able to exercise to your usual degree for the first couple of weeks, it can help deplete your glycogen stores. Therefore, increasing ketone production and aiding in pushing you into such a state of ketosis sooner rather than afterward.

Many researches have shown that not only does working out while in a fasted state increase ketone levels, but if you efficiently exercise while on the ketogenic diet, the rate that ketones are produced is increased as well. One study found that when on the ketogenic diet if you exercise before such a meal rather than afterward, the blood ketone levels can be one-hundred and 37% to 300 and 14% higher.

Prioritize Sleep

If you're sleep deprived or oversleeping, your whole body will quickly increase the production of stress hormones. Not only can this affect your overall stress level, but it can entirely prevent you from losing weight and sometimes even cause weight gain. Therefore, it is crucial to ensure that you're sleeping the recommended number of hours. Studies have shown that less than 7 hours or more than nine hours will increase these stress hormones; therefore, it is best to find what suits your needs within that period quickly.

Cook Large Batches of Food

While cooking can be significantly limited on the ketogenic diet with the addition of pre-cooked meats & microwave-steamed vegetables, that does not mean you won't ever need to cook. Although, if you're limited on time or energy, cooking in large batches using a Slow Cooker can save you energy, time, and money. Cook more than you need, then store it in the fridge or freezer. If you desire, you can cook 2 or 3 servings at a time to keep in the refrigerator, or you can easily make enough food to last you two or three weeks and store it in the freezer. It is perfectly fit for people on the go, as you have to remove it from the fridge and thaw it out in the microwave.

Get Your Carbohydrates from Vegetables

While you can quickly get some of your daily net carbohydrates from dairy, nuts, or other items, you should try to keep most of your carbohydrates coming from low-starch vegetables and low-sugar fruits. Cabbage, kale, avocado, broccoli, olives, strawberries, blackberries – there are some excellent fruit and vegetable options on the ketogenic diet, and it is crucial not to forsake these to quickly eat "low-carb" packaged foods, as low-carbohydrate tortillas. You need nutrition and fiber that comes from these unique fruits and vegetables.

Invest in a Kitchen Scale

Accurately tracking your entire food intake for your macro ratio is incredibly crucial on the ketogenic diet, especially during the beginning phase. A lot of people may eyeball what they think is the correct proportion, but it is inaccurate and results in them being kicked out of ketosis. People will be frustrated by not understanding why their weight has stalled, only to quickly learn it is because they were not weighing and tracking their food. For instance, if you eyeball what you think is the correct amount of almond butter, you could accidentally consume an extra two tablespoons over a day. While two tablespoons might not seem like much, it contains 200 calories and six net carbohydrates.

A kitchen scale is the most precise method in which to track how much food you're consuming, and they are simple to use. Thankfully, these scales are relatively inexpensive, and you can quickly get an inexpensive one between ten and 25 dollars.

Take Exogenous Ketones

Exogenous ketones can help you increase the number of ketone bodies you have and make the process of going into ketosis easier and quicker. In fact, including some exogenous ketones in your diet can significantly improve your ketogenic journey by giving you more energy and helping your whole body adapt to the entire process of ketosis sooner than it otherwise would.

The best type of exogenous ketones and the most common on the market is beta-hydroxybutyrate, otherwise known as BHB. These are the most effective form of ketones which your whole body can use as fuel and energy.

While a lot of people dread the idea of the keto flu, especially if they are busy with work or family, the addition of exogenous ketones has helped a lot of people avoid this phenomenon. They might be such a little pricey, but if you can afford it, then it could be worth adding exogenous ketones to your diet for at least the first two weeks of the ketogenic diet.

Keep Snacks on Hand

The final thing you want is to be tired and hungry, needing a snack but with nothing to eat quickly. Therefore, to help you stick to your diet and prevent overeating in the evenings, it is best to keep snacks on hand. Some great snacks are cheese, boiled eggs, sandwich meat, nuts, beef jerky, fat bombs, recently prepared guacamole, or pre-cooked bacon.

CHAPTER 3:

Slow Cooker Tips & Tricks

If you have ever tossed a bunch of different ingredients into your Slow Cooker in the morning and thought about how delicious your dinner was going to be all day long, only to come home to a pot of mush, you might feel like giving up. However, don't give up just yet. Here are the top tips and tricks that you can use to ensure you are the master of your Slow Cooker in no time flat:

Start with frozen meat, which is at room temperature. It is because you do want to brown the outside of the meat in advance; before you put it in your slow cooker. When you caramelize the outside of the meat, you are going to get a deep, delicious flavor in your dish. It also suggested that when you do brown the meat, you do so only after you have seasoned it. It will create a fantastic flavor.

Don't forget about the brown bits. The brown bits are the tiny morsels that are left in the pan after the meat has browned. They are packed full of flavor. You will want them in your Slow Cooker. You can deglaze your pan by adding some stock, water, or even wine to the pan. Cook over medium heat while carefully scraping the browned bits off of the bottom of the pan with a wooden spoon. Most of these are going to dissolve that you can use to make a nice sauce.

If you do use wine in your Slow Cooker, don't cook with any wine that you would not drink. Each of your ingredients should be quality ingredients. The Slow Cooker is not a magic machine that is going to turn low-quality ingredients into high-quality food. Imagine how bad a cake would taste if you used old poor-quality chocolate.

If you add tomatoes to your recipes, it is essential to choose tomatoes that are not going to turn out mushy. Choose whole canned tomatoes instead of crushed. If you want the tomatoes to be in smaller pieces, chop them up before you put them in your Slow Cooker. You can also use dried tomatoes but never do you want to use fresh tomatoes in your Slow Cooker. They will turn into mush.

Don't freak out if you look into the Slow Cooker and find that there is too much liquid. Transfer some of that liquid to a saucepan. You can make gravy out of it or use it to glaze the food.

If you open up your Slow Cooker and find that your meat is perfectly cooked, but your vegetables are overcooked, remove the vegetables that are overcooked. Never serve the dish with overcooked vegetables. Serve the meat with a side of freshly cooked vegetables. You can also puree the overcooked vegetables and mix them in with the sauce.

Make sure that you understand how your Slow Cooker works. The high setting is only used when cooking foods for a shorter time. You do not want to leave your Slow Cooker on the high setting for 10 or 12 hours because you are going to come back to a burned mess. Make sure that you always check to ensure you are using the right setting.

You will find that some of the foods that you make in your Slow Cooker are going to taste better the following day. It is because flavors have been able to develop as the food sits so many meat dishes and chilies are going to be better the day after you make them.

The great thing about Slow Cooker is that it works very well with fattier cuts of meat. When you cook them on low and for a long time, the fat is going to make sure that the meat will not become dry. Since fattier cuts are generally the cheaper cuts, this is a great thing when it comes to your budget. It doesn't mean that you should not cook lean meats in your Slow Cooker. It is okay for you to cook meats like chicken breast in the Slow Cooker, but it is advisable to do this on days when you know you are going to be around.

When you are using it, it is essential to make sure that the food you add to it is appropriately layered. Most of the time, the source of heat will be at the bottom of the Slow Cooker. It means that you need to place foods on the bottom of the Slow Cooker that will take more time to cook, such as root vegetables or severe cuts of meat. The more delicate vegetables should be at the top of the slow cooker or added within the last 30 minutes to ensure that they do not turn into mush.

Every time that you lift that lid, it will add about 30 minutes to the cooking time, so don't do it. Having a glass lid, allows you to see how the food is doing. So, do not open the Slow Cooker until the end of the cooking time, then, if you need to, you can add other spices or ingredients.

Herbs and dairy should always be added at the end of the cooking process. You will only stir in items like sour cream right before you serve the dish. If you do this too early, the dairy product will curdle and ruin your entire dish.

Some vegetables that you add, such as onions, may add too much liquid to your recipe; if you find this, remove the lid from the Slow Cooker for about 30 minutes and turn it on high. It is going to boil off the extra liquid.

Not all Slow Cooker is the same, so if while you are working through these recipes, you find that they are not cooking for the exact time that the recipe says they should, it is okay. What that means is that your recipes may get done a bit sooner or a bit afterward than what the recipe says they will. It is only because all Slow Cooker is different. While others may run a bit hot, yours may take a bit longer to heat up. If you notice that one recipe takes a bit longer to cook or that most of the recipes do, make a note of that, and then you will know in the future that you will need to add a bit more time when cooking in the Slow Cooker.

CHAPTER 4:

Breakfast

Cherry Tomatoes Thyme Asparagus Frittata

Preparation time: 15 minutes

Cooking time: 6 hours

Servings: 6

Ingredients:

2 tablespoons unsalted butter, ghee, or extra-virgin olive oil

12 large eggs

¼ cup heavy (whipping) cream

1 tablespoon minced fresh thyme

½ teaspoon kosher salt

¼ teaspoon freshly ground black pepper

1½ cups shredded sharp white Cheddar cheese, divided

½ cup grated Parmesan cheese

16 cherry tomatoes

16 asparagus spears

Directions:

Glaze the inside of the slow cooker with the butter.

In the slow cooker, beat the eggs, then whisk in the heavy cream, thyme, salt, and pepper.

Add ¾ cup of Cheddar cheese and the Parmesan cheese and stir to mix.

Sprinkle the remaining ¾ cup of Cheddar cheese over the top. Scatter the cherry tomatoes over the frittata.

Arrange the asparagus spears decoratively over the top. Cook within 6 hours on low or 3 hours on soaring. Serve.

Nutrition:

Calories: 370

Fat: 29g

Carbs: 4g

Protein: 24g

Healthy Low Carb Walnut Zucchini Bread

Preparation time: 15 minutes

Cooking time: 3 hours & 10 minutes

Servings: 12

Ingredients:

3 eggs

1/2 cup walnuts, chopped

2 cups zucchini, shredded

2 tsp vanilla

1/2 cup pure all-purpose sweetener

1/3 cup coconut oil, softened

1/2 tsp baking soda

1 1/2 Tsp baking powder

2 tsp cinnamon

1/3 cup coconut flour

1 cup almond flour

1/2 Tsp salt

Directions:

Mix the almond flour, baking powder, cinnamon, baking soda, coconut flour, and salt in a bowl. Set aside.

Whisk eggs, vanilla, sweetener, and oil in another bowl.

Put dry batter to the wet and fold well. Add walnut and zucchini and fold well.

Pour batter into the silicone bread pan. Place the bread pan into the slow cooker on the rack.

Cook on high within 3 hours. Cut the bread loaf into the slices and serve.

Nutrition:

Calories: 174

Fat: 15.4 g

Carb: 5.8 g

Protein: 5.3 g

Savory Creamy Breakfast Casserole

Preparation time: 15 minutes

Cooking time: 6 hours

Servings: 8

Ingredients:

1 tablespoon unsalted butter, Ghee

10 large eggs, beaten

1 cup heavy (whipping) cream

1½ cups shredded sharp Cheddar cheese, divided

½ cup grated Romano cheese

½ teaspoon kosher salt

¼ teaspoon freshly ground black pepper

8 ounces thick-cut ham, diced

¾ head broccoli, cut into small florets

½ onion, diced

Directions:

Grease the slow cooker with the butter.

Whisk the eggs, heavy cream, ½ cup of Cheddar cheese, the Romano cheese, salt, and pepper inside the slow cooker.

Stir in the ham, broccoli, and onion. Put the remaining 1 cup of Cheddar cheese over the top.

Cook within 6 hours on low or 3 hours on high. Serve hot.

Nutrition:

Calories: 465 Fat: 36g Carbs: 7g Protein: 28g

Low-Carb Hash Brown Breakfast Casserole

Preparation time: 15 minutes

Cooking time: 6 hours

Servings: 6

Ingredients:

1 tablespoon unsalted butter, Ghee

12 large eggs

½ cup heavy cream

1 teaspoon kosher salt

½ teaspoon ground black pepper

½ teaspoon ground mustard

1 head cauliflower, shredded or minced

1 onion, diced

10 ounces cooked sausage links, sliced

2 cups shredded Cheddar cheese, divided

Directions:

Grease the slow cooker with the butter.

Beat the eggs, then whisk in heavy cream, 1 teaspoon of salt, ½ teaspoon of pepper, and the ground mustard in a large bowl.

Spread about one-third of the cauliflower in an even layer in the bottom of the cooker.

Layer one-third of the onions over the cauliflower, then one-third of the sausage, and top with ½ cup of Cheddar cheese. Season with salt and pepper. Repeat twice.

Pour the egg batter evenly over the layered ingredients, then sprinkle the remaining ½ cup Cheddar cheese on top—Cook within 6 hours on low. Serve hot.

Nutrition:

Calories: 523 Fat: 40g Carbs: 7g Protein: 33g

Onion Broccoli Cream Cheese Quiche

Preparation time: 15 minutes

Cooking time: 2 hours & 25 minutes

Servings: 8

Ingredients:

9 eggs

2 cups cheese, shredded and divided

8 oz cream cheese

1/4 Tsp onion powder

3 cups broccoli, cut into florets

1/4 Tsp pepper

3/4 Tsp salt

Directions:

Add broccoli into the boiling water and cook for 3 minutes. Drain well and set aside to cool.

Add eggs, cream cheese, onion powder, pepper, and salt in mixing bowl and beat until well combined.

Spray slow cooker from inside using cooking spray.

Add cooked broccoli into the slow cooker then sprinkle half cup cheese.

Pour egg mixture over broccoli and cheese mixture.

Cook on high within 2 hours and 15 minutes.

Once it is done, then sprinkle the remaining cheese and cover for 10 minutes or until cheese melted. Serve.

Nutrition:

Calories 296 Fat 24.3 g Carb 3.9 g

Protein 16.4 g

Delicious Thyme Sausage Squash

Preparation time: 15 minutes

Cooking time: 6 hours

Servings: 4

Ingredients:

2 tablespoons extra-virgin olive oil

14 ounces smoked chicken sausage, thinly sliced

¼ cup chicken broth

1 onion, halved and sliced

½ medium butternut squash, peeled, diced

1 small green bell pepper, strips

½ small red bell pepper, strips

½ small yellow bell pepper, strips

2 teaspoons snipped fresh thyme or ½ teaspoon dried thyme, crushed

½ teaspoon kosher salt

½ teaspoon freshly ground black pepper

1 cup shredded Swiss cheese

Directions:

Combine the olive oil, sausage, broth, onion, butternut squash, bell peppers, thyme, salt, and pepper in the slow cooker. Toss to mix. Cook within 6 hours on low.

Before serving, sprinkle the Swiss cheese over the top, cover, and cook for about 3 minutes more to melt the cheese.

Nutrition:

Calories: 502

Fat: 38g

Carbs: 12g

Protein: 27g

Mexican Style Breakfast Casserole

Preparation time: 15 minutes

Cooking time: 5 hours

Servings: 5

Ingredients:

5 eggs

6 ounces pork sausage, cooked, drained

½ cup 1% milk

½ teaspoon garlic powder

2 jalapeños, deseeded, finely chopped

½ teaspoon ground cumin

½ teaspoon ground coriander

1 ½ cups chunky salsa

1 ½ cup pepper Jack cheese, shredded

Salt to taste

Pepper to taste

¼ cup fresh cilantro

Directions:

Coat the slow cooker with cooking spray. Mix the eggs, salt, pepper, plus milk in a bowl.

Add garlic powder, cumin, coriander, and sausage and mix well.

Pour the mixture into the slow cooker. Set the slow cooker on 'Low' within 4-5 hours or on 'High' for 2-3 hours. Place toppings of your choice and serve.

Nutrition:Calories: 320 Fat: 24.1 g Carb: 5.2 g

Protein: 17.9 g

Almond Lemon Blueberry Muffins

Preparation time: 15 minutes

Cooking time: 3 hours

Servings: 3

Ingredients:

1 cup almond flour

1 large egg

3 drops stevia

¼ cup fresh blueberries

¼ teaspoon lemon zest, grated

¼ teaspoon pure lemon extract

½ cup heavy whipping cream

2 tablespoons butter, melted

½ teaspoon baking powder

Directions:

Whisk the egg into a bowl. Add the rest of the fixing, and mix.

Pour batter into lined or greased muffin molds. Pour up to ¾ of the cup.

Pour 6 ounces of water into the slow cooker. Place an aluminum foil at the bottom, and the muffin molds inside.

Set the slow cooker on 'High' within 2-3 hours. Let it cool in the cooker for a while.

Remove from the cooker. Loosen the edges of the muffins. Invert on to a plate and serve.

Nutrition:

Calories: 223 Fat: 21g

Carb: 5g Protein: 6 g

Healthy Veggie Omelet

Preparation time: 15 minutes

Cooking time: 1 hour & 40 minutes

Servings: 4

Ingredients:

6 eggs

1 tsp parsley, dried

1 tsp garlic powder

1 bell pepper, diced

1/2 cup onion, sliced

1 cup spinach

1/2 cup almond milk, unsweetened

4 egg whites

Pepper

Salt

Directions:

Grease the slow cooker from inside using cooking spray.

Whisk egg whites, eggs, parsley, garlic powder, almond milk, pepper, and salt in a large bowl.

Stir in bell peppers, spinach, and onion. Pour egg batter into the slow cooker.

Cook on high within 90 minutes or until egg sets. Cut into the slices and serve.

Nutrition:

Calories: 200 Fat: 13.9 g

Carb: 5.8 g Protein 13.4 g

Arugula Cheese Herb Frittata

Preparation time: 15 minutes

Cooking time: 3 hours & 10 minutes

Servings: 6

Ingredients:

8 eggs

3/4 cup goat cheese, crumbled

1/2 cup onion, sliced

1 1/2 cups red peppers, roasted and chopped

4 cups baby arugula

1 tsp oregano, dried

1/3 cup almond milk

Pepper

Salt

Directions:

Grease the slow cooker using a cooking spray. Whisk eggs, oregano, and almond milk in a mixing bowl.

Put pepper and salt. Arrange red peppers, onion, arugula, and cheese into the slow cooker.

Pour egg batter into the slow cooker over the vegetables. Cook on low within 3 hours. Serve hot and enjoy.

Nutrition:

Calories: 178

Fat: 12.8 g

Carb: 6 g

Protein: 11.4 g

Yummy Cauliflower Crust Breakfast Pizza

Preparation time: 15 minutes

Cooking time: 5 hours

Servings: 4

Ingredients:

2 large eggs

3 cups riced cauliflower

1 cup grated Parmesan cheese

8 ounces goat cheese, divided

½ teaspoon kosher salt

1 tablespoon extra-virgin olive oil

Grated zest of 1 lemon

Directions:

Beat the eggs, cauliflower, Parmesan cheese, 2 ounces of goat cheese, and the salt until well mixed in a large bowl.

Grease the slow cooker using the olive oil. Press the cauliflower batter in an even layer around the cooker's bottom and extend slightly up the sides.

Stir the remaining 6 ounces of goat cheese and the lemon zest in a small bowl. Dollop spoonsful onto the cauliflower crust, distributing it evenly.

Set the lid on the slow cooker, but prop it slightly open with a chopstick or wooden spoon. Cook within 6 hours on low or 3 hours on high, until the edges are slightly browned.

When finished, turn off the cooker but let the pizza sit in it 30 minutes before serving. Serve warm.

Nutrition:

Calories: 389

Fat: 29g

Carbs: 6g

Protein: 24g

Parmesan Zucchini Paprika & Ricotta Frittata

Preparation time: 15 minutes

Cooking time: 6 hours

Servings: 6

Ingredients:

2 medium zucchinis, shredded

1 teaspoon kosher salt, divided

1 tablespoon extra-virgin olive oil

12 large eggs

3 tablespoons heavy (whipping) cream

3 tablespoons finely chopped fresh parsley

1 tablespoon fresh thyme

½ teaspoon paprika

½ teaspoon freshly ground black pepper

6 ounces ricotta cheese

12 cherry tomatoes, halved

½ cup grated Parmesan cheese

Directions:

Toss the shredded zucchini with ½ teaspoon of salt in a colander set in the sink. Let the zucchini sit for a few minutes, then squeeze out the excess liquid with your hands.

Grease the slow cooker with olive oil.

Beat the eggs, heavy cream, parsley, thyme, paprika, pepper, and the remaining ½ teaspoon of salt in a large bowl.

Put the zucchini and stir. Transfer the mixture to the prepared insert.

Using a large spoon, dollop the ricotta cheese into the egg mixture, distributing it evenly.

Top with the tomatoes and sprinkle the Parmesan cheese over the top. Set to cook within 6 hours on low or 3 hours on high. Serve at room temperature.

Nutrition:

Calories: 291

Fat: 22g

Carbs: 4g

Protein: 18g

Scrambled Eggs with Smoked Salmon

Preparation time: 15 minutes

Cooking time: 2 hours

Servings: 6

Ingredients:

smoked salmon ¼ lb.

eggs12 pcs fresh

heavy cream½ cup

almond flour¼ cup

Salt and black pepper at will

Butter2 tablespoons

fresh chives at will

Directions:

Cut the slices of salmon. Set aside for garnish. Chop the rest of the salmon into small pieces.

Take a medium bowl, whisk the eggs and cream together. Add half of the chopped chives, season eggs with salt and pepper. Add flour.

Dissolve the butter over medium heat, then pour into the mixture. Grease the Slow Cooker with oil or cooking spray.

Add salmon pieces to the mixture, pour it into the Slow Cooker. Set to cook on low within 2 hours.

Garnish the dish with remaining salmon, chives. Serve warm and enjoy!

Nutrition:

Calories: 263

Carbs: 0g

Fat: 0g

Protein: 0g

Garlic-Parmesan Asparagus Crock Pot

Preparation time: 15 minutes

Cooking time: 1 hour

Servings: 6

Ingredients:

olive oil extra virgin2 tablespoons

minced garlic2 teaspoons

egg 1 pcs fresh

garlic salt1/2 teaspoon

fresh asparagus12 ounces

Parmesan cheese1/3 cup

Pepper at will

Directions:

Peel the garlic and mince it. Wash the asparagus. Shred the Parmesan cheese.

Take a medium-sized bowl combine oil, garlic, cracked egg, and salt together. Whisk everything well.

Cover the green beans and coat them well.

Spread the cooking spray over the Slow Cooker's bottom, put the coated asparagus, season with the shredded cheese. Toss.

Cook on high within 1 hour. Once the time is over, you may also season with the rest of the cheese. Serve.

Nutrition:

Calories: 88

Carbs: 7g

Fat: 9g

Protein: 7g

Persian Omelet Crock Pot

Preparation time: 15 minutes

Cooking time: 3 hours

Servings: 14

Ingredients:

olive oil 2 tablespoons

butter 1 tablespoons

red onion 1 large

green onions 4 pcs

garlic 2 cloves

spinach 2 oz

fresh chives ¼ cup

cilantro leaves ¼ cup

parsley leaves ¼ cup

fresh dill 2 tablespoons

Kosher salt and black pepper at will

pine nuts ¼ cup

eggs 9 large

whole milk ¼ cup

Greek yogurt 1 cup

Directions:

Take a saucepan to melt the butter. Add red onion, stirring occasionally; it takes about 8-9 minutes.

Add green onions, garlic, continue cooking for 4 minutes. Put the spinach, chives, parsley, cilantro, add salt and pepper at will. Remove the skillet, add the pine nuts.

Take a bowl, crack the eggs, add milk, and a little pepper and whisk. Mix the eggs with veggie mixture.

Open the Slow Cooker and spread the cooking spray over the bottom and sides. Pour the mix into the Slow Cooker. Cook on low for 3 hours. Serve with Greek yogurt. Bon Appetite!

Nutrition:

Calories: 220 Carbs: 9g Fat: 16g Protein: 12g

Broccoli and Cheese Stuffed Squash

Preparation time: 15 minutes

Cooking time: 3 hours

Servings: 7

Ingredients:

squash 1 pcs, halves

broccoli florets 2 cups

garlic 3 pcs

red pepper flakes 1 teaspoon

Italian season 1 teaspoon

mozzarella cheese 1/2 cup

Parmesan cheese 1/3 cup

cooking spray

salt and pepper at will

Directions:

Grease the Slow Cooker. Put the squash halves in the Slow Cooker.

Add a little bit of water at room temperature to the bottom of the Slow Cooker.

Put on low within 2 hours, until squash is mild. Take off the squash and let it cool for about 15 minutes.

Take a medium skillet, add pepper flakes and a little bit oil and cook for 20 seconds, stir it continuously.

Add broccoli, minced garlic to the skillet, continue to stir thoroughly, until the broccoli is tender.

Take the squash and using a fork; take off the flesh of the squash. Add it to the medium bowl and conjoin with the broccoli mixture.

Shred the Parmesan cheese carefully, put salt and pepper at will, add seasoning to the mixture. Mix well and fill the squash.

Put the filled squash again in the Slow Cooker, dress with mozzarella cheese each squash half.

Cover and cook on low within 1 hour. Remove the dish and serve.

Nutrition:

Calories: 230 Carbs: 22g Fat: 6g Protein: 21g

Garlic Butter Keto Spinach

Preparation time: 15 minutes

Cooking time: 1 hour

Servings: 4

Ingredients:

salted butter 2 tablespoons

garlic, minced 4 cloves

baby spinach 8 oz

Pinch of salt

lemon juice 1 teaspoons

Directions:

Heat-up a little skillet, add the butter, melt. Sautee the garlic until a bit tender.

Spray the cooking spray over the bottom of the Slow Cooker.

Put the spinach into the Slow Cooker, season with salt and lemon juice, tender garlic, butter.

Put to cook on low within 1 hour. Garnish with fresh lemon wedges. Serve hot.

Nutrition:

Calories: 38 Carbs: 2g Fat: 3g Protein: 2g

Keto Crock Pot Tasty Onions

Preparation time: 15 minutes

Cooking time: 6 hours

Servings: 4

Ingredients:

Onions 4 (or 5) large pcs, sliced

Butter or coconut oil 4 tablespoon

coconut aminos 1/4 cup

Splenda (optional)

Salt and pepper

Directions:

Place the onion slices into the Slow Cooker. Top the onion slices with coconut amino and butter; you might add Splenda at will.

Cook it on low during 6-7 hours. Serve over the grilled vegetables.

Nutrition:

Calories: 38

Carbs: 9g

Fat: 0g

Protein: 0g

Crock Pot Benedict Casserole

Preparation time: 15 minutes

Cooking time: 4 hours

Servings: 7

Ingredients:

For the Casserole

English muffin 1 large, cut into portions

Canadian bacon1 lb. thick-cut

eggs 10 large

milk 1 cup

salt and pepper

for garnish

For the Sauce

egg 6 yolks

lemon juice 1 1/2 tablespoon

unsalted butter, melted1 1/2 sticks

salt

pinch of cayenne

Directions:

For the muffin: Using a medium-sized skillet, melt the butter. Add coconut and almond flour, egg, salt, and stir everything well. Add baking soda. Grease the Slow Cooker with cooking spray. Pour the mixture, put on low for 2 hours. Remove once done.

Grease again the Slow Cooker with cooking spray, cut the muffin into equal pieces, put on the bottom.

Slice the bacon, sprinkle half of it over top of the muffin pieces.

Whisk milk, eggs, season with salt and black pepper in a large bowl.

Pour the egg batter evenly over the muffin pieces and top with the rest of the bacon.

Cook on low within 2 hours in the slow cooker. Remove, and keep the muffins covered before serving.

To make the sauce, set up a double boiler, put the egg yolks, squeeze lemon juice in a bowl, and mix.

Put your bowl over the double boiler, continue whisking carefully; the bowl mustn't get too hot.

Put in the melted butter while continuing to whisk.

Season with salt and pepper. You may also add a little bit more lemon juice or cayenne.

Serve and enjoy.

Nutrition:

Calories: 286

Carbs: 16g

Fat: 19g

Protein: 14g

Crustless Crock Pot Spinach Quiche

Preparation time: 15 minutes

Cooking time: 2 hours

Servings: 11

Ingredients:

frozen spinach10 oz package

butter or ghee1 tablespoon

red bell pepper1 medium

Cheddar cheese1 1/2 cups

eggs8 pcs

homemade sour cream1 cup

fresh chives2 tablespoons

sea salt1/2 teaspoon

ground black pepper1/4 teaspoon

ground almond flour   1/2 cup

baking soda1/4 teaspoon

Directions:

Let the frozen spinach thaw and drain it well. Chop finely. Wash the pepper and slice it. Remove the seeds.

Grate the cheddar cheese and set aside. Chop the fresh chives finely.

Grease the slow cooker with cooking spray.

Take a little skillet, heat the butter over high heat on the stove, sauté the pepper until tender, for about 6 minutes. Mix the eggs, sour cream, salt, plus pepper in a large bowl.

Add grated cheese and chives and continue to mix. In another medium-sized bowl, combine almond flour with baking soda.

Pour into the egg mixture, add peppers to the egg's mixture, pour gently into the slow cooker.

Set to cook on high within 2 hours then Serve.

Nutrition:

Calories: 153

Carbs: 19g

Fat: 3g

Protein: 9g

Broccoli Gratin with Parmesan and Swiss Cheese

Preparation time: 15 minutes

Cooking time: 1 hour

Servings: 7

Ingredients:

bite-size broccoli flowerets8 cups

Swiss cheese1 1/2 cups

mayo 8 teaspoon

lemon juice1 1/2 tablespoon

Dijon mustard3/4 teaspoon

green onions3 tablespoon

Parmesan cheese1/4 cup

black pepper and salt to taste

Directions:

Wash broccoli and cut into small florets. Grate both parmesan and Swiss cheese into a bowl. Set aside.

Squeeze juice of a lemon into a cup. Wash and chop the green onions.

Grease with cooking spray or olive oil (optional) over the bottom of the slow cooker.

Put broccoli florets in a single layer. Mix in a separate bowl lemon juice, mustard, mayo, black pepper, add to the mixture green onion and grated cheese.

Put the mixture over the broccoli, cover, and cook on low 1 hour. Serve hot.

Nutrition:

Calories: 210

Carbs: 44g

Fat: 2g

Protein: 5g

Crock Pot Cream Cheese French Toast

Preparation time: 15 minutes

Cooking time: 2 hours

Servings: 9

Ingredients:

cream cheese 1 (8-oz) package

slivered almonds ¼ cup

keto bread 1 loaf

eggs 4 pcs

almond extract 1 teaspoon

sweetener 1 tablespoon

milk 1 cup

butter 2 tablespoon

Cheddar cheese ½ cup

Maple syrup, at will, for dressing

Directions:

Mix cream cheese with almonds in a large bowl. Slice the keto bread into 2-inch slices. Try to make a 1/2-inch slit (horizontal) at the bottom of every piece to make a pocket.

Fill all the slices with cream mixture. Set aside. In a little bowl, mix eggs, extract the sweetener in milk. Coat the keto slices into the mix.

Grease with cooking spray the slow cooker over the bottom and sides, then put the coated keto slices on the slow cooker's base. Put on the top of each separate piece additional shredded cheese.

Cook on low for 2 hours. Serve hot.

Nutrition:

Calories: 280

Carbs: 34g

Fat: 8g

Protein: 19g

Keto Crock Pot Turkey Stuffed Peppers

Preparation time: 15 minutes

Cooking time: 6 hours

Servings: 7

Ingredients:

olive oil1 tablespoon

ground turkey1 lb.

onion1 pcs

garlic1 clove

green bell peppers4 pcs

tomato sauce/pasta sauce (low carb)24 oz jar

water1/2 cup

Directions:

Peel and cut the small onion, peel the garlic, and press or mince it.

Wash the bell peppers, cut off the tops and clean them accurately.

Take a medium bowl, put their ground turkey, cut onion, pressed or minced garlic, and add pasta sauce.

Separate the compound into four equal parts, place the mixtures into the prepared cleaned peppers.

Spread the olive oil over the slow cooker bottom, and sides put the peppers inside, and top them with sauce.

Add a little water into the slow cooker, cook on low for 6-7 hours.

Serve with remaining sauce and enjoy.

Nutrition:

Calories: 245 Carbs: 26g

Fat: 7g Protein: 19g

Crock Pot Keto English Muffin

Preparation time: 15 minutes

Cooking time: 2 hours

Servings: 6

Ingredients:

almond flour3 tablespoons

coconut flour 1/2 tablespoon

butter 1 tablespoon

egg 1 large

sea salt1 pinch

baking soda1/2 teaspoons

salt

Directions:

Take a medium-sized skillet, melt the butter. It usually takes 20-30 seconds.

Pour coconut and almond flour, egg, salt into the melted butter and stir everything well.

Remove skillet from the heat and add baking soda.

Coat the slow cooker with cooking spray. Pour the mixture.

Put on low for 2 hours. Check the readiness with a fork.

Remove the baked muffin from the slow cooker and eat with bacon slices, cheese, or other breakfast staples.

Nutrition:

Calories: 188

Carbs: 3g

Fat: 17g

Protein: 7g

Cauliflower Casserole with Tomato and Goat Cheese

Preparation time: 15 minutes

Cooking time: 3 hours

Servings: 12

Ingredients:

cauliflower florets 6 cups

olive oil 4 teaspoons

dried oregano 1 teaspoon

salt 1/2 teaspoon

ground pepper 1/2 teaspoons

goat cheese crumbled 2 oz.

The Sauce:

olive oil 1 teaspoon

garlic 3 cloves

crushed tomatoes 1 (28 oz.) can

bay leaves 2 pcs

salt 1/4 teaspoon

minced flat-leaf parsley 1/4 cup

Directions:

Grease the slow cooker with cooking spray, put the cauliflower on its bottom, add olive oil, oregano, and pepper. Salt if desired.

Cook on the low setting within 2 hours until the cauliflower florets get tender and a little bit brown color.

For making the sauce: Take a medium-sized skillet, heat the olive oil, add garlic and cook 1 minute, stir it thoroughly all the time.

Add the crushed tomatoes and bay leaves; let it simmer for some minutes. Remove the bay leaves, dress with pepper and salt.

Put the sauce over the cauliflower florets in the slow cooker once the time is over.

Spread the Goat cheese over the dish, cover the slow cooker, and continue cooking for 1 hour on low. Serve warm!

Nutrition:

Calories: 170

Carbs: 10g

Fat: 13g

Protein: 7g

Greek Eggs Breakfast Casserole

Preparation time: 15 minutes

Cooking time: 6 hours

Servings: 9

Ingredients:

eggs (whisked) 12 pcs

milk ½ cup

salt ½ teaspoon

black pepper 1 teaspoon

Red Onion 1 tablespoon

Garlic 1 teaspoon

Sun-dried tomatoes ½ cup

spinach 2 cups

Feta Cheese ½ cup crushed

pepper at will

Directions:

Whisk the eggs in a bowl.

Add to the mixture milk, pepper, salt, and stir to combine. Add the minced onion and garlic.

Add dried tomatoes and spinach. Pour all the batter into the slow cooker, add Feta cheese.

Set to cook on the low setting within 5-6 hours. Serve.

Nutrition:

Calories: 253

Carbs: 1g

Fat: 17g

Protein: 22g

Crock Pot Turkish Breakfast Eggs

Preparation time: 15 minutes

Cooking time: 4 hours

Servings: 9

Ingredients:

olive oil 1 tablespoon

onions 2 pcs, chopped

red bell pepper 1 pcs, sliced

red chili 1 small

cherry tomatoes 8 pcs

keto bread 1 slice

eggs 4 pcs

milk 2 tablespoon

small bunch of parsley, chopped

natural yogurt 4 tablespoon

pepper at will

Directions:

Grease the slow cooker using oil.

Heat-up, the oil, add the onions, pepper, and chili in a large skillet, then stir. Cook until the veggies begin to soften.

Transfer it in the Slow Cooker, then add the cherry tomatoes and bread, stir everything well.

Cook on low for 4 hours—season with fresh parsley and yogurt.

Nutrition:

Calories: 123

Carbs: 17g

Fat: 5g

Protein: 1g

Cheesy Garlic Brussels Sprouts

Preparation time: 15 minutes

Cooking time: 3 hours

Servings: 6

Ingredients:

1 tablespoon unsalted butter

2½ pounds Brussels sprouts, trimmed and halved

¾ cup grated Parmesan cheese

2 tablespoons heavy cream

1/8 teaspoon freshly grated nutmeg

4 cloves garlic, thinly sliced

4 ounces cream cheese, cubed

½ teaspoon kosher salt

¼ teaspoon ground black pepper

Directions:

Coat the insert of a 4- to – 6-quart crockpot with the butter. Add the garlic, cream cheese, Brussels sprouts, pepper, and salt.

Toss to mix very well—cover and cook on the low, about 2 to 3 hours.

Turn off the slow cooker. Stir in cream, parmesan, and nutmeg until the cheeses thaw and the Brussels sprouts are coated in a creamy sauce.

Taste, season with more pepper if required. Serve.

Nutrition:

Calories: 159

Fat: 9.5g

Saturated fat: 5.5g

Carbs: 14.1g

Fiber: 5.4g

Sugars: 3.7 g

Protein: 7.7g

Sodium: 279.8 mg

Blueberry Pancake

Preparation time: 15 minutes

Cooking time: 40 minutes

Servings: 8

Ingredients:

1½ cups milk

2 large eggs

1 teaspoon vanilla

2 cups all-purpose flour

2½ teaspoon baking powder

2 tablespoons white sugar

¼ cup fresh blueberries

Directions:

Toss the eggs, vanilla, and milk together in a small bowl. Stir flour, sugar, and baking powder together in a large bowl until well-mixed.

Add the wet fixings to the dry and stir just until mixed.

Pour the batter into the slow cooker. Add the blueberries.

Set the timer at 40 minutes on low.

Check to confirm if the pancake is cooked through by pressing the top. Serve and enjoy with syrup, fruit, or whipped cream.

Nutrition:

Calories: 174

Carbs: 30g

Protein: 6g

Fat: 2g

Cholesterol: 45mg

Sodium: 37mg

Potassium: 266mg

Sugar: 5g

Sausage and Peppers

Preparation time: 15 minutes

Cooking time: 6 hours

Servings: 8

Ingredients:

6 medium cloves garlic

2 large yellow onions

4 green bell peppers, cleaned and thinly sliced

28 ounces canned unsalted crushed tomatoes

¼ cup of cold water

1 bay leaf

2 pounds uncooked Italian Sausage Links, mild or spicy

1 tablespoon kosher salt

1 teaspoon Italian seasoning

¼ teaspoon dried oregano

½ teaspoon crushed red pepper flakes

Directions:

Thinly slice the garlic. Peel the onions and halve, then cut.

Add the chopped garlic and sliced onion into the slow cooker.

Remember to spray the slow cooker with oil. Cut the bell peppers in half.

Remove the ribs and any seeds in them. Then slice thinly.

Add the sliced bell peppers, Italian seasoning, salt, crushed red pepper flakes, dried oregano, 1 can crushed tomatoes, and ¼ cup of water to the slow cooker.

Toss to coat and liquid is uniformly distributed. Take out almost half of the peppers and the onion mixture to a bowl.

Immerse the uncooked sausage in the middle and then add the peppers and the onions back to the slow cooker.

Put the bay leaf, then cover, set to low, and cook for 6 hours. Serve hot.

Nutrition:

Calories: 456

Fat: 36g

Cholesterol: 86mg

Sodium: 1838mg

Potassium: 746mg

Carbs: 15g

Fiber: 4g

Sugar: 7g

Protein: 19g

Breakfast Sausage Casserole

Preparation time: 15 minutes

Cooking time: 3 hours

Servings: 6

Ingredients:

1 lb. pork sausage

½ cup chopped green bell pepper

½ cup chopped red bell pepper

1 tablespoon ghee

12 large eggs

½ cup of coconut milk

1 tablespoon nutritional yeast

1 teaspoon dry rubbed sage

1 teaspoon dried thyme

½ teaspoon garlic powder

½ teaspoon ground black pepper

½ teaspoon salt

½ cup sliced red onion

Directions:

Heat-up a medium cast-iron skillet over medium heat for 2 minutes. Add the pork sausage, then break it into small crumbles.

Cook for 3 minutes. Stir in the black pepper, sea salt, thyme, sage, and garlic powder.

Cook for an additional 5 minutes. Turn the heat off.

Stir in the bell peppers and the chopped onion. Coat the bowl of the slow cooker with ghee.

Add the pork and vegetable mixture into the bottom of the crockpot.

Whisk the coconut milk, nutritional yeast, and the eggs until the eggs are well incorporated together in a large bowl. Pour it into the crockpot on top of the pork mixture.

Cook on low for 2 to 3 hours. Chop into 6 servings.

Nutrition:

Calories: 77 Carbs: 2g Fat: 5g

Protein: 5g

Stuffed Breakfast Peppers

Preparation time: 15 minutes

Cooking time: 45 minutes

Servings: 6

Ingredients:

3 bell peppers halved and seeded

4 eggs

½ cup milk

¾ teaspoon salt

2 tablespoons chopped green onion

¼ cup chopped frozen spinach thawed, squeezed dry

¾ cup shredded cheddar cheese divided

½ cup finely chopped ham

Directions:

Line slow cooker with tin foil. Arrange the peppers in the slow cooker and fill with the remaining fixings. Cook on low within 3-4 hours. Serve.

Nutrition:

Calories: 180

Carbs: 3g

Protein: 8g

Fat: 15g

Cholesterol: 205mg

Sodium: 430mg

Fiber: 1g

Sugar: 2g

Cheese and Sausage Breakfast

Preparation time: 15 minutes

Cooking time: 2 hours

Servings: 8

Ingredients:

2 tablespoon butter, softened

8 oz. breakfast sausage

1 lb. sweet potatoes, peeled and cubed

12 eggs

1 cup milk

¾ teaspoon salt

¼ teaspoon black pepper

4 oz. shredded mild cheddar cheese

Directions:

Coat the slow cooker and inside of the foil collar using softened butter.

Sauté in a large skillet over medium heat, the breakfast sausage until cooked through and browned, about 5 to 8 minutes.

Put the sweet potatoes into a microwave-safe bowl. Add 1 tablespoon water and cover bowl with a damp paper towel—microwave on high within 3 to 4 minutes.

Arrange the sausage and sweet potatoes in the bottom of the slow cooker.

Toss eggs, black pepper, milk, and salt to combine. Add the cheese; stir to mix very well.

Pour the egg/cheese mixture over sausage and sweet potatoes.

Then put 2 layers of paper towels below the slow cooker lid before.

Cook on high for 2 hours. Slice and serve.

Nutrition:

Calories: 326

Carbs: 14g

Protein: 18g

Fat: 22g

Cholesterol: 291mg

Sodium: 650mg

Potassium: 408mg

Fiber: 2g

Sugar: 4g

Mushrooms, Cauliflower, and Zucchini Toast

Preparation time: 15 minutes

Cooking time: 7 hours

Servings: 8

Ingredients:

3-pound boneless beef chuck roast

2 cups keto compliant beef broth

5-7 radishes, cut into halves

1½ cups cauliflower florets

½ cup chopped celery

1/3 cup zucchini rounds

¼ cup chopped orange bell pepper

1 teaspoon xanthan gum (optional to thicken the gravy)

2 sprigs fresh rosemary

Fresh parsley (for garnish)

1 teaspoon Himalayan sea salt

½ teaspoon freshly ground black pepper

1 teaspoon garlic powder

½ teaspoon dried Italian seasoning

1 tablespoon avocado oil or ghee

1 small onion chopped

½ cup sliced mushrooms

1 tablespoon tomato paste

1 teaspoon keto compliant Worcestershire sauce

2 teaspoons coconut aminos

Directions:

Season the roast with Italian seasoning, black pepper, garlic powder, and salt. Let it stand alone for about 27 to 30 minutes.

Add oil to a large skillet on medium-high heat. Add the roast; sear until brown, about 4 minutes on all sides.

Add the diced mushrooms and onions; let them cook for about 1 to 2 minutes until sweet-smelling.

Transfer the roast and the onions to the bottom of a slow cooker, then pour in the broth; then cook on high for 4 hours or low for 7 hours.

Add the vegetables: zucchini, celery, turnips, bell peppers, and cauliflower. Set it again for about 1 hour.

Transfer then shred into chunks with 2 forks.

Sprinkle with diced parsley if preferred. Serve hot with gravy.

Nutrition:

Calories: 345

Total Fat: 21g

Carbs: 4g

Fiber: 1g

Protein: 34g

Pesto Scrambled Eggs

Preparation time: 5 minutes

Cooking time: 4 hours

Servings: 3

Ingredients:

3 large eggs, beaten

1 tablespoon butter

1 tablespoon organic green pesto sauce

2 tablespoon sour cream, full-fat

Salt and pepper to taste

Directions:

In a mixing bowl, combine all fixings.

Cook in the slow cooker on high within 2 hours or on low for 4 hours.

Halfway before the cooking time, use a fork to break the eggs into small pieces. Continue cooking until eggs are well done. Serve.

Nutrition:

Calories: 167 Carbohydrates: 3.3g

Protein: 20.4g Fat: 41.5g

Sugar: g Sodium: 721mg Fiber: 0.7g

Kale and Cheese Omelet

Preparation time: 5 minutes

Cooking time: 4 hours

Servings: 2

Ingredients:

5 eggs, beaten

2 tablespoons onion, chopped

2 teaspoons olive oil

3 ounces kale, chopped

1/3 cup white cheese, grated

Directions:

Mix all fixings in a bowl. Put it in the crockpot. Cook on high within 2 hours or on low for 3 hours.

Nutrition:

Calories: 372 Carbohydrates: 2.1g

Protein: 24.5g Fat: 36.2g

Sugar: 0.2g Sodium: 362mg Fiber: 1.3g

Egg Casserole with Italian Cheeses, Sun-Dried Tomatoes, and Herbs

Preparation time: 5 minutes

Cooking time: 4 hours

Servings: 8

Ingredients:

10 eggs

2 tablespoons milk

3 tablespoons sun-dried tomatoes, chopped

2 tablespoons onion, minced

2 tablespoons basil, chopped

1 tablespoon thyme leaves

Salt and pepper to taste

1 cup mixed Italian cheeses, grated

Directions:

Mix all items in a bowl. Put it inside your slow cooker, and set to cook on high for 2 hours or low for 3 hours.

Nutrition:

Calories: 140 Carbohydrates: 3.87g

Protein: 10.93g

Fat: 8.89g

Sugar: 1.27g

Sodium: 309mg

Fiber: 0.3g

Kale, Mushrooms, And Caramelized Onions

Preparation time: 10 minutes

Cooking time: 4 hours

Servings: 6

Ingredients:

2 teaspoons olive oil

½ tablespoon onion, caramelized

1 red bell pepper, diced

1 cup mushrooms, sliced

2 cups kale, chopped

1 teaspoon dried thyme

10 large eggs, beaten

¼ cup milk

2 cups cheese, shredded

Salt and pepper to taste

Directions:

Place all fixings in the slow cooker. Cook on high within 3 hours or on low for 4 hours.

Nutrition:

Calories: 223

Carbohydrates: 4.6g

Protein: 32.1g

Fat: 36.3g

Sugar: 0.8g

Sodium: 471mg

Fiber: 2.1g

Egg and Cheese Casserole with Chayote Squash

Preparation time: 5 minutes

Cooking time: 4 hours

Servings: 4

Ingredients:

1 teaspoon olive oil

1 red onion, diced

2 small chayote squash, grated

½ small red bell pepper, diced

10 large eggs, beaten

¼ cup low-fat cottage cheese

2 tablespoons milk

½ teaspoon ground cumin

2 cups grated cheesed

Salt and pepper to taste

Directions:

Combine all fixings in a mixing bowl. Pour into the slow cooker.

Cook on high within 3 hours or on low for 4 hours.

Nutrition:

Calories: 209

Carbohydrates: 6.3g

Protein: 35.2g

Fat: 33.6g Sugar: 1.5g

Sodium: 362mg

Fiber: 3.2g

Sausage and Kale Strata

Preparation time: 5 minutes

Cooking time: 4 hours

Servings: 12

Ingredients:

12 eggs, beaten

2 ½ cups milk

Salt and pepper to taste

2 tablespoons fresh oregano, minced

2 pounds breakfast sausages, sliced

1 bunch kale, torn into pieces

16 ounces white mushrooms, sliced

2 ½ cups Monterey Jack cheese, grated

Directions:

Mix all fixings in a large mixing bowl until well combined.

Pour into the slow cooker and close the lid. Set to cook on high within 3 hours or low for 4 hours.

Nutrition:

Calories: 231

Carbohydrates: 4.5g

Protein: 32.3g

Fat: 37.4g

Sugar: 0.6g

Sodium: 525mg

Fiber: 3.2g

Egg Cake Recipe with Peppers, Kale, and Cheddar

Preparation time: 10 minutes

Cooking time: 4 hours

Servings: 6

Ingredients:

1 dozen eggs, beaten

¼ cup milk

¼ cup almond flour

1 clove of garlic, minced

Salt and pepper to taste

1 cup kale, chopped

1 red bell pepper, chopped

¾ cup mozzarella cheese, grated

1 green onion, chopped

Directions:

In a mixing bowl, combine all fixings.

Pour into the slow cooker. Cook on high within 4 hours or on high for 6 hours. Serve.

Nutrition:

Calories: 527

Carbohydrates: 3.1g

Protein: 42.3g

Fat: 45.6g

Sugar: 0.5g

Sodium: 425mg

Fiber: 2.4g

Feta Cheese and Kale Breakfast Casserole

Preparation time: 5 minutes

Cooking time: 4 hours

Servings: 6

Ingredients:

10 ounces kale, chopped

2 teaspoons olive oil

¾ cup feta cheese, crumbled

12 eggs, beaten

Salt and pepper to taste

Directions:

Mix all fixings in a large mixing bowl until well combined.

Put the batter inside the slow cooker, then cook on high for 3 hours or low for 4 hours.

Nutrition:

Calories: 397

Carbohydrates: 4g

Protein: 32.2g

Fat: 29.4g

Sugar: 0.6g

Sodium: 425mg

Fiber: 3.2g

Cauliflower and Ham Casserole

Preparation time: 5 minutes

Cooking time: 4 hours

Servings: 6

Ingredients:

1 head cauliflower, grated

1 cup ham, cubed

½ cup mozzarella cheese, grated

½ cup cheddar cheese, grated

1 onion, chopped

Salt and pepper to taste

10 eggs, beaten

Directions:

Mix all fixings in a bowl. Pour into the slow cooker.

Cook on high within 3 hours or on low for 4 hours.

Nutrition:

Calories: 418

Carbohydrates: 5.2g

Protein: 28.1g

Fat: 42.4g

Sugar: 0.5g

Sodium: 831mg

Fiber: 2.1g

Sausage-Stuffed Eggplants

Preparation time: 10 minutes

Cooking time: 6 hours

Servings: 6

Ingredients:

12 ounces sausage links, chopped

2 cloves of garlic, minced

2 tablespoons rosemary, fresh

Salt and pepper to taste

3 small eggplants, sliced

6 slices mozzarella cheese

Directions:

Mix all items in a bowl. Line a foil at the bottom of the slow cooker.

Grease with cooking spray. Pour into the slow cooker and cook on low for 6 hours or on high for 4 hours.

Nutrition:

Calories: 471

Carbohydrates: 6.3g

Protein: 16.83g

Fat: 38.9g

Sugar: 0.4g

Sodium: 1107mg

Fiber: 3.8g

Zucchini Sausage Breakfast "Bake"

Preparation time: 5 minutes

Cooking time: 4 hours

Servings: 12

Ingredients:

1-pound Italian sausages, chopped

½ cup coconut flour

2 teaspoons baking powder

1 teaspoon salt

½ teaspoon pepper

8 ounces cream cheese

10 large eggs

2 small zucchinis, grated and excess water squeezed

4 cloves of garlic, minced

1 cup cheese, shredded

Directions:

Mix all fixings in a bowl. Set in the slow cooker; cook within 3 hours on high or on low for 4 hours.

Nutrition:

Calories: 344

Carbohydrates: 6.3g

Protein: 21g

Fat: 27g Sugar: 0.4g

Sodium: 736mg

Fiber: 4g

Cheddar Jalapeno Breakfast Sausages

Preparation time: 5 minutes

Cooking time: 6 hours

Servings: 12

Ingredients:

12 medium-sized breakfast sausages

1 jalapeno pepper, chopped

½ cup cheddar cheese, grated

¼ cup heavy cream

Salt and pepper to taste

Directions:

Mix all items in a bowl, then put it into the slow cooker.

Set to cook on low for 6 hours or on high for 4 hours.

Garnish with parsley on top.

Nutrition:

Calories: 472

Carbohydrates: 1.2g

Protein: 32.6g

Fat: 42.4g

Sugar: 0g

Sodium: 731mg

Fiber: 0.4g

Chocolate Peanut Butter Breakfast Bars

Preparation time: 15 minutes

Cooking time: 6 hours

Servings: 12

Ingredients:

4 ounces cream cheese, softened

1 large egg, beaten

2 cups almond flour

½ cup chunky peanut butter

½ cup heavy cream

3 tablespoons stevia sweetener

1 teaspoon vanilla extract

½ cup dark chocolate chips

Directions:

Mix the cream cheese, egg, almond flour, peanut butter, heavy cream, stevia, vanilla extract, and chocolate chips in a large mixing bowl using a hand mixer.

Put the bottom of the slow cooker with foil and grease with cooking spray.

Pour the batter inside the slow cooker and cook for 5 hours or on low or 3 hours on high.

Nutrition:

Calories: 170 Carbohydrates: 4.4g

Protein: 8.1g Fat: 20.5g

Sugar: 1.2g Sodium: 732mg Fiber: 1.7g

CHAPTER 5:

Vegan & Vegetarian

Homemade Vegetable Stock

Preparation time: 15 minutes

Cooking time: 12 hours & 30 minutes

Servings: 4

Ingredients:

4 quarts cold filtered water

12 whole peppercorns

3 peeled and chopped carrots

3 chopped celery stalks

2 bay leaves

4 smashed garlic cloves

1 large quartered onion

2 tablespoons apple cider vinegar

Any other vegetable scraps

Directions:

Put everything in your slow cooker and cover. Do not turn on; let it sit for 30 minutes.

Cook on low for 12 hours. Strain the broth and discard the solids.

Before using, keep the stock in a container in the fridge for 2-3 hours.

Nutrition:

Calories: 11

Protein: 0g

Carbs: 3g

Fat: 0g

Fiber: 0g

Cream of Zucchini Soup

Preparation time: 15 minutes

Cooking time: 2 hours & 10 minutes

Servings: 4

Ingredients:

3 cups vegetable stock

2 pounds chopped zucchini

2 minced garlic cloves

¾ cup chopped onion

¼ cup basil leaves

1 tablespoon extra-virgin olive oil

Salt and pepper to taste

Directions:

Heat-up olive oil in a skillet. When hot, cook garlic and onion for about 5 minutes.

Pour into your slow cooker with the rest of the fixings. Close the lid.

Cook on low for 2 hours. Puree the soup with an immersion blender. Serve.

Nutrition:

Calories: 96

Protein: 7g

Carbs: 11g

Fat: 5g

Fiber: 2.3g

Tomato Soup

Preparation time: 15 minutes

Cooking time: 4 hours

Servings: 4

Ingredients:

1 can crushed tomatoes

1 cup vegetable broth

½ cup heavy cream

2 tablespoons chopped parsley

½ teaspoon onion powder

½ teaspoon garlic powder

Salt and pepper to taste

Directions:

Put all the fixings except heavy cream in the slow cooker, then cook on low for 4 hours.

Blend then stir in the cream using an immersion blender. Taste and season with more salt and pepper if necessary.

Nutrition:

Calories: 165

Protein: 3g

Carbs: 15g

Fat: 13g

Fiber: 3.7g

Vegetable Korma

Preparation time: 15 minutes

Cooking time: 8 hours

Servings: 4

Ingredients:

1 head's worth of cauliflower florets

¾ can of full-fat coconut milk

2 cups chopped green beans

½ chopped onion

2 minced garlic cloves

2 tablespoons curry powder

2 tablespoons coconut flour

1 teaspoon garam masala

Salt and pepper to taste

Directions:

Add vegetables into your slow cooker. Mix coconut milk with seasonings.

Pour into the slow cooker. Sprinkle over coconut flour and mix until blended.

Close and cook on low for 8 hours. Taste and season more if necessary. Serve!

Nutrition:

Calories: 206

Protein: 5g

Carbs: 18g

Fat: 14g

Fiber: 9.5g

Zoodles with Cauliflower-Tomato Sauce

Preparation time: 15 minutes

Cooking time: 3 hours & 31 minutes

Servings: 4

Ingredients:

5 large spiralized zucchinis

Two 24-ounce cans of diced tomatoes

2 small heads' worth of cauliflower florets

1 cup chopped sweet onion

4 minced garlic cloves

½ cup veggie broth

5 teaspoons Italian seasoning

Salt and pepper to taste

Enough water to cover zoodles

Directions:

Put everything but the zoodles into your slow cooker. Cook on high for 3 ½ hours.

Smash into a chunky sauce with a potato masher or another utensil.

To cook the zoodles, boil a large pot of water. When boiling, cook zoodles for just 1 minute, then drain—Season with salt and pepper. Serve sauce over zoodles!

Nutrition:

Calories: 113 Protein: 7g Carbs: 22g

Fat: 2g Fiber: 10.5g

Spaghetti Squash Carbonara

Preparation time: 15 minutes

Cooking time: 8 hours & 10 minutes

Servings: 4

Ingredients:

2 cups of water

One 3-pound spaghetti squash

½ cup coconut bacon

½ cup fresh spinach leaves

1 egg

3 tablespoons heavy cream

3 tablespoons unsweetened almond milk

½ cup grated Parmesan cheese

1 teaspoon garlic powder

Salt and pepper to taste

Directions:

Put squash in your cooker and pour in 2 cups of water. Close the lid.

Cook on low for 8-9 hours. When the spaghetti squash cools, mix egg, cream, milk, and cheese in a bowl.

When the squash is cool enough for you to handle with oven mitts, cut it open lengthwise and scrape out noodles. Mix in the egg mixture right away.

Add spinach and seasonings. Top with coconut bacon and enjoy!

Nutrition:

Calories: 211 Protein: 5g Carbs: 26g

Fat: 11g Fiber: 5.1g

Summery Bell Pepper + Eggplant Salad

Preparation time: 15 minutes

Cooking time: 7 hours

Servings: 4

Ingredients:

One 24-ounce can of whole tomatoes

2 sliced yellow bell peppers

2 small eggplants (smaller ones tend to be less bitter)

1 sliced red onion

1 tablespoon paprika

2 teaspoons cumin

Salt and pepper to taste

A squeeze of lime juice

Directions:

Mix all the fixings in your slow cooker. Close the lid. Cook on low for 7-8 hours.

When time is up, serve warm, or chill in the fridge for a few hours before eating.

Nutrition:

Calories: 128 Protein: 5g Carbs: 27g Fat: 1g

Fiber: 9.7g

Stuffed Eggplant

Preparation time: 15 minutes

Cooking time: 1 hour & 30 minutes

Servings: 6

Ingredients:

1 seeded and chopped green bell pepper

1 tbsp. tomato paste

1 tsp. cumin

1 tsp. raw coconut sugar

2 chopped red onions

3 tbsp. chopped parsley

4 chopped tomatoes

4 minced garlic cloves

4 tbsp. olive oil

6 eggplants

Directions:

Remove eggplant skins with a vegetable peeler. Slice eggplants lengthwise and sprinkle with salt. Set aside for half an hour to sweat.

Place eggplants into your slow cooker. Cook on high 20 minutes.

Sauté onions in a heated pan with olive oil. Stir bell pepper and garlic with onions and sauté for an additional 1 to 2 minutes.

Pour mixture into eggplants into the slow cooker—Cook 20 minutes on high.

Put pepper plus salt and add parsley, tomato paste, cumin, sugar, and tomato. Cook another 10 minutes, stir well and serve!

Nutrition:

Calories: 180

Carbs: 2g

Fat: 13g

Protein: 9g

Bacon Cheddar Broccoli Salad

Preparation time: 15 minutes

Cooking time: 2 hours

Servings: 15

Ingredients:

Dressing:

¼ C. sweetener of choice

1 C. keto mayo

2 tbsp. organic vinegar

Broccoli Salad:

½ diced red onion

4 ounces cheddar cheese

½ pound bacon, cooked and chopped

1 large head broccoli

1/8 C. sunflower seeds

1/8 C. pumpkin seeds

Directions:

For the dressing, whisk all dressing components together, adjusting taste pepper and salt, and add to your slow cooker. Set to a low setting to cook for 2 hours until everything is combined. Serve warm!

Nutrition:

Calories: 189

Carbs: 8g

Fat: 21g

Protein: 8g

Cracked-Out Keto Slaw

Preparation time: 15 minutes

Cooking time: 1 hour & 35 minutes

Servings: 2

Ingredients:

½ C. chopped macadamia nuts

1 tbsp. sesame oil

1 tsp. chili paste

1 tsp. vinegar

2 garlic cloves

2 tbsp. tamari

4 C. shredded cabbage

Directions:

Toss cabbage with chili paste, sesame oil, vinegar, and tamari. Add to slow cooker.

Add minced garlic and mix well. Set to cook on high 1 ½ hours.

Stir in macadamia nuts. Cook 5 minutes more. Garnish with sesame seeds before serving.

Nutrition:

Calories: 360 Carbs: 5g Fat: 33g Protein: 7g

Zucchini Pasta

Preparation time: 15 minutes

Cooking time: 2 hours

Servings: 4

Ingredients:

¼ C. olive oil

½ C. basil

½ tsp. red pepper flakes

1-pint halved cherry tomatoes

1 sliced red onion

2 pounds spiralized zucchini

4 minced garlic cloves

Directions:

Sauté onion and garlic 3 minutes till fragrant in olive oil.

Add zucchini noodles to your slow cooker and season with pepper and salt—Cook 60 minutes on high heat.

Mix in tomatoes, basil, onion, garlic, and red pepper. Cook another 20 minutes.

Add parmesan cheese to slow cooker. Mix thoroughly and cook 10 minutes to melt the cheese. Devour!

Nutrition:

Calories: 181 Carbs: 6g Fat: 13g Protein: 5g

Twice Baked Spaghetti Squash

Preparation time: 15 minutes

Cooking time: 6 hours

Servings: 4

Ingredients:

¼ tsp. Pepper

¼ tsp. salt

½ C. grated parmesan cheese

1 tsp. oregano

2 minced garlic cloves

2 small spaghetti squashes

2 tbsp. butter

4 slices Provolone cheese

Directions:

Cut spaghetti squash in half lengthwise, discarding innards. Set gently into your pot.

Cook on high heat for 4 hours.

Take squash innards and mix with parmesan cheese and butter. Then mix in pepper, salt, garlic, and oregano.

Add squash innards mixture to the middle of cooked squash halves.

Cook on high for another 1-2 hours till middles are deliciously bubbly.

Nutrition:

Calories: 230 Carbs: 4g Fat: 17g Protein: 12g

Mushroom Risotto

Preparation time: 15 minutes

Cooking time: 4 hours

Servings: 4

Ingredients:

¼ C. vegetable broth

1-pound sliced Portobello mushrooms

1-pound sliced white mushrooms

1/3 C. grated parmesan cheese

2 diced shallots

3 tbsp. chopped chives

3 tbsp. coconut oil

4 ½ C. riced cauliflower

4 tbsp. butter

Directions:

Heat-up oil and sauté mushrooms 3 minutes till soft. Discard liquid and set it to the side.

Add oil to skillet and sauté shallots 60 seconds.

Pour all recipe components into your pot and mix well to combine.

Cook 3 hours on high heat. Serve topped with parmesan cheese.

Nutrition:

Calories: 438 Carbs: 5g Fat: 17g Protein: 12g

Vegan Bibimbap

Preparation time: 15 minutes

Cooking time: 45 minutes

Servings: 4

Ingredients:

½ cucumber, sliced into strips

1 grated carrot

1 sliced red bell pepper

1 tbsp. soy sauce

1 tsp. sesame oil

10-ounces riced cauliflower

2 tbsp. rice vinegar

2 tbsp. sesame seeds

2 tbsp. sriracha sauce

4-5 broccoli florets

7-ounces tempeh, sliced into squares

Liquid sweetener

Directions:

In a bowl, combine tempeh squares with 1 tbsp soy sauce and 2 tbsp vinegar. Set aside to soak. Slice veggies.

Add carrot, broccoli, and peppers to slow cooker. Cook on high 30 minutes.

Add cauliflower rice to the slow cooker; cook 5 minutes.

Add sweetener, oil, soy sauce, vinegar, and sriracha to slow cooker. Don't hesitate to add a bit of water if you find the mixture to be too thick.

Nutrition:

Calories: 119 Carbs: 0g Fat: 18g Protein: 8g

Avocado Pesto Kelp Noodles

Preparation time: 15 minutes

Cooking time: 1 hour & 30 minutes

Servings: 2

Ingredients:

Pesto:

¼ C. basil

½ C. extra-virgin olive oil

1 avocado

1 C. baby spinach leaves

1 tsp. salt

1-2 garlic cloves

1 package of kelp noodles

Directions:

Add kelp noodles to slow cooker with just enough water to cover them. Cook on high 45-60 minutes.

In the meantime, combine pesto ingredients in a blender, blending till smooth and incorporated.

Stir in pesto and heat noodle mixture 10 minutes.

Nutrition:

Calories: 321 Carbs: 1g Fat: 32g Protein: 2g

Vegan Cream of Mushroom Soup

Preparation time: 15 minutes

Cooking time: 1 hour & 40 minutes

Servings: 2

Ingredients:

¼ tsp sea salt

½ diced yellow onion

½ tsp. extra-virgin olive oil

1 ½ C. chopped white mushrooms

1 2/3 C. unsweetened almond milk

1 tsp. onion powder

2 C. cauliflower florets

Directions:

Add cauliflower, pepper, salt, onion powder, and milk to slow cooker. Stir and set to cook on high 1 hour.

With olive oil, sauté onions and mushrooms together 8 to 10 minutes till softened.

Allow cauliflower mixture to cool off a bit and add to blender. Blend until smooth. Then blend in mushroom mixture.

Pour back into the slow cooker and heat 30 minutes.

Nutrition:

Calories: 281

Carbs: 3g Fat: 16g Protein: 11g

Creamy Curry Sauce Noodle Bowl

Preparation time: 15 minutes

Cooking time: 2 hours

Servings: 4

Ingredients:

½ head chopped cauliflower

1 diced red bell pepper

1 pack of Kanten Noodles

2 chopped carrots

2 handfuls of mixed greens

Chopped cilantro

Curry Sauce:

¼ C. avocado oil mayo

¼ C. water

¼ tsp./ ginger

½ tsp. pepper

1 ½ tsp. coriander

1 tsp. cumin

1 tsp turmeric

2 tbsp. apple cider vinegar

2 tbsp. avocado oil

2 tsp. curry powder

Directions:

Add all ingredients, minus curry sauce components, to your slow cooker. Set to cook on high 1-2 hours.

In the meantime, add all of the curry sauce ingredients to a blender. Puree until smooth.

Pour over veggie and noodle mixture. Stir well to coat.

Nutrition:

Calories: 110

Carbs: 1g

Fat: 9g

Protein: 7g

Spinach Artichoke Casserole

Preparation time: 15 minutes

Cooking time: 4 hours

Servings: 10

Ingredients:

½ tsp. pepper

¾ C. coconut flour

¾ C. unsweetened almond milk

1 C. grated parmesan cheese

1 tbsp. baking powder

1 tsp. salt

3 minced garlic cloves

5-ounces chopped spinach

6-ounces chopped artichoke hearts

8 eggs

Directions:

Grease the inside of your slow cooker.

Whisk ½ of parmesan cheese, pepper, salt, garlic, artichoke hearts, spinach, eggs, and almond milk.

Add baking powder and coconut flour, combining well.

Spread into the slow cooker. Sprinkle with remaining parmesan cheese.

Cook within 2 to 3 hours on high, or you can cook 4 to 6 hours on a lower heat setting.

Nutrition:

Calories: 141

Carbs: 7g

Fat: 9g

Protein: 10g

Asparagus with Lemon

Preparation time: 15 minutes

Cooking time: 2 hours

Servings: 2

Ingredients:

1 lb. asparagus spears

1 tbsp lemon juice

Directions:

Prepare the seasonings: 2 crushed cloves of garlic and salt and pepper to taste.

Put the asparagus spears on the bottom of the crockpot. Add the lemon juice and the seasonings.

Cook on low for 2 hours.

Nutrition:

Calories: 78

Fat: 2 g

Carbs: 3.7 g

Protein: 9 g

Veggie-Noodle Soup

Preparation time: 15 minutes

Cooking time: 8 hours

Servings: 2

Ingredients:

1/2 cup chopped carrots, chopped

1/2 cup chopped celery, chopped

1 tsp Italian seasoning

7 oz zucchini, cut spiral

2 cups spinach leaves, chopped

Directions:

Except for the zucchini and spinach, add all the ingredients to the crockpot.

Add 3 cups of water.

Cover and cook within 8 hours on low. Add the zucchini and spinach at the last 10 minutes of cooking.

Nutrition:

Calories: 56 Fat: 0.5 g

Carbs: 0.5 g Protein: 3 g

Zucchini and Yellow Squash

Preparation time: 15 minutes

Cooking time: 6 hours

Servings: 2

Ingredients:

2/3 cup zucchini, sliced

2/3 cups yellow squash, sliced

1/3 tsp Italian seasoning

1/8 cup butter

Directions:

Place zucchini and squash on the bottom of the slow cooker.

Sprinkle with the Italian seasoning with salt, pepper, and garlic powder to taste. Top with butter.

Cover and cook within 6 hours on low.

Nutrition:

Calories: 122

Fat: 9.9 g

Carbs: 3.7 g

Protein: 4.2 g

Gluten-Free Zucchini Bread

Preparation time: 15 minutes

Cooking time: 3 hours

Servings: 2

Ingredients:

1/2 cup coconut flour

1/2 tsp baking powder and baking soda

1 egg, whisked

1/4 cup butter

1 cup zucchini, shredded

Directions:

Combine all dry ingredients and add a pinch of salt and sweetener of choice. Combine the dry ingredients with the eggs and mix thoroughly.

Fold in zucchini and spread inside the slow cooker. Cover and cook within 3 hours on high.

Nutrition:

Calories: 174

Fat: 13 g

Carbs: 2.9 g

Protein: 4 g

Eggplant Parmesan

Preparation time: 40 minutes

Cooking time: 4 hours

Servings: 2

Ingredients:

1 large eggplant, 1/2-inch slices

1 egg, whisked

1 tsp Italian seasoning

1 cup marinara

1/4 cup Parmesan cheese, grated

Directions:

Put salt on each side of the eggplant, then let stand for 30 minutes.

Spread some of the marinara on the bottom of the slow cooker and season with salt and pepper, garlic powder, and Italian seasoning.

Spread the eggplants on a single the slow cooker and pour over some of the marinara

sauce. Repeat up to 3 layers. Top with Parmesan. Cover and cook for 4 hours. l

Nutrition:

Calories: 159 Fat: 12 g

Carbs: 8 g Protein: 14 g

Zucchini Lasagna

Preparation time: 15 minutes

Cooking time: 4 hours

Servings: 2

Ingredients:

1 large egg, whisked

1/8 cup Parmesan cheese, grated

1 cup spinach, chopped

2 cups tomato sauce

2 zucchinis, 1/8-inch thick, pre-grilled

Directions:

Mix egg with spinach and parmesan. Spread some of the tomato sauce inside the slow cooker and season with salt and pepper. lo

Spread the zucchini on a single the slow cooker and pour over some of the tomato sauce. Repeat until 3 layers. Top with Parmesan. Cover and cook for 4 hours.

Nutrition:

Calories: 251

Fat: 13.9 g

Carbs: 4.8 g

Protein: 20.8 g

Cauliflower Bolognese on Zucchini Noodles

Preparation time: 15 minutes

Cooking time: 4 hours

Servings: 2

Ingredients:

1 cauliflower head, floret cuts

1 tsp dried basil flakes

28 oz diced tomatoes

1/2 cup vegetable broth

5 zucchinis, spiral cut

Directions:

Place ingredients in the slow cooker except for the zucchini. Season with 2 garlic cloves, 3.4 diced onions, salt, pepper to taste, and desired spices. Cover and cook for 4 hours.

Smash florets of the cauliflower with a fork to form "Bolognese."

Transfer the dish on top of the zucchini noodles.

Nutrition:

Calories: 164 Fat: 5 g Carbs: 6 g Protein: 12 g

Garlic Ranch Mushrooms

Preparation time: 15 minutes

Cooking time: 2 hours

Servings: 2

Ingredients:

1 package of Ranch Dressing

4 packages of whole mushrooms

1 cube butter, melted

Directions:

Place 5 cloves of garlic at the bottom of the slow cooker and pour in the melted butter.

Add in the mushrooms and pour the dressing—season with salt and pepper to taste.

Cover and cook on high within 2 hours.

Nutrition:

Calories: 97

Fat: 20 g

Carbs: 3 g

Protein: 10 g

Easy Creamed Spinach

Preparation time: 15 minutes

Cooking time: 3 hours

Servings: 2

Ingredients:

10 oz spinach, defrosted

3 tbsp Parmesan cheese

3 oz cream cheese

2 tbsp sour cream

Directions:

Combine all the fixings in the slow cooker.

Add some seasonings: salt and pepper to taste and half a teaspoon of onion and garlic powder. Mix thoroughly—cover and cook within 3 hours on low.

Nutrition:

Calories: 165

Fat: 13.22 g

Carbs: 3.63 g

Protein: 7.33 g

Garlic Tomato, Zucchini, and Yellow Squash

Preparation time: 15 minutes

Cooking time: 6 hours

Servings: 3

Ingredients:

1 medium yellow squash, quartered, sliced

1 medium zucchini, quartered, sliced

1 tomato, cut into wedges

½ teaspoon Italian seasoning

¼ teaspoon of sea salt

2 tablespoons parmesan cheese or Asiago cheese, grated

Pepper to taste

½ teaspoon garlic powder

2 tablespoons cold butter, cubed

Directions:

Add squash, tomato, and zucchini in the slow cooker. Sprinkle salt, garlic powder, garlic slices, pepper, and Italian seasoning.

Place butter cubes all over the vegetables, then sprinkle cheese on top. Close the lid. Cook on 'Low' for 4-6 hours or until tender. Stir and serve.

Nutrition:

Calories126 Fat 10.2g Carbohydrate 6g

Protein 4.9g

Parmesan Zucchini and Tomato Gratin

Preparation time: 15 minutes

Cooking time: 4 hours

Servings: 3

Ingredients:

3 small zucchinis, sliced

1 small onion, chopped

1 medium tomato, sliced

¼ cup parmesan cheese, shredded

1 tablespoon garlic, minced

½ teaspoon garlic powder

1 teaspoon dried basil

1 tablespoon olive oil + extra to drizzle

¼ teaspoon salt

Directions:

Place a skillet over medium heat. Put the oil, then onions, and cook until soft. Add garlic and cook until fragrant.

Transfer into the slow cooker. Place alternate layers of zucchini slices and a tomato slice.

Drizzle olive oil all over the top layer. Sprinkle dried herbs, salt, garlic powder, and finally, Parmesan cheese. Close the lid. Cook on 'Low' for 3-4 hours or until tender.

Nutrition:

Calories 89 Fat 5.5g Carbohydrate 9.1g

Protein 3.1g

Slow-Cooked Summer Vegetables

Preparation time: 15 minutes

Cooking time:

45 minutes

Servings: 5

Ingredients:

1 cup okra slices

1 medium onion, chopped into chunks

1 medium zucchini, sliced

½ cup grape tomatoes

1 yellow bell pepper, sliced

½ cup mushroom, sliced

¼ cup olive oil

¼ cup balsamic vinegar

½ tablespoon fresh thyme, chopped

1 tablespoon fresh basil, chopped

Directions:

Put all the fixings into the slow cooker and stir well. Close the lid. Cook on 'High' for 45 minutes. Serve.

Nutrition:

Calories 125 Fat 10.4g Carbohydrate 7.9g

Protein 1.8g

Cheesy Cauliflower Garlic Bread

Preparation time: 15 minutes

Cooking time: 4 hours

Servings: 6

Ingredients:

1 ½ pounds cauliflower, grated to a rice-like texture

4 cups mozzarella cheese, shredded, divided

3 teaspoons garlic

2 teaspoons red pepper flakes

Pepper to taste

6 teaspoons Italian seasoning

6 tablespoons coconut flour

1 teaspoon salt

4 large eggs, beaten

Cooking spray

Directions:

Grease the instant pot with cooking spray. Add all the ingredients (left out 2 cups of cheese and garlic) into a bowl and mix it until well.

Transfer into the slow cooker. Scatter garlic and remaining cheese on top.

Close the lid. Cook on 'High' for 2-4 hours or until brown and crisp. Cut slices and serve.

Nutrition:

Calories 184 Fat 11.2g

Carbohydrate 9.5g Protein 13.7g

Cheesy Cauliflower Gratin

Preparation time: 15 minutes

Cooking time: 4 hours & 10 minutes

Servings: 3

Ingredients:

2 cups cauliflower florets

3 tablespoons heavy whipping cream

3 deli slices pepper Jack cheese

2 tablespoons butter

Salt to taste

Pepper to taste

Directions:

Add cauliflower, cream, butter, salt, and pepper into the slow cooker. Close the lid. Cook on 'Low' for 3-4 hours or until tender.

When done, mash with a fork. Taste and adjust the seasoning if necessary.

Place cheese slices on top. Cover and cook within 10 minutes or until cheese melts. Serve right away.

Nutrition:

Calories 216 Fat 19.3g

Carbohydrate 4g Protein 5.7g

Creamy Ricotta Spaghetti Squash

Preparation time: 15 minutes

Cooking time: 6 hours

Servings: 8

Ingredients:

2 spaghetti squash, halved, deseeded

2 teaspoons garlic powder

4 tablespoons fresh basil or parsley, chopped

2 cups part-skim ricotta cheese

2 teaspoons lemon zest, grated

Salt to taste

Pepper to taste

Cooking spray

Directions:

Spray the cut part of the spaghetti squash with cooking spray. Place it in the slow cooker with the cut side facing down.

Close the lid. Cook on 'Low' for 4-6 hours or until tender. When done, using a fork, scrape the squash, and add into a bowl.

Add ricotta cheese, lemon zest, garlic powder, salt, pepper, and basil and mix well.

Nutrition:

Calories112 Fat 5.4g

Carbohydrate 9.1g Protein 7.7g

Creamy Keto Mash

Preparation time: 15 minutes

Cooking time: 2 hours

Servings: 8

Ingredients:

2 large heads cauliflower, chopped into small floret's

4 cloves garlic, minced

1 large onion, chopped

8 tablespoons butter or ghee+ extra to top

1 cup cream cheese or sour cream

½ cup of water

Salt to taste

Pepper to taste

Directions:

Place the cauliflower florets in the slow cooker. Pour about ½ a cup of water.

Close the lid. Cook on 'Low' for 1-2 hours or until tender.

Place a skillet over medium heat. Add 2 tablespoons butter or ghee. When it melts, add onions and garlic and sauté until the onions are translucent.

Add remaining butter and stir, then remove from heat. Transfer into a blender. Add cauliflower and blend until smooth or blend in the food processor. Add cream cheese and pulse until well combined.

Transfer into a bowl, then add salt and pepper to taste. Top with butter plus ghee and serve.

Nutrition:

Calories 219 Fat 21.7g

Carbohydrate 4.3g Protein 3.1g

Keto Zupa Toscana Soup

Preparation time: 10 minutes

Cooking time: 4 hours

Servings: 10

Ingredients:

1 lb. hot or mild ground Italian sausage

1 medium onion, finely chopped

1 tbsp oil

36 oz. veggie stock

3 minced garlic cloves

1 large head cauliflower

3 cups diced kale

¼ tsp mashed red pepper flakes

½ cup heavy cream

1 tsp salt

½ tsp pepper

Directions:

Heat-up a skillet and brown the ground sausage over medium heat until ready.

Remove the sausage with a slotted spoon then transfer to a 6-qt slow cooker. Throw away the grease.

Using the same skillet, pour the oil into the skillet then sauté the onions for 3 to 4 minutes or until transparent.

Pour the onions, veggie stock, kale, cauliflower florets, pepper, mashed red pepper flakes, and salt into the slow cooker then mix until well combined.

Cook for 4 hours on high or 8 hours on low. Pour in the heavy cream then stir until well mixed.

Serve immediately.

Nutrition:

Calories: 246

Carbs: 7g

Protein: 14g

Fat: 19g

Keto Spinach-Feta Quiche

Preparation time: 20 minutes

Cooking time: 7 to 8 hours

Servings: 4

Ingredients:

2 cups fresh spinach

8 eggs

2 cups of milk

½ cup shredded Parmesan cheese

¾ cup crumbled feta cheese

¼ cup shredded cheddar cheese

2 garlic cloves, minced

¼ tsp salt

Directions:

Mix the eggs plus milk in a large bowl.

Add the spinach, feta cheese, garlic, Parmesan cheese, and salt, then stir until well combined.

Put the batter into the greased slow cooker then sprinkle cheddar cheese on top.

Cover then cook for 7 to 8 hours on low.

Nutrition:

Calories: 337

Carbs: 9.4g

Protein: 25g

Fat: 22.4g

Cheesy Zucchini-Asparagus Frittata

Preparation time: 30 minutes

Cooking time: 1 hour 10 minutes

Servings: 6

Ingredients:

8 oz. asparagus, trimmed then sliced diagonally into 2" pieces

3 tbsp olive oil

1 medium-size zucchini, cut into ½" thickness

2 medium-size shallots, diced

12 large eggs

1 cup Parmesan cheese, grated

¼ cup minced fresh basil (or flat-leaf parsley leaves)

Fresh ground black pepper

Sea salt

Directions:

Heat-up oil in a medium-size skillet over medium-high heat then add the asparagus, shallots, and zucchini. Cook for some minutes until the asparagus starts to soften and the zucchini a bit browned.

Remove the veggies from heat then let it cool for 10 minutes. Grease the bottom and sides about 2" up of your 5 to 7 qt oval slow cooker using a cooking spray and then pour the cooled veggies into the slow cooker.

Beat the eggs, basil, and parmesan together in a medium-size bowl, then add a small salt and some black pepper. Put the batter inside the slow cooker, then mix until the veggies are well mixed.

Cover the cooker then cook for 60 to 70 minutes on high until ready. Slice into 4 portions, then use a spatula to lift it out into plates. Serve at once.

Nutrition:

Calories: 520

Carbs: 4g

Protein: 41g

Fat: 37g

Slow-Cooked Yellow Squash Zucchini

Preparation time: 5 minutes

Cooking time: 6 hours

Servings: 6

Ingredients:

2 medium yellow squash, sliced and quartered

2 medium zucchinis, sliced and quartered

¼ tsp pepper

1 tsp Italian seasoning

1 tsp powdered garlic

¼ cup Asiago or Parmesan cheese, grated

¼ cup butter, cubed

½ tsp sea salt

Directions:

Combine the sliced yellow squash and zucchini in your slow cooker. Sprinkle Italian seasoning, pepper, sea salt, and garlic powder on top.

Place the butter pieces, and cheese on top. Cover the cooker then cook for 4 to 6 hours on low.

Nutrition:

Calories: 122 Carbs: 5.4g

Protein: 4.2g Fat: 9.9g

Cabbage, Kielbasa, and Onion Soup

Preparation Time: 5 Minutes

Cooking Time: 8 Hours

Servings: 6

Ingredients:

2 ½ lb. cabbage head, cut into wedges

1 cup vegetable broth

1 onion, thinly sliced

1 tbsp. brown mustard

½ tsp black pepper

1 lb. kielbasa, sliced into 3-inch pieces

½ tsp kosher salt

Cooking spray, as required

Directions:

Put all the items in the slow cooker, excluding the kielbasa, and combine them well.

Make sure that the cabbage is well coated with the seasoning broth mixture.

Now, top it with the kielbasa and cover the slow cooker.

Cook for 7 hours on low heat. Stir it again and cook it for an additional 1 hour.

Nutrition:

Calories: 278 Carbs: 11g

Protein: 11.8g Fat: 21g

Parmesan Mushrooms

Preparation Time: 5 Minutes

Cooking Time: 4 Hours

Servings: 4

Ingredients:

16 oz. cremini mushrooms, fresh

½ oz. ranch dressing mix

2 tbsp. parmesan cheese, add more if desired

½ cup butter, melted and unsalted

Directions

Place the mushrooms in the slow cooker.

Combine melted butter and ranch dressing in a small-sized bowl. Stir in the butter mixture over the mushrooms and mix well.

Now, toss the parmesan cheese over the top. Cover the slow cooker and cook for 4 hours on low heat.

Nutrition:

Calories: 240

Carbs: 4g

Protein: 4.9g

Fat: 24g

Mashed Garlic Cauliflower

Preparation Time: 5 Minutes

Cooking Time: 6 Hours

Servings: 6

Ingredients:

2 medium cauliflower head, sliced into florets

3 tbsp. butter

4 garlic cloves

2 tsp Celtic sea salt

8 to 10 cups of water

½ tsp black pepper

Dill, to taste

Directions:

Place the garlic and cauliflower along with a sufficient amount of water in the slow cooker.

Cook within 6 hours on low heat or until the cauliflower becomes tender.

Discard the water then place the cauliflower in the food processor. Add butter, then pulse until it is mashed.

Now, to this, stir in the seasoning and check for taste. Finally, toss the herbs into it and serve it immediately.

Nutrition:

Calories: 58

Carbs: 0.5g

Protein: 0.2g

Fat: 1.4g

Broccoli Cheddar Soup

Preparation Time: 10 Minutes

Cooking Time: 6 to 8 hours

Servings: 20

Ingredients:

1 ½ lb. broccoli

2 tbsp. butter

1 medium onion, chopped

2 leeks, rinsed and trimmed

2 cups heavy cream

1 cauliflower, medium head

2 cups parmesan cheese, grated

5 garlic cloves, minced

4 cups of sharp cheddar cheese, shredded

32 oz. chicken broth

Salt and pepper, to taste

Directions:

Heat-up a medium-sized skillet over medium heat. Stir in the onion, garlic, butter, salt, and pepper and cook until the onions become translucent and caramelized.

After that, take the slow cooker and heat it on high and then toss the cauliflower, leeks, and broccoli to it.

Pour in the heavy cream, broth along with salt and pepper, and combine them well.

Stir in the caramelized onions and mix well until well incorporated.

Cook in the slow cooker within 5 to 6 hours on high heat. Once it is cooked, mash the vegetables.

Finally, add the parmesan and cheddar cheese, salt plus pepper, and cook them for another additional hour. Serve.

Nutrition:

Calories: 235 Carbs: 5g

Protein: 13g Fat: 18g

Elbows Casserole

Preparation Time: 5 Minutes

Cooking Time: 5 ½ Hours

Servings: 4

Ingredients:

1 packet low carb elbows or ravioli, cooked

¼ cup Romano cheese, preferably grated

¼ cup black olives, sliced

2 cup low carb BBQ sauce

2 cup mushrooms, preferably sliced

1 cup of small curd cottage cheese

Directions:

Coat your slow cooker with oil.

Spoon the BBQ sauce into it and then top with ½ of the cooked elbows, half of the Romano cheese and mushrooms along with 2 tbsp of the olives.

Continue layering with the remaining ingredients.

Cook within 5 ½ hours on low heat or until cooked.

Sprinkle with the cottage cheese and cook again for another half an hour.

Nutrition:

Calories: 400 Carbs: 9.6g

Protein: 10.5g Fat: 30.5g

Cheesy Beer Dip Salsa

Preparation Time: 5 Minutes

Cooking Time: 4 Hours

Servings: 5 ½ cups

Ingredients:

16 oz. salsa

2/3 cup beer

1 lb. American cheese, shredded

8 oz. cream cheese, sliced

8 oz. Monterey jack cheese, shredded

Directions:

Begin by combining all the ingredients until they are properly mixed.

Cover the slow cooker and cook for 4 hours on low heat. Serve immediately.

Nutrition:

Calories: 177

Carbs: 5g

Protein: 9g

Fat: 14g

Brussels Sprout Dip

Preparation Time: 10 minutes

Cooking Time: 1 to 2 hours

Servings: 4

Ingredients:

1 lb. Brussels sprouts, quartered

¼ cup parmesan cheese, grated

1 garlic clove, unpeeled

¼ cup sour cream

1 tbsp. olive oil

½ tsp thyme, chopped

¾ cup mozzarella, shredded

4 oz. cream cheese, room temperature

Salt and pepper, to taste

¼ cup mayonnaise

Directions:

Combine Brussels sprouts with pepper, olive oil, and salt and then spread them in a baking sheet in a single layer along with garlic.

Roast in a preheated oven at 400 degrees F for about 25 to 30 minutes while flipping them repeatedly.

Place all the other remaining ingredients into the slow cooker and stir well. Stir in the Brussels sprouts. Cook within 1 to 2 hours on high heat or until the cheese has melted.

Nutrition:

Calories: 196 Carbs: 6g

Protein: 13g Fat: 33g

Braised Cabbage

Preparation Time: 5 Minutes

Cooking Time: 5 Hours

Servings: 2

Ingredients:

1 green cabbage head, tough ends discarded and cut into 12 wedges

½ cup bone broth

1 sweet onion, preferably large and chopped

¼ cup bacon fat, melted

4 garlic cloves

Celtic sea salt, preferably coarse

caraway seeds

Directions:

Heat the slow cooker on high heat and then add melted bacon fat and onions to it.

After that, place the cabbage wedges in a layer in the slow cooker. Spoon the broth over it along with the salt and caraway seeds.

Cover the slow cooker, then cook within 1 hour. In between, stir the cabbage once to shift the top ones to the bottom. Pour in more stock if required.

Cook it again for another 4 hours on high heat. Once cooked, you can add some apple cider vinegar if you like.

Nutrition:

Calories: 122 Carbs: 2g

Protein: 8.7g Fat: 3.4g

CHAPTER 6:

Appetizers & Snacks

Asparagus Bacon Bouquet

Preparation time: 15 minutes

Cooking time: 4 hours

Servings: 4

Ingredients:

8 asparagus spears, trimmed

8 slices bacon

1 tsp black pepper

Extra virgin olive oil

Directions:

Coat slow cooker with extra virgin olive oil.

Slice spears in half, and sprinkle with black pepper

Wrap three spear halves with one slice bacon, and set inside the slow cooker.

Cook for 4 hours on medium.

Nutrition:

Calories 345

Carbs 2 g

Fat 27 g

Protein 22 g

Sodium 1311 mg

Sugar 0 g

Creamy Asiago Spinach Dip

Preparation time: 15 minutes

Cooking time: 4 hours

Servings: 6

Ingredients:

6 cups spinach, wash, chopped

½ cup artichoke hearts

½ cup cream cheese

½ cup Asiago cheese, grated

½ cup almond milk

1 tsp black pepper

Extra virgin olive oil

Directions:

Coat slow cooker with olive oil.

Place cream cheese and almond milk in a blender, and mix until smooth.

Finely chop spinach, add to blender along with salt and black pepper, and mix.

Place spinach mixture in a blender, add artichoke hearts and mix in with a spatula.

Sprinkle Asiago cheese on top, and cook on medium for 4 hours.

Serve dip with a selection of veggies like broccoli florets and carrot sticks.

Nutrition:

Calories 214

Carbs 4 g

Fat 19 g

Protein 8 g

Sodium 380 mg

Sugar 1 g

Madras Curry Chicken Bites

Preparation time: 15 minutes

Cooking time: 7 hours

Servings: 4

Ingredients:

1 lb. chicken breasts, skinless, boneless

4 cloves garlic, grated

1 tsp ginger, grated

2 cups low-sodium chicken stock

2 lemons, juiced

1 tsp coriander, crushed

1 tsp cumin

½ tsp fenugreek

1 tbsp curry powder

½ tsp cinnamon

1½ tsp salt

1 tsp black pepper

Extra virgin olive oil

Directions:

Cube chicken breast into ½" pieces, and sprinkle with ½ tsp salt and ½ tsp black pepper.

Heat 3 tbsp extra virgin olive oil in a skillet, add chicken breasts, and brown.

Place chicken breasts in a slow cooker.

Add chicken stock, garlic, lemon juice, spices, and salt.

Cook on low for 7 hours.

Nutrition:

Calories 234

Carbs 3 g

Fat 8 g

Protein 38 g

Sodium 782 mg

Sugar 0 g

Spiced Jicama Wedges with Cilantro Chutney

Preparation time: 15 minutes

Cooking time: 4 hours

Servings: 8

Ingredients:

1 lb. jicama, peeled

1 tsp paprika

½ tsp dried parsley

2 tsp salt

2 tsp black pepper

Extra virgin olive oil

Cilantro Chutney

1 tsp dill chopped

¼ cup cilantro

½ tsp salt

1 tsp paprika

1tsp black pepper

2 lemons, juiced

¼ cup extra virgin olive oil

Directions:

Slice jicama into 1" wedges, and submerge in a bowl of cold water for 20 minutes.

Place the paprika, oregano, salt, black pepper in a bowl, and toss with jicama.

Add 5 tbsp extra virgin olive oil into a bowl and coat well.

Place jicama in the slow cooker, and cook on high for 4 hours.

Combine ingredients for chutney in blender, mix, and refrigerate until jicama wedges are ready to serve.

Nutrition:

Calories 94

Carbs 5.2 g

Fat 8 g

Protein 1 g

Sodium 879 mg

Sugar 1 g

Teriyaki Chicken Wings

Preparation time: 15 minutes

Cooking time: 4 hours

Servings: 4

Ingredients

2 lb. chicken wings

2 tsp ginger, grated

4 cloves garlic, grated

¼ cup of soy sauce

4 dates, pitted

Extra virgin olive oil

Directions

Processed the dates in a food processor along with 2 tbsp soy sauce, and mix until pasty.

Combine ginger, garlic, soy sauce, and dates in a bowl, add chicken wings, coat, and refrigerate overnight.

Coat slow cooker with a little sesame oil, add chicken wings and cook on high for 4 hours.

Nutrition:

Calories 354

Carbs 5.5 g

Fat 16 g

Protein 45 g

Sodium 730 mg

Sugar 0 g

Portabella Pizza Bites

Preparation time: 15 minutes

Cooking time: 5 hours

Servings: 8

Ingredients:

8 Portabella Mushrooms

½ lb. ground pork

1 medium onion, diced

4 cloves garlic, grated

2 cups crushed tomato

½ cup Mozzarella, shredded

¼ cup Parmesan

½ tsp oregano

1 tsp salt

1 tsp black pepper

Garnish

½ cup parsley, chopped

Directions:

Coat 6 qt. slow cooker with extra virgin olive oil

Heat 3 tbsp extra virgin olive oil in a skillet, add pork, brown.

Mix crushed tomato with salt, black pepper, oregano, parmesan, and garlic.

Spoon a little tomato-parmesan mixture into each mushroom, add a little ground pork, and sprinkle with Mozzarella.

Place each mushroom in a slow cooker. Cook pizza bites on medium for 5 hours.

Sprinkle a little parsley on top before serving.

Nutrition:

Calories 106

Carbs 5.6 g

Fat 3 g

Protein 13 g

Sodium 421 mg

Sugar 2 g

Candied Walnuts

Preparation time: 15 minutes

Cooking time: 2 hours & 30 minutes

Servings: 16

Ingredients:

½ cup unsalted butter

1-pound walnuts

½ cup Splenda, granular

1½ teaspoons ground cinnamon

¼ teaspoon ground allspice

¼ teaspoon ground ginger

1/8 teaspoon ground cloves

Directions:

Set a slow cooker on high and preheat for about 15 minutes. Add butter and walnuts and stir to combine.

Add the Splenda and stir to combine well. Cook, covered, for about 15 minutes.

Uncover the slow cooker and stir the mixture. Set to cook on low, uncovered, within 2 hours, stirring occasionally.

Transfer the walnuts to a bowl. In another small bowl, mix spices.

Sift spice mixture over walnuts and toss to coat evenly. Set aside to cool before serving.

Nutrition:

Calories: 227 Carbohydrates: 10.5g

Protein: 6.9g Fat: 22.5g

Sugar: 7g Sodium: 42mg

Fiber: 2.1g

Flavorful Pecans

Preparation time: 15 minutes

Cooking time: 2 hours & 30 minutes

Servings: 16

Ingredients:

1-pound pecan halves

¼ cup butter, melted

1 teaspoon dried oregano

1 teaspoon dried basil

1 teaspoon dried thyme

1 tablespoon red chili powder

½ teaspoon onion powder

¼ teaspoon garlic powder

¼ teaspoon cayenne pepper

Salt, to taste

Directions:

Combine all fixings in a large slow cooker.

Cook in the slow cooker on high and cook, covered, for about 15 minutes.

Uncover the slow cooker and stir the mixture.

Cook on low, uncovered, within 2 hours, mixing occasionally.

Transfer the pecans into a bowl and keep aside to cool before serving.

Nutrition:

Calories: 225

Carbohydrates: 4.5g

Protein: 3.2g

Fat: 23.2g

Sugar: 1.1g

Sodium: 37mg

Fiber: 3.3g

Herb Flavored Almonds

Preparation time: 15 minutes

Cooking time: 2 hours

Servings: 16

Ingredients:

2 cups of raw almonds

1 tablespoon olive oil

1 tablespoon dried rosemary

1 tablespoon dried thyme

Salt

ground black pepper

Directions:

Mix all the fixings in a large slow cooker.

Cook in the slow cooker on high and cook, covered, for about 1½ hours, stirring after every 30 minutes. Cool before serving.

Nutrition:

Calories: 77 Carbohydrates: 2.8g

Protein: 2.5g Fat: 6.9g

Sugar: 0.5g

Sodium: 12mg

Fiber: 1.6g

Ultra-Spicy Almonds

Preparation time: 15 minutes

Cooking time: 2 hours & 30 minutes

Servings: 32

Ingredients:

2½ tablespoons coconut oil

4 cups of raw almonds

3 garlic cloves, minced

1 teaspoon smoked paprika

2 teaspoons red chili powder

1 teaspoon ground cumin

1 teaspoon onion powder

Salt

ground black pepper

Directions:

Set a slow cooker on high and preheat for about 25 minutes.

Add all ingredients and stir to combine.

Cook on low, uncovered, for about 2 hours, stirring occasionally.

Then, in high and cook, uncovered, within 30 minutes.

Cool before serving.

Nutrition:

Calories: 80

Carbohydrates: 2.9g

Protein: 2.6g

Fat: 7.1g

Sugar: 0.6g

Sodium: 6mg

Fiber: 1.6g

Tastier Nuts Combo

Preparation time: 15 minutes

Cooking time: 2 hours

Servings: 32

Ingredients:

1 cup hazelnuts, toasted and skins removed

1 cup whole almonds, toasted

1 cup pecan halves, toasted

1 cup whole cashews

½ cup Erythritol

1/3 cup butter, melted

½ teaspoon ground cinnamon

½ teaspoon ground ginger

¼ teaspoon ground cloves

¼ teaspoon cayenne pepper

Directions:

In a large slow cooker, add all fixings and stir to combine.

Set on low, covered, cook for about 2 hours, stirring once after 1 hour.

Uncover the slow cooker and stir nuts again.

Transfer nuts onto a sheet of buttered foil to cool for at least 1 hour before serving.

Nutrition:

Calories: 101

Carbohydrates: 3.1g

Protein: 2.1g

Fat: 0.6g

Sugar: 0.6g

Sodium: 14mg

Fiber: 1.2g

Zesty Chicken Wings

Preparation time: 15 minutes

Cooking time: 7 hours & 12 minutes

Servings: 8

Ingredients:

For Sauce:

¼ cup low-sodium soy sauce

¼ cup fresh lime juice

2 tablespoons Erythritol

1 teaspoon Sriracha

1 teaspoon ginger powder

2 garlic cloves, minced

1 teaspoon fresh lime zest, grated finely

For Wings:

2 pounds grass-fed chicken wings

4 teaspoons arrowroot starch

1 tablespoon water

Directions:

For the sauce: Put all sauce fixings in a large bowl, and beat until well combined.

Put chicken wings at the bottom of a slow cooker, and top with sauce evenly.

Set on low setting and cook, covered, for about 6-7 hours.

Dissolve arrowroot starch in water in a small bowl.

Uncover the slow cooker and stir in arrowroot mixture until well combined.

Cook on high, covered, for about 10-12 minutes.

Serve immediately.

Nutrition:

Calories: 456

Carbohydrates: 12.6g

Protein: 66.8g

Fat: 16.9g

Sugar: 8.6g

Sodium: 1084mg

Fiber: 0.2g

Buffalo Chicken Meatballs

Preparation time: 15 minutes

Cooking time: 2 hours & 5 minutes

Servings: 4

Ingredients:

1-pound ground grass-fed chicken

1 organic egg

1/3 cup almond meal

2 scallions, sliced thinly

2 garlic cloves, minced

Salt

black pepper, ground

¾ cup sugar-free buffalo sauce

Directions:

Preheat the oven to 400 degrees F.

In a bowl, add all ingredients except buffalo sauce and mix until well combined.

Make 1½-inch balls from chicken mixture.

Arrange meatballs onto a baking sheet and bake for about 5 minutes.

Remove from oven and transfer meatballs into a slow cooker with buffalo sauce, stir.

Cook on low, then covered, for about 2 hours. Serve immediately.

Nutrition:

Calories: 283

Carbohydrates: 3g

Protein: 36.1g

Fat: 13.5g

Sugar: 0.6g

Sodium: 224mg

Fiber: 1.2g

Foolproof Beef Meatballs

Preparation time: 15 minutes

Cooking time: 7 hours & 5 minutes

Servings: 8

Ingredients:

2 pounds ground lean grass-fed beef

2 organic eggs, beaten

1 medium yellow onion, chopped

2 garlic cloves, minced

¼ cup fresh parsley leaves, chopped

½ teaspoon red pepper flakes, crushed

¼ teaspoon cayenne pepper

Salt

ground black pepper

2 tablespoons olive oil

Directions:

Mix all items except oil in a bowl. Make desired size balls from the mixture.

Heat-up oil over medium-high heat in a large skillet, then cook meatballs for 4-5 minutes or until golden brown from all sides.

Transfer the meatballs into a greased slow cooker.

Cook in the slow cooker on low, covered, for about 7 hours. Serve hot.

Nutrition:

Calories: 264

Carbohydrates: 10.8g

Protein: 36.1g

Fat: 11.7g

Sugar: 0.7g

Sodium: 508mg

Fiber: 0g

Super-Tasty Pork Meatballs

Preparation time: 15 minutes

Cooking time: 6 hours & 20 minutes

Servings: 8

Ingredients:

2 pounds lean ground pork

1 cup Cheddar cheese, shredded

1 large organic egg

¼ cup yellow onion, chopped

¼ teaspoon ground allspice

1 tablespoon water

4 tablespoons unsalted butter

1½ cups heavy whipping cream

1½ cups homemade chicken broth

1 tablespoon Worcestershire sauce

1 tablespoon Dijon mustard

Directions:

Warm-up, the oven to 400 degrees F, then line a large baking dish with parchment paper.

In a large bowl, add ground pork, cheddar cheese, egg, onion, allspice, and water and mix until well combined.

Make 1½-inch balls from pork mixture.

Arrange the meatballs onto a prepared baking dish and bake for about 20 minutes.

Meanwhile, in a small skillet, add butter, heavy cream, and broth and bring to a gentle boil over medium heat.

Adjust to low and simmer for about 20 minutes, stirring occasionally.

Stir in Worcestershire sauce and mustard and remove from heat.

In a slow cooker, add sauce and meatballs and stir.

Cook in the slow cooker on low, covered, for about 4-6 hours. Serve immediately.

Nutrition:

Calories: 358

Carbohydrates: 1.9g

Protein: 29.2g

Fat: 25.8g

Sugar: 0.8g

Sodium: 398mg

Fiber: 0.2g

Inspiring Sausage Sliders

Preparation time: 15 minutes

Cooking time: 5 hours

Servings: 10

Ingredients:

2 cups sugar-free ketchup

¼ cup Erythritol

1 tablespoon Worcestershire sauce

2 teaspoons mustard

1 teaspoon hot sauce

1 medium yellow onion, chopped finely

½ cup homemade chicken broth

2 pounds pork sausage, cut into ½-inch rounds

Directions:

In a large slow cooker, add all items and stir to combine.

Cook on low, covered, for about 4-5 hours.

Serve immediately.

Nutrition:

Calories: 365

Carbohydrates: 13.7g

Protein: 19g

Fat: 26.2g

Sugar: 11.8g

Sodium: 1280mg

Fiber: 0.5g

Potluck Party Peppers

Preparation time: 15 minutes

Cooking time: 9 hours

Servings: 10

Ingredients:

1½ pounds mini sweet peppers, seeded and tops removed

1-pound ground Italian sausage

1 (24-ounce) jar sugar-free spaghetti sauce

8-ounce mozzarella cheese, shredded

Directions:

Stuff each pepper evenly with sausage.

Lightly greased slow cooker, arrange peppers. Cook on low, covered, for about 6-8 hours.

Uncover the crockpot and top each pepper with mozzarella cheese.

Cook, covered for about 10 minutes. Serve hot.

Nutrition:

Calories: 248

Carbohydrates: 9.6g

Protein: 15.6g

Fat: 16g

Sugar: 7.5g

Sodium: 824mg

Fiber: 1.8g

Perfect Eggplant Tapenade

Preparation time: 15 minutes

Cooking time: 9 hours

Servings: 2

Ingredients:

2 cups eggplants, chopped

1 cup tomatoes, chopped

3 garlic cloves, minced

2 teaspoons capers

2 teaspoons fresh lemon juice

1 teaspoon dried basil

Salt, to taste

Pinch of ground black pepper

Directions:

In a slow cooker, add eggplant, tomatoes, garlic, and capers and mix well.

Cook on low, covered, for about 7-9 hours.

Uncover the slow cooker and stir in the remaining ingredients. Serve hot.

Nutrition:

Calories: 46

Carbohydrates: 10.1g

Protein: 2g

Fat: 0.4g

Sugar: 5g

Sodium: 170mg

Fiber: 4.2g

Swiss Style Cheese Fondue

Preparation time: 15 minutes

Cooking time: 3 hours & 10 minutes

Servings: 6

Ingredients:

1 clove garlic, cut in half

2½ cups homemade chicken broth

3 tablespoons fresh lemon juice

16 ounces Swiss cheese, shredded

8 ounces Cheddar cheese, shredded

3 tablespoons almond flour

Pinch of ground nutmeg

Pinch of paprika

Pinch of ground black pepper

Directions:

Rub a pan evenly with cut garlic halves. Add broth and place pan over medium heat.

Cook until mixture is just beginning to bubble. Adjust to low, then stir in lemon juice.

Meanwhile, in a bowl, mix cheeses and flour. Slowly, add cheese mixture to broth, stirring continuously.

Cook until cheese mixture becomes thick, stirring continuously. Transfer the cheese mixture to a greased crockpot and sprinkle with nutmeg, paprika, and black pepper.

Cook in the slow cooker on low, covered, for about 1-3 hours.

Nutrition:

Calories: 479 Carbohydrates: 6.1g

Protein: 32.6g Fat: 36g

Sugar: 1.8g Sodium: 700mg

Fiber: 0.5g

Tex-Mex Cheese Dip

Preparation time: 15 minutes

Cooking time: 1 hour & 30 minutes

Servings: 6

Ingredients:

8 ounces Velveeta cheese, cubed

¾ cup diced tomatoes with green chili peppers

1 teaspoon taco seasoning

Directions:

In a slow cooker, place Velveeta cheese cubes.

Cook on low and cook, covered, for about 30-60 minutes, stirring occasionally.

Uncover the slow cooker and stir in tomatoes and taco seasoning. Cook, covered, for about 30 minutes

Serve hot.

Nutrition:

Calories: 114 Carbohydrates: 5.2g

Protein: 7g Fat: 8.1g

Sugar: 3.4g

Sodium: 577mg

Fiber: 0.3g

2-Ingredient Cheese Dip

Preparation time: 15 minutes

Cooking time: 2 hours

Servings: 20

Ingredients:

16 ounces Velveeta cheese, cubed

1 (16-ounce) jar salsa

Directions:

In a large slow cooker, place cheese and salsa and stir gently to combine.

Cook on high, covered, for about 2 hours, stirring occasionally. Serve hot.

Nutrition:

Calories: 71 Carbohydrates: 3.9g

Protein: 4.4g Fat: 4.9g

Sugar: 2.3g Sodium: 460mg Fiber: 0.4g

Garlic Parmesan Chicken Wings

Preparation Time: 10 Minutes

Cooking Time: 3 Hours 20 Minutes

Servings: 8

Ingredients:

1 cup Parmesan Cheese, shredded

4 lb. Chicken Wings

¼ tsp. Black Pepper, grounded

½ cup Butter, preferably organic

1 tsp. Sea Salt

6 Garlic cloves, finely minced

Directions:

Begin by placing the chicken wings in the bottom portion of the slow cooker. After that, butter a large skillet over medium heat, and to this, add the garlic.

Sauté the garlic for 30 to 50 seconds or until aromatic. Spoon in the oil over the chicken wings and coat them well.

Now, cook them for 3 hours on low heat. Toward the end time, preheat the oven to broil.

Line the baking sheet using a parchment paper. Once the chicken is cooked, transfer them to the baking sheet in a single layer.

Broil it within 5 minutes or until the chicken is golden brown in color and crispy. Bring the baking sheet out after 5 minutes and top it with the cheese.

Return the sheet to oven and bake for another 2 minutes or until melted.

Nutrition:

Calories: 426 Fat: 34g

Carbohydrates: 1g Proteins: 27g

Candied Pecans

Preparation Time: 5 Minutes

Cooking Time: 3 Hours

Servings: 12

Ingredients:

1 cup Sukrin Gold

1 Egg White, medium-sized

4 cups Pecan

¼ cup Water

2 tsp. Vanilla Extract

1 ½ tbsp. Cinnamon

Directions:

First, butter the insides of the slow cooker and transfer the pecans to it.

After that, mix vanilla extract and egg white in a mixing bowl until just combined and foamy.

Spoon this egg mixture over the pan. Stir them so that they coat the pecans well. Now, combine the cinnamon with the Sukrin Gold until well incorporated.

Pour the batter over the pecans and stir them again.

Then, close the lid and cook for 3 hours on low heat while stirring them every quarter of an hour.

Once the time is up, transfer the pecans to a baking sheet in a single layer and allow it to cool. Serve and enjoy.

Nutrition:

Calories: 257

Fat: 26g

Carbohydrates: 4g

Proteins: 4g

Cocoa Nuts

Preparation Time: 5 Minutes

Cooking Time: 1 Hour

Servings: 6

Ingredients:

½ cup Walnuts

2 tbsp. Swerve

½ cup Almonds, slivered

2 tbsp. Butter softened

½ cup Pecans, halved

2 tbsp. Cocoa Powder, unsweetened

1 tsp. Vanilla Extract

Directions:

First, place all the ingredients needed to make this snack in a large mixing bowl. Mix well until well combined.

Transfer the nut mixture to the slow cooker— Cook within 1 hour on high heat.

Once the cooking time is up, place them on a baking sheet and cool before storing.

Nutrition:

Calories: 218

Fat: 21g Carbohydrates: 2g

Proteins: 4g

Thai Curry Nuts

Preparation Time: 5 Minutes

Cooking Time: 1 Hour & 30 Minutes

Servings: 8

Ingredients:

4 cups Nuts, raw

½ tsp. Salt

¼ cup Coconut Oil

1 tbsp. Curry Paste

1 tbsp. Swerve Sweetener

Directions:

Start by heating the crockpot to high heat. Add coconut oil to crockpot and once the oil has melted, stir in curry paste, salt, and sugar. Mix well.

Once the spice paste has dissolved, add the raw nuts. Stir them well so that the syrup coats the nuts well. Then, cover the lid and cook for 1 ½ hour on high heat.

Finally, transfer the nuts to a baking sheet and allow them to cool completely before storing.

Nutrition:

Calories: 547

Fat: 57g

Carbohydrates: 5g

Proteins: 5.41g

Pumpkin Spiced Nuts

Preparation Time: 15 Minutes

Cooking Time: 2 Hours

Servings: 4

Ingredients:

1 cup Walnuts, raw & halved

2 Egg Whites, large

2 cups Almonds, raw & unsalted

1 ½ tbsp. Pumpkin Pie Spice

2 cups Cashews, raw & unsalted

1 cup Brazil Nuts, raw & unsalted

1 ½ cup Coconut Sugar

Directions:

First, grease the insides of the slow cooker with oil or butter.

After that, combine the nuts with the pumpkin pie spice and coconut sugar. Mix well.

Then, add the egg whites into it until everything comes together. Now, transfer the nut mixture to the slow cooker.

Cook for 2 hours on low heat. Make sure to stir them every 45 minutes or so.

Once the nuts are done with cooking, place them on a baking sheet and allow it to cool completely.

Nutrition:

Calories: 382

Fat: 34.66g

Carbohydrates: 7g

Proteins: 10.92g

Turkey Meatballs

Preparation Time: 15 Minutes

Cooking Time: 6 Hours

Servings: 20

Ingredients:

1lb. Turkey

3 Garlic cloves, crushed

½ tsp. Onion Powder

1 tbsp Red Wine Vinegar

½ tsp. Rosemary

1 lb. Turkey sausage, grounded

1 Egg, large & organic

½ tsp. Thyme

1 tsp. Salt

½ of 1 Onion, large & diced

½ tsp. Garlic powder

1 tsp. Basil

1 × 28 oz Can have crushed Tomatoes

½ tsp. Oregano

½ cup Almond Meal

Directions:

First, you need to mix turkey and sausage in a large bowl until well combined.

After that, stir together onion powder, basil, almond meal, oregano, garlic powder, and rosemary in another bowl until mixed well.

Then, put the almond meal batter to the meat mixture and give everything a good stir.

Mix in the egg until well incorporated. Now, form a ball out of this mixture and place them on the baking sheet.

Place them in the oven and broil them for 2 to 3 minutes. Once broiled, add the meatballs to the crockpot.

Top the meatballs with garlic, onion, vinegar, tomatoes, and salt.

Close the lid and cook them for 6 hours on low heat. Finally, garnish them with basil before serving.

Nutrition:

Calories: 95

Fat: 7.14g

Carbohydrates: 1.85g

Proteins: 10.18g

Bok Choy Brownies

Preparation Time: 10 Minutes

Cooking Time: 4 Hours

Servings: 8

Ingredients:

1 packet of Bok Choy, trimmed and stems coarsely chopped

½ cup Swerve Sweetener

2 Eggs, large & organic

½ tsp. Salt

1 tsp. Baking powder

1 cup Almond Flour

1 tsp. Vanilla Extract

½ cup Cocoa Powder

1/3 cup Coconut Oil

½ tsp. Espresso powder

Directions:

To begin with, grease the insides of the slow cooker. Heat saltwater in a saucepan over medium heat and place the bok choy into it.

Simmer for 5 minutes or until the stems are cooked well.

Now, transfer the cooked bok choy to a blender and blend until it becomes a smooth puree. Mix all the dry fixing in a large mixing bowl.

Add the wet fixing one by one until everything comes together. Put the batter inside the slow cooker and close the lid.

Cook within 4 hours on low heat or until the center is set and a toothpick inserted comes clean.

Allow them to cool in the slow cooker itself and then slice them into small pieces. Serve warm or cold.

Nutrition:

Calories: 235 Fat: 20.82g

Carbohydrates: 5.39g Proteins: 6.68g

Lemon Custard

Preparation Time: 10 Minutes

Cooking Time: 3 Hours

Servings: 4

Ingredients:

5 Egg yolks, large & organic

1 tsp. Vanilla Extract

2 cups Whipping Cream

1 tbsp. Lemon zest

½ tsp. Liquid Stevia

¼ cup Lemon Juice, freshly squeezed

Directions:

Combine egg yolks, liquid stevia, lemon juice, and zest and vanilla extract in a medium-sized mixing bowl.

Once well combined, add whipping cream to the bowl and stir them again. Divide the mixture into 4 ramekins.

After that, place a rack into the slow cooker and arrange the ramekins on it. Put water inside the slow cooker, so it reaches halfway up the sides of the ramekins.

Cook within 3 hours on low heat. Finally, remove the ramekins from the slow cooker and allow them to cool at room temperature.

Chill them in the refrigerator.

Nutrition:

Calories: 319

Fat: 30g

Carbohydrates: 3g

Proteins: 7g

Buffalo Chicken Dip

Preparation Time: 10 Minutes

Cooking Time: 2 Hours

Servings: 8

Ingredients:

1 tbsp. Ranch Seasoning

3 cups cooked chicken, diced

1 cup Hot Sauce

4 oz. Blue Cheese, crumbled

1 cup Sour Cream

½ cup Green Onion, thinly sliced

1 × 8 oz. Cream Cheese, chopped into cubes

2 cups Mozzarella Cheese, shredded

Directions:

Start by greasing the insides of the slow cooker. Stir in all the remaining ingredients into the slow cooker and mix well.

Cook for 2 hours on high heat or until the cheese is melted. Garnish with green onions and serve it along with celery stalks.

Nutrition:

Calories: 344

Fat: 25.3g

Carbohydrates: 5.3g

Proteins: 22.39g

CHAPTER 7:

Lunch

Amazing Sour Cream Chicken

Preparation time: 15 minutes

Cooking time: 6 hours

Servings: 4

Ingredients:

1 cup of sour cream

½ cup of chicken stock

1 can of diced green chilies and tomatoes

1 batch of taco seasoning

2 pounds of chicken breast

Directions:

Put all the items to the slow cooker. Cook on low for 6 hours. Divide onto plates and serve.

Nutrition:

Calories: 262

Fat: 13 g

Fiber: 2.5 g

Protein: 32 g

Carbs: 23 g

Mouth-Watering Minced Pork Zucchini Lasagna

Preparation time: 15 minutes

Cooking time: 8 hours

Servings: 4

Ingredients:

4 medium zucchinis

1 diced small onion

1 minced clove of garlic

2 cups of minced lean ground pork

2 cans of Italian diced tomatoes

2 tablespoons of olive oil

2 cups of shredded Mozzarella cheese

1 large egg

1 tablespoon of dried basil

Salt and pepper

2 tablespoons of butter

Directions:

Slice the zucchini lengthwise into 6 slices. Heat-up the olive oil in a saucepan, then sauté the garlic and onions for 5 minutes.

Put the minced meat, cook for a further 5 minutes, put the tomatoes, and cook for an additional 5 minutes. Add the seasoning and mix thoroughly.

Mix the egg plus cheese in a small bowl, and whisk. Grease the crockpot using the butter, and then begin to layer the lasagna. First, layer with the zucchini slices, add the meat mixture, then top with the cheese. Repeat and finish with the cheese—Cook for 8 hours on low.

Nutrition:

Carbs: 10 g

Protein: 23 g

Fat: 30 g

Calories: 398

Fantastic Lemon Thyme Chicken

Preparation time: 15 minutes

Cooking time: 4 hours

Servings: 4

Ingredients:

10-15 cloves of garlic

2 sliced lemons

½ teaspoon of ground pepper

1 teaspoon of thyme

3 ½-pound whole chicken

Directions:

Arrange the lemon and garlic on the base of a slow cooker. Mix the spices and use them to season the chicken.

Put the chicken in the slow cooker. Cook on low within 4 hours. Remove, let it cool within 15 minutes, and then serve.

Nutrition:

Calories: 120 Fat: 8 g

Carbs: 1 g Fiber: 0 g Protein: 12 g

Beautiful BBQ Ribs

Preparation time: 15 minutes

Cooking time: 8 hours

Servings: 4

Ingredients:

3 pounds of pork ribs

1 tablespoon of olive oil

1 can of tomato paste, 28 ounces

½ cup of hot water

½ cup of vinegar

6 tablespoons of Worcestershire sauce

4 tablespoons of dry mustard

1 tablespoon of chili powder

1 teaspoon of ground cumin

1 teaspoon of powdered sweetener of your choice

Salt and pepper

Directions:

Heat the olive oil in a large frying pan and brown the ribs, then put in the crockpot.

Combine the remainder of the fixing in a small bowl, whisk thoroughly and pour over the ribs—Cook for 8 hours on low.

Nutrition:

Carbs: 14 g

Protein: 38 g

Fat: 28 g

Calories: 410

Delightful Balsamic Oregano Chicken

Preparation time: 15 minutes

Cooking time: 4 hours

Servings: 6

Ingredients:

6 pieces of boneless, skinless chicken

2 cans of diced tomatoes

1 large onion, thinly sliced

4 cloves of garlic

½ cup of balsamic vinegar

1 tablespoon of olive oil

1 tablespoon of dried oregano

1 teaspoon of dried rosemary

1 teaspoon of dried basil

½ teaspoon of thyme

Salt and pepper

Directions:

Combine all the fixing except the chicken in a small bowl. Mix them thoroughly. Put the chicken inside the slow cooker, then pour the remaining ingredients over the top.

Cook on high for 4 hours.

Nutrition:

Calories: 190

Fat: 6 g

Carbs: 5 g

Fiber: 1 g

Protein: 26 g

Scrumptious Bay Leaf Pork Roast Shoulder

Preparation time: 15 minutes

Cooking time: 8 hours

Servings: 4

Ingredients:

3 pounds of whole pork shoulder

1 can of Italian diced tomatoes

1 diced sweet onion

3 chopped cloves of garlic

4 tablespoons of lard

1 cup of water

1 bay leaf

¼ teaspoon of ground cloves

Salt and pepper

Directions:

Put all the items in the slow cooker. Cook for 8 hours on low.

Nutrition:

Carbs: 10 g

Protein: 33 g

Fat: 30 g

Calories: 421

Tantalizing Chicken Breast with Artichoke Stuffing

Preparation time: 15 minutes

Cooking time: 4 hours

Servings: 4

Ingredients:

4 boneless, skinless chicken breasts

3 cups of finely chopped spinach

½ cup of chopped roasted red peppers

¼ cup of sliced black olives

1 cup of chopped canned artichoke hearts

4 ounces of reduced-fat feta cheese

1 teaspoon of dried oregano

1 teaspoon of garlic powder

1 ½ cups of low-sodium chicken broth

Salt and pepper

Directions:

Cut deep in the center of the chicken and season it with salt and pepper.

In a small bowl, combine the garlic, feta, oregano, peppers, spinach, and artichoke hearts.

Stuff the artichoke mixture into the cut in the chicken and put it into the slow cooker.

Cook within low for 4 hours.

Nutrition:

Calories: 222 Fat: 7 g Carbs: 4 g

Fiber: 0 g Protein: 52 g

Gorgeous Coconut Turmeric Pork Curry

Preparation time: 15 minutes

Cooking time: 8 hours

Servings: 4

Ingredients:

2.2 pounds of cubed pork shoulder

1 tablespoon of coconut oil

1 tablespoon of olive oil

1 diced yellow onion

2 cloves of minced garlic

2 tablespoons of tomato paste

1 can of coconut milk, 12 ounces

1 cup of water

½ cup of white wine

1 teaspoon of turmeric

1 teaspoon of ginger powder

1 teaspoon of curry powder

½ teaspoon of paprika

Salt and pepper

Directions:

Heat-up 1 tablespoon of olive oil in a saucepan and sauté the garlic and onions for 3 minutes.

Add the pork and brown it, and then add the tomato paste.

Mix the remaining ingredients in the crockpot and then add the pork.

Cook for 8 hours on low. Divide onto plates and serve

Nutrition:

Carbs: 7 g

Protein: 30 g

Fat: 31 g Calories: 425

Tantalizing Pork Chops with Cumin Butter and Garlic

Preparation time: 15 minutes

Cooking time: 4 hours

Servings: 4

Ingredients:

3.5 pounds of pork sirloin chops with the bone

½ cup of salsa

3 tablespoons of butter

5 tablespoons of lime juice

½ teaspoon of ground cumin

¾ teaspoon of garlic powder

¾ teaspoon of salt

¾ teaspoon of black pepper

Directions:

Combine the spices and season the pork chops.

Melt the butter in a saucepan and brown the pork chops for 3 minutes on each side.

Put it inside the slow cooker and pour the salsa over the top.

Cook on high within 3-4 hours. Divide onto plates and serve.

Nutrition:

Calories: 364

Fat: 17 g

Carbs: 3 g

Fiber: 0 g

Protein: 51 g

Crockpot Beef Roast

Calories: 234

Carbohydrates: 2.4g

Protein: 33.1g

Fat: 10.3g

Sugar: 0.9 g

Sodium: 758.2mg

Fiber: 0.5g

Preparation time: 20 minutes

Cooking time: 10 hours

Servings: 6

Ingredients:

2-pounds beef chuck roast, trimmed of excess fat

1 ½ tsp. salt

¾ tsp. black pepper

2 tbsps. fresh basil, chopped

4 cloves of garlic, minced

2 bay leaves

1 large yellow onion, chopped

2 c. beef stock

Directions:

Pat dry the beef roast with a paper towel and rub with salt, pepper, and chopped basil.

Take inside the crockpot and spread the onion, garlic, and bay leaves.

Pour over the beef stock, then cook on low within 10 hours until tender.

Nutrition:

Chipotle Barbecue Chicken

Preparation time: 20 minutes

Cooking time: 8 hours

Servings: 5

Ingredients:

¼ c. water

1 14-ounce boneless chicken breasts, skin removed

1 14-ounce boneless chicken thighs, skin removed

Pepper and salt to taste

2 tbsp chipotle Tabasco sauce

1 c. tomato sauce

1/3 c. apple cider vinegar

1 onion, chopped

4 tbsp unsalted butter

2 tbsp yellow mustard

¼ tsp garlic powder

½ c. water

Directions:

Take all ingredients in a crockpot. Stir everything so that the chicken is coated with the sauce.

Cook within 8 hours, low. Serve.

Nutrition:

Calories: 482

Carbohydrates: 3g

Protein:29.4 g

Fat: 18.7g

Sugar: 0g

Sodium: 462mg

Fiber: 0.3g

Spicy Shredded Chicken Lettuce Wraps

Preparation time: 15 minutes

Cooking time: 10 hours

Servings: 8

Ingredients:

4 chicken breast, skin and bones removed

1 c. tomato salsa

1 tsp. onion powder

1 can dice green chilies

1 tbsp. Tabasco sauce

2 tbsps. freshly squeezed lime juice

Pepper and salt to taste

2 large heads iceberg lettuce, rinsed

Directions:

Take the chicken breast in the crockpot.

Pour over the tomato salsa, onion powder, green chilies, Tabasco sauce, and lime juice. Season with pepper and salt to taste.

Close the lid and cook for 10 hours. Shred the chicken meat using a fork.

Take on top of lettuce leaves. Garnish with sour cream, tomatoes, or avocado slices if needed.

Nutrition:

Calories: 231

Carbohydrates: 3g

Protein: 23 g

Fat: 12g

Sugar: 0.5g

Sodium: 375mg

Fiber: 2g

Bacon Cheeseburger Casserole

Preparation time: 50 minutes

Cooking time: 4 hours

Servings: 8

Ingredients:

2-pounds ground beef

½ onion, sliced thinly

½ tsp. salt

½ tsp. black pepper

1 15-ounce can cream of mushroom soup

1 15-ounce can cheddar cheese soup

pounds bacon, cooked and crumbled

2 c. cheddar cheese, grated

Directions:

Cook the ground beef plus the onions in a skillet over medium heat. Season with pepper and salt to taste.

Take the beef in the crockpot and add the cream of mushroom soup and cheese soup.

Pour in the bacon and half of the cheddar cheese. Give a stir. Cook on low for 4 hours.

Put the remaining cheese on top an hour before it is done cooking.

Nutrition:

Calories: 322 Carbohydrates: 2g

Protein: 36g Fat: 21g

Sugar: 0g Sodium: 271mg Fiber: 1.3g

Crockpot Ranch Chicken

Preparation time: 55 minutes

Cooking time: 7 hours

Servings: 6

Ingredients:

2 pounds boneless chicken breasts

3 tbsp dry ranch dressing mix

3 tbsp butter

4 ounces cream cheese

Directions:

Take the chicken in the crockpot. Pour the ranch dressing and rub on the chicken.

Add the butter and cream cheese—Cook within 7 hours, low.

Shred the chicken before serving.

Nutrition:

Calories: 266

Carbohydrates: 0g

Protein: 33g

Fat:12.9g

Sugar: 0g

Sodium: 167mg

Fiber: 0g

Coconut Cilantro Shrimp Curry

Preparation time: 40 minutes

Cooking time: 23 hours & 10 minutes

Servings: 4

Ingredients:

1 can light coconut milk

15-ounces water

½ c. Thai red curry sauce

2 ½ tsp lemon juice

1 tsp. garlic powder

¼ c. cilantro

Pepper and salt to taste

1-pound shrimps head removed only

Directions:

Take the coconut milk, water, and curry sauce in the crockpot.

Stir in the lemon juice, garlic powder, and cilantro—season with pepper and salt to taste.

Cook on high for 23 hours. Add the shrimps and cook on high for 10 minutes.

Nutrition:

Calories: 211

Carbohydrates: 2g

Protein: 18.2g

Fat: 22g Sugar: 0g

Sodium: 135mg

Fiber: 0.8g

Crockpot Butter Masala Chicken

Preparation time: 45 minutes

Cooking time: 7 hours

Servings: 8

Ingredients:

1 tbsp. olive oil

9 cloves of garlic, crushed

2 tsp. garam masala

2-pounds boneless chicken breasts, cut into strips

1 can light coconut milk

1 can tomato paste

½ tsp. cayenne pepper

1 tsp. dried coriander

1 tbsp. paprika

1 tsp. turmeric powder

1 tsp. cumin powder

1 ½ tsp salt

Directions:

Heat-up the olive oil in a skillet over medium flame and sauté the garlic for 1 minute. Put the garam masala, then cook for another minute or until fragrant. Set aside.

Take the chicken in the crockpot and add the garlic and garam masala mixture. Stir to coat the chicken meat. Put the rest of the fixing, and cook on low for 7 hours.

Nutrition:

Calories: 520 Carbohydrates: 2.3g

Protein: 32.7g Fat: 28g

Sugar: 0g Sodium: 342mg

Fiber: 0.8g

Kashmiri Lamb Curry

Preparation time: 40 minutes

Cooking time: 7 hours

Servings: 6

Ingredients:

¼ c. unsweetened coconut meat, shredded

3 long green fresh chili peppers

4 dried red chili peppers

1 tsp. garam masala

1 tsp. cumin seeds

5 cloves of garlic, crushed

1-piece ginger root, peeled and grated

2-pounds lamb meat

2 large onions, sliced

3 tomatoes, chopped

6 tbsps. vegetable oil

½ ground turmeric

1 c. plain yogurt

¼ c. cilantro, chopped

1 c. water

Pepper and salt to taste

Directions:

Take the chilies, garam masala, cumin seeds, garlic, ginger, tomatoes, and coconut in a blender and pulse until smooth. Set aside.

In a skillet, heat vegetable oil and sauté the onions and lamb meat for 3 minutes.

Transfer the meat mixture to the crockpot. Pour in chili paste mixture on top of the lamb.

Add the turmeric, yogurt, cilantro, and water—season with pepper and salt.

Cook within 7 hours, low, until tender.

Nutrition:

Calories: 489 Carbohydrates: 3g

Protein: 25g Fat: 40g

Sugar: 0g Sodium: 166mg

Fiber: 2.5g

Chicken with Bacon Gravy

Preparation time: 35 minutes

Cooking time: 7 hours

Servings: 4

Ingredients:

1 ½ pounds chicken breasts, bones, and skin removed

¼ tsp. pepper

1 tsp. salt

1 tsp. minced garlic

1 tsp. dried thyme

6 slices of bacon, cooked and crumbled

1 ½ c. water

2/3 c. heavy cream

Directions:

Take all ingredients except the heavy cream in the crockpot, then cook within 6 hours, low.

Put the heavy cream and continue cooking for another hour.

Nutrition:

Calories: 359

Carbohydrates: 0.9g

Protein: 21g

Fat: 25g

Sugar: 0g

Sodium: mg

Fiber:0 g

Garlic Butter Chicken with Cream Cheese

Preparation time: 20 minutes

Cooking time: 6 hours

Servings: 8

Ingredients:

2 ½ pounds chicken breast

1 stick of butter, softened

8 cloves of garlic, sliced in half

1 onion, sliced

1 ½ tsp. salt

8 ounces cream cheese

1 c. chicken stock

Directions:

Take the chicken in the crockpot and add the butter. Stir in the garlic and onions. Season with salt.

Cook on low for 6 hours. Meanwhile, prepare the cream cheese sauce by mixing cream cheese and chicken stock in a saucepan, medium flame and stir until the sauce has reduced. Pour over the chicken.

Nutrition:

Calories: 463

Carbohydraes: 2 g Protein: 22.4g

Fat: 35g

Sugar: 0g

Sodium: 674mg

Fiber: 0.6g

Cheesy Adobo Chicken

Preparation time: 30 minutes

Cooking time: 8 hours

Servings: 6

Ingredients:

1 pound of chicken breasts, bones removed but the skin on

1 tbsp butter

½ c. tomatoes, sliced

2 tbsp adobo sauce

½ c. milk

¾ c. cheddar cheese, shredded

Directions:

Take all ingredients in the crockpot. Mix, then cook on low within 8 hours. Use a fork to shred the chicken. Serve.

Nutrition:

Calories: 493 Carbohydrates: 0g

Protein: 25.8g Fat: 33.9g Sugar: 0g

Sodium: 375mg Fiber: 0g

Ketogenic Chicken Tikka Masala

Preparation time: 25 minutes

Cooking time: 8 hours

Servings: 6

Ingredients:

1 ½ pounds chicken thighs, bone-in, and skin-on

2 tsp onion powder

2 tbsp olive oil

5 tsp garam masala

3 tbsps. tomato paste

1-inch ginger root, grated

3 cloves of garlic

2 tsp smoked paprika

1 c. heavy cream

1 c. tomatoes, diced

1 c. coconut milk

Salt to taste

Fresh cilantro for garnish

Directions:

Take all ingredients except the cilantro in the crockpot. Mix everything until the spices are incorporated well.

Cook within 8 hours, low. Garnish with cilantro once cooked.

Nutrition:

Calories: 493

Carbohydrates:4.3g

Protein: 26.6g

Fat: 41.2g

Sugar: 1g

Sodium: 457mg

Fiber: 2g

Balsamic Chicken Thighs

Preparation time: 30 minutes

Cooking time: 8 hours

Servings: 8

Ingredients:

1 tsp. dried basil

2 tsp minced onion

1 tsp garlic powder

½ tsp salt

½ tsp black pepper

8 boneless chicken breasts

1 tbsp EVOO

4 cloves of garlic, minced

½ c. balsamic vinegar

Parsley for garnish

Directions:

In a small bowl, mix the dried basil, onion, garlic, salt, and pepper. Rub the spice mixture onto the chicken. Set aside

Take olive oil in the crockpot and sprinkle minced garlic. Arrange the chicken piece on top of the oil and garlic

Pour balsamic vinegar. Cook on low for 8 hours. Garnish with parsley once cooked.

Nutrition:

Calories: 133 Carbohydrates: 5.6g

Protein: 20.1g Fat: 4g Sugar: 3g

Sodium: 832mg

Fiber: 0.1g

Chicken Lo Mein

Preparation time: 40 minutes

Cooking time: 2 hours & 30 minutes

Servings: 6

Ingredients:

1 ½ pounds chicken, sliced into strip

1 tbsp coconut aminos

½ tsp sesame oil

½ tsp garlic paste

2 cloves of garlic, minced

1 tsp ginger, minced

bunch bok choy washed and sliced

12 ounces kelp noodles

Pepper and salt to taste

¾ c. chicken broth

1 tbsp. rice vinegar

1 tsp. red pepper chili flakes

Directions:

In a small bowl, mix the chicken, coconut aminos, sesame oil, and garlic paste. Let it marinate for 30 minutes inside the fridge.

Cook the marinated chicken in the crockpot on high for 2 hours. Set aside.

Take the garlic, ginger, and bok choy at the bottom of the crockpot. Add the chicken and kelp noodles on top—season with pepper and salt to taste.

Mix the chicken broth, rice vinegar, and red pepper flakes in a bowl.

Pour over the chicken mixture and cook for 30 minutes on high.

Nutrition:

Calories: 174

Carbohydrates: 3.1g

Protein: 24.5g

Fat: 8.1g

Sugar: 0.5g

Sodium: 436mg

Fiber: 1.6g

Ethiopian Doro Watt Chicken

Preparation time: 35 minutes

Cooking time: 8 hours

Servings: 6

Ingredients:

1 tsp chili powder

1 tsp sweet paprika

½ tsp ground ginger

1 tbsp salt

1 tsp ground coriander

1/8 tsp ground cardamom

1/8 tsp allspice

1/8 tsp fenugreek powder

1/8 tsp nutmeg

1 whole chicken, sliced into different parts

½ c. butter

1 clove of garlic, minced

1/2 c. water

2 large onions, chopped

8 hard-boiled eggs

Directions:

Combine the first 9 items in a bowl. Use this spice mix and rub it on the chicken parts. Marinate within 30 minutes in the fridge.

Take the butter in the crockpot and add the onion and garlic. Take the chicken pieces. Arrange the hard-boiled eggs randomly on top of the chicken.

Pour water, then cook on low within 8 hours.

Nutrition:

Calories: 315 Carbohydrates:4g

Protein: 19g Fat: 25g Sugar: 0g

Sodium: 698mg Fiber: 0.8g

Mexican Chicken Soup

Preparation time: 15 minutes

Cooking time: 8 hours

Servings: 6

Ingredients:

6 cups chicken broth

4 teaspoons garlic

0.25 cups jalapeno

1 tablespoon cumin

1 tablespoon chili powder

0.5 cups cilantro

2 tablespoons lime juice

1.5 cups carrots

0.66 cups onion

0.5 cups Roma tomato

0.75 cups tomato juice

1 teaspoon coriander

2 teaspoons sea salt

4 cups chicken breast

Directions:

Chop herbs and vegetables. Put everything in the cooker. Low cook for 8 hours. Serve.

Nutrition:

Calories 296

Fat 16 grams

Protein 27 grams

Carbs 10 grams

Apricot Pulled Pork

Preparation time: 15 minutes

Cooking time: 11 hours

Servings: 10

Ingredients:

3 pounds pork

1 cup barbecue sauce

6 ounces dried apricots

10 pounds apricot spread that does not contain any sugar

1 sweet onion

Directions:

Put the pork in the cooker. Add the barbecue, apricots, spread, and onions. Low cook for 11 hours.

Nutrition:

Calories 458

Fat 30 grams

Protein 33 grams

Carbs 15 grams

Chicken Kale Soup

Preparation time: 15 minutes

Cooking time: 6 hours

Servings: 6

Ingredients:

1 tablespoon olive oil

14 ounces chicken broth

0.5 cups olive oil

5 ounces kale

Salt to taste

2 pounds of chicken

0.33 cups onion

32 ounces chicken stock

0.25 cups lemon juice

Directions:

Cook the chicken until it achieves approximately 165F. Do this in a pan.

Shred and put it into the cooker.

Process the onion, broth, and oil and put it into the cooker. Add other ingredients and mix.

Low cook for 6 hours. Serve.

Nutrition:

Calories 261

Fat 21 grams

Protein 14 grams

Carbs 2 grams

Creamy Italian Chicken

Preparation time: 15 minutes

Cooking time: 6 hours

Servings: 8

Ingredients:

2 pounds of chicken

10.5 ounces chicken soup, cream and canned

1 teaspoon garlic powder

0.25 cups onion

2 tablespoons dressing mix, Italian

8 ounces cream cheese

Directions:

Cube the chicken. Place it in the cooker.

Dice and add onions. Stir in cream cheese: mix garlic, soup, and dressing mix.

Pour into the cooker. Low cook for 6 hours.

Nutrition:

Calories 255

Fat 14 grams

Protein 23 grams

Carbs 7 grams

Mississippi Roast

Preparation time: 15 minutes

Cooking time: 8 hours

Servings: 6

Ingredients:

2 pounds roast beef

1 pack dressing mix, ranch

0.5 cups butter, salted

3 tablespoons olive oil

1 yellow onion

1 cup au jus

6 pepperoncini

Directions:

Sear the roast. Cover with chopped onion. Pour in au jus.

Sprinkle ranch mix. Evenly disperse the butter.

Evenly place pepperoncini. Low cook for 8 hours.

Nutrition:

Calories 608

Fat 49 grams

Protein 30 grams

Carbs 8 grams

Taco Soup

Preparation time: 15 minutes

Cooking time: 4 hours

Servings: 8

Ingredients:

2 pounds sausage, ground

20 ounces Rotel

4 cups chicken broth

0.5 cups cheddar

16 ounces cream cheese

2 tablespoons seasoning, taco

2 tablespoons cilantro

Directions:

Brown the sausage. In the cooker, add the Rotel, cream cheese, and seasoning.

Toss in the sausage. Pour in chicken broth.

Low cook for 4 hours. Stir in cilantro. Let sit 10 minutes.

Top with cheddar. Serve.

Nutrition:

Calories 547

Fat 43 grams

Protein 33 grams

Carbs 5 grams

Chicken and Vegetables

Preparation time: 15 minutes

Cooking time: 8 hours

Servings: 8

Ingredients:

2 pounds chicken that does not contain any skin or bones

2 cups green beans

1 cup chicken broth

2 teaspoons herb blend

2 cups carrots

2 onions

4 teaspoons Worcestershire sauce

Pepper and salt

Directions:

Prepare and chop the vegetables. Put the chicken in the cooker.

Add the vegetables. Pour the broth and Worcestershire sauce. Low cook for 8 hours.

Nutrition:

Calories 160

Fat 3 grams

Protein 23 grams

Carbs 13 grams

Chicken Gyros

Preparation time: 15 minutes

Cooking time: 8 hours

Servings: 8

Ingredients:

0.5 an onion

2 pounds ground chicken

0.5 cups breadcrumbs, low-carb

1 teaspoon thyme

0.25 teaspoons nutmeg

1 tablespoon olive oil

3 garlic cloves

2 eggs

1 lemon

0.25 teaspoons cinnamon

12 pita bread

Toppings:

Tomato

Greek yogurt, plain

Cucumber

Lemon

Directions:

Process the garlic and onion. Mix the above with the eggs, lemon, cinnamon, salt, chicken, breadcrumbs, thyme, and nutmeg.

Roll into a ball. Put in a cooker—drizzle olive oil.

Low cook for 8 hours. Once finished, put on pita and apply toppings.

Nutrition:

Calories 248

Fat 13 grams

Protein 23 grams

Carbs 10 grams

Chili Colorado

Preparation time: 15 minutes

Cooking time: 10 hours

Servings: 12

Ingredients:

2.5 pounds beef

3 cloves garlic

27 ounces green chilies, canned

1 teaspoon salt

0.5 teaspoons chili powder

1 onion

43.5 ounces tomatoes, canned

1 teaspoon ground cumin

1 teaspoon pepper

Directions:

Put the meat in the cooker. Add the garlic and onion.

Add the tomatoes and chilies. Add the seasonings.

Low cook for 10 hours. Serve.

Nutrition:

Calories 164

Fat 3 grams

Protein 20 grams

Carbs 10 grams

Beef Chimichangas

Preparation time: 15 minutes

Cooking time: 12 hours

Servings: 16

Ingredients:

3 pounds beef, boneless

10 ounces green chilies and tomatoes, canned

3 ounces garlic

3 tablespoons seasoning, taco

3 garlic cloves

16 flour tortillas

Toppings:

Refried beans

Sour cream

Guacamole

Lettuce

Cheese

Salsa

Directions:

Prepare the meat. Add it to the cooker after applying seasoning. Add chilies and tomatoes. Toss in garlic.

Low cook for 12 hours. Shred the beef. Once removed, add it and all desired toppings to tortillas. Fry folded tortillas. Serve.

Nutrition:

Calories 249

Fat 18 grams

Protein 14 grams

Carbs 3 grams

Pizza Casserole

Preparation time: 15 minutes

Cooking time: 4 hours

Servings: 3

Ingredients:

2 chicken breasts without bones

2 garlic cloves

1 teaspoon seasoning, Italian

Dash pepper

8 ounces tomato sauce

1 bay leaf

0.25 teaspoons salt

0.5 cups mozzarella

Directions:

Put the chicken in the cooker. Add other ingredients, except cheese.

Low cook for 4 hours. After cooking, top with cheese.

Nutrition:

Calories 228

Fat 9 grams

Protein 31 grams

Carbs 5 grams

Cheesy Cauliflower Bread

Preparation time: 15 minutes

Cooking time: 3 hours

Servings: 8

Ingredients:

12 ounces cauliflower, chopped

2 cups mozzarella

0.5 teaspoons salt

2 cloves garlic

2 eggs

2 tablespoons coconut flour

0.5 teaspoons pepper

0.25 cups basil, fresh

Directions:

Whisk half of the cheese plus the flour, pepper, cauliflower, salt, and eggs.

Press the above into the cooker. Add the remaining cheese plus the garlic.

High cook for 3 hours. Garnish with basil.

Nutrition:

Calories 224

Fat 15 grams

Protein 15 grams

Carbs 6 grams

CHAPTER 8:

Dinner

Moist and Spicy Pulled Chicken Breast

Preparation time: 15 minutes

Cooking time: 6 hours

Servings: 8

Ingredients:

1 teaspoon dry oregano

1 teaspoon dry thyme

1 teaspoon dried rosemary

1 teaspoon garlic powder

1 teaspoon sweet paprika

½ teaspoon chili powder

Salt and pepper to taste

4 tablespoons butter

5.5 pounds of chicken breasts

1 ½ cups ready-made tomato salsa

2 Tablespoons of olive oil

Directions:

Mix dry seasoning, sprinkle half on the bottom of crockpot.

Place the chicken breasts over it, sprinkle the rest of the spices.

Pour the salsa over the chicken. Cover, cook on low for 6 hours.

Nutrition:

Calories: 42 Carbs: 1g Fat: 1g Protein: 9g

Whole Roasted Chicken

Preparation time: 15 minutes

Cooking time: 8 hours

Servings: 6

Ingredients:

1 whole chicken (approximately 5.5 pounds)

4 garlic cloves

6 small onions

1 Tablespoon olive oil, for rubbing

2 teaspoons salt

2 teaspoons sweet paprika

1 teaspoon Cayenne pepper

1 teaspoon onion powder

1 teaspoon ground thyme

2 teaspoons fresh ground black pepper

4 Tablespoons butter, cut into cubes

Directions:

Mix all dry ingredients well.

Stuff the chicken belly with garlic and onions.

On the bottom of the crockpot, place four balls of aluminum foil.

Set the chicken on top of the balls. Rub it generously with olive oil.

Cover the chicken with seasoning, drop in butter pieces. Cover, cook on low for 8 hours.

Nutrition:

Calories: 120 Carbs: 1g Fat: 6g Protein: 17g

Pot Roast Beef Brisket

Preparation time: 15 minutes

Cooking time: 12 hours

Servings: 10

Ingredients:

6.6 pounds beef brisket, whole

2 Tablespoons olive oil

2 Tablespoons apple cider vinegar

1 teaspoon dry oregano

1 teaspoon dry thyme

1 teaspoon dried rosemary

2 Tablespoons paprika

1 teaspoon Cayenne pepper

1 tablespoon salt

1 teaspoon fresh ground black pepper

Directions:

In a bowl, mix dry seasoning, add olive oil, apple cider vinegar.

Place the meat in the crockpot, generously coat with seasoning mix.

Cover, cook on low for 12 hours.

Remove the brisket, place it on a pan. Sear it under the broiler for 2-4 minutes, observe it, so the meat doesn't burn.

Wrap it using a foil, then let it rest for 1 hour. Slice and serve.

Nutrition:

Calories: 280 Carbs: 4g Fat: 20g Protein: 20g

Seriously Delicious Lamb Roast

Preparation time: 15 minutes

Cooking time: 8 hours

Servings: 8

Ingredients:

12 medium radishes, scrubbed, washed, and cut in half

Salt and pepper to taste

1 red onion, diced

2 garlic cloves, minced

1 lamb joint (approximately 4.5 pounds) at room temperature

2 Tablespoons olive oil

1 teaspoon dry oregano

1 teaspoon dry thyme

1 sprig fresh rosemary

4 cups heated broth, your choice

Directions:

Place cut radishes along the bottom of the crockpot. Season. Add onion and garlic. Blend the herbs plus olive oil in a small bowl until it forms to paste. Place the meat on top of the radishes. Knead the paste over the meat. Heat the stock, pour it around the meat.

Cover, cook on low for 8 hours. Let it rest for 20 minutes. Slice and serve.

Nutrition:

Calories: 206 Carbs: 4g Fat: 9g Protein: 32g

Lamb Provençal

Preparation time: 15 minutes

Cooking time: 8 hours

Servings: 4

Ingredients:

2 racks lamb, approximately 2 pounds

1 Tablespoon olive oil

2 Tablespoons fresh rosemary, chopped

1 Tablespoon fresh thyme, chopped

4 garlic cloves, minced

1 teaspoon dry oregano

1 lemon, the zest

1 teaspoon minced fresh ginger

1 cup (Good) red wine

Salt and pepper to taste

Directions:

Preheat the crockpot on low.

In a pan, heat 1 tablespoon olive oil. Brown the meat for 2 minutes per side.

Mix remaining ingredients in a bowl.

Place the lamb in the crockpot, pour the remaining seasoning over the meat.

Cover, cook on low for 8 hours.

Nutrition:

Calories: 140 Carbs: 3g Fat: 5g Protein: 21g

Greek Style Lamb Shanks

Preparation time: 15 minutes

Cooking time: 6 hours

Servings: 8

Ingredients:

3 Tablespoons butter

4 lamb shanks, approximately 1 pound each

2 Tablespoons olive oil

8-10 pearl onions

5 garlic cloves, minced

2 beef tomatoes, cubed

¼ cup of green olives

4 bay leaves

1 sprig fresh rosemary

1 teaspoon dry thyme

1 teaspoon ground cumin

1 cup fresh spinach

¾ cup hot water

½ cup red wine, Merlot or Cabernet

Salt and pepper to taste

Directions:

Liquify the butter in a pan, then cook the shanks on each side.

Remove, then add oil, onions, garlic. Cook for 3-4 minutes. Add tomatoes, olives, spices, then stir well. Put the liquids and return the meat. Boil for 1 minute.

Transfer everything to the slow cooker.

Cover, cook on medium-high for 6 hours.

Nutrition:

Calories: 250

Carbs: 3g

Fat: 16g

Protein: 22g

Homemade Meatballs and Spaghetti Squash

Preparation time: 15 minutes

Cooking time: 8 hours

Servings: 8

Ingredients:

1 medium-sized spaghetti squash, washed, halved

1 Tablespoon butter, to grease the crockpot

2.2 pounds lean ground beef

2 garlic cloves

1 red onion, chopped

½ cup almond flour

2 Tablespoons of dry Parmesan cheese

1 egg, beaten

1 teaspoon ground cumin

Salt and pepper to taste

4 cans diced Italian tomatoes

1 small can tomato paste, 28 ounces

1 cup hot water

1 red onion, chopped

¼ cup chopped parsley

½ teaspoon each, salt and sugar (optional)

1 bay leaf

Directions:

Grease the crockpot, place both squash halves open side down in the crockpot.

Mix meatball ingredients in a bowl—form approximately 20 small meatballs.

In a pan, heat the o live oil. Fry the meatballs within 2-3 minutes per side. Transfer to the crockpot.

In the small bowl, add the tomatoes, tomato paste, oil, water, onion, and parsley, add ½ teaspoon each of salt and sugar. Mix well.

Pour the marinara sauce in the crockpot around the squash halves.

Cover, cook on low for 8 hours.

Nutrition:

Calories: 235

Carbs: 12g

Fat: 14g

Protein: 15g

Beef and Cabbage Roast

Preparation time: 15 minutes

Cooking time: 8 hours

Servings: 10

Ingredients:

1 red onion, quartered

2 garlic cloves, minced

2-3 stocks celery, diced (approximately 1 cup)

4-6 dry pimento berries

2 bay leaves

5.5 pounds beef brisket (two pieces)

1 teaspoon chili powder

1 teaspoon ground cumin

2 cups broth, beef + 2 cups hot water

Salt and pepper to taste

1 medium cabbage (approximately 2.2 pounds), cut in half, then quartered

Directions:

Add all ingredients, except cabbage, to the crockpot in order of the list.

Cover, cook on low for 7 hours.

Uncover, add the cabbage on top of the stew. Re-cover, cook for 1 additional hour.

Nutrition:

Calories: 150

Carbs: 8g

Fat: 3g

Protein: 22g

Simple Chicken Chili

Preparation time: 15 minutes

Cooking time: 6 hours

Servings: 8

Ingredients:

1 Tablespoon butter

1 red onion, sliced

1 bell pepper, sliced

2 garlic cloves, minced

3 pounds boneless chicken thighs

8 slices bacon, chopped

1 teaspoon chili powder

Salt and pepper to taste

1 cup chicken broth

¼ cup of coconut milk

3 Tablespoons tomato paste

Directions:

Add all ingredients to the crockpot, starting with the butter.

Cover, cook on low for 6 hours.

Strip the chicken using a fork in the crockpot. Serve.

Nutrition:

Calories: 210

Carbs: 32g

Fat: 4g

Protein: 14g

Beef Shoulder in BBQ Sauce

Preparation time: 15 minutes

Cooking time: 10 hours

Servings: 12

Ingredients:

8 pounds beef shoulder, whole

1 Tablespoon butter

1 yellow onion, diced

1 garlic bulb, peeled and minced

4 Tablespoons red wine vinegar

2 Tablespoons Worcestershire sauce

4 Tablespoons Swerve (or a suitable substitute)

1 Tablespoon mustard

1 teaspoon salt

1 teaspoon fresh ground black pepper

Directions:

In a bowl, mix seasoning. Set aside.

Liquify the butter in a pan, add the meat. Brown on all sides. Transfer to crockpot.

Fry the onion within 2-3 minutes in the same pan, then pour over the meat.

Pour in the seasoning. Cover, cook on low for 10 hours.

Remove, cover it with foil, then let it rest for 1 hour.

Turn the crockpot on high, reduce the remaining liquid by half and serve with the shredded beef.

Nutrition:

Calories: 140 Carbs: 5g Fat: 9g Protein: 8g

Dressed Pork Leg Roast

Preparation time: 15 minutes

Cooking time: 8 hours

Servings: 14

Ingredients:

8 pounds pork leg

1 Tablespoon butter

1 yellow onion, sliced

6 garlic cloves, peeled and minced

2 Tablespoons ground cumin

2 Tablespoons ground thyme

2 Tablespoons ground chili

1 teaspoon salt

1 teaspoon fresh ground black pepper

1 cup hot water

Directions:

Butter the crockpot. Slice crisscrosses along the top of the pork leg.

Arrange onion slices and minced garlic along the bottom of the crockpot.

Place meat on top of vegetables.

In a small bowl, mix the herbs. Rub it all over the pork leg.

Add the water. Cover, cook on high for 8 hours.

Remove and transfer, cover with foil. Let it rest for 1 hour.

Shred the meat and serve.

Nutrition:

Calories: 143

Carbs: 0g

Fat: 3g

Protein: 28g

Rabbit & Mushroom Stew

Preparation time: 15 minutes

Cooking time: 6 hours

Servings: 6

Ingredients:

1 rabbit, in portion size pieces

2 cups spicy Spanish sausage, cut into chunks

2 Tablespoons butter, divided

1 red onion, sliced

1 cup button mushrooms, washed and dried

1 teaspoon cayenne pepper

1 teaspoon sweet paprika

1 teaspoon salt

1 teaspoon fresh ground black pepper

1 cup chicken broth+1 cup hot water

Directions:

Butter the slow cooker.

In a large pan, melt the butter, add the rabbit pieces, brown on all sides. Transfer to a slow cooker.

In the same pan, sauté the onions, sausage chunks, and spices for 2-3 minutes. Set the chicken broth, heat on high for 1 minute, then pour the mixture over the rabbit.

Add the mushrooms. Adjust the seasoning, if needed. Add the water. Cover, cook on high for 6 hours. Serve.

Nutrition:

Calories: 122 Carbs: 19g Fat: 1g Protein: 10g

Italian Spicy Sausage & Bell Peppers

Preparation time: 15 minutes

Cooking time: 6 hours

Servings: 5

Ingredients:

2 Tablespoons butter

2 red onions, sliced

4 bell peppers, sliced

2 regular cans Italian tomatoes, diced

2.2 pounds spicy Italian sausage

1 teaspoon dry oregano

1 teaspoon dry thyme

1 teaspoon dry basil

1 teaspoon sweet paprika

1 teaspoon salt

1 teaspoon fresh ground black pepper

Directions:

Grease with butter the slow cooker. Add the sliced onions and peppers. Salt.

Pour the tomatoes over it, then add seasoning. Mix it in.

Arrange sausages in the middle of the pepper and onion mixture.

Add ¼ cup hot water. Cover, cook on low for 6 hours. Serve.

Nutrition:

Calories: 180

Carbs: 19g

Fat: 6g

Protein: 12g

Chicken in Salsa Verde

Preparation time: 15 minutes

Cooking time: 6 hours

Servings: 4

Ingredients:

2.2 pounds of chicken breasts

3 bunches parsley, chopped

¾ cup olive oil

¼ cup capers, drained and chopped

3 anchovy fillets

1 lemon, juice, and zest

2 garlic cloves, minced

1 teaspoon salt

1 teaspoon fresh ground black pepper

Directions:

Place the chicken breasts in the crockpot.

Blend the rest of the fixing in a blender, then pour over the chicken.

Cover, cook on low for 6 hours. Shred with a fork and serve.

Nutrition:

Calories: 145 Carbs: 5g

Fat: 2g

Protein: 26g

Salmon Poached in White Wine and Lemon

Preparation time: 15 minutes

Cooking time: 2 hours

Servings: 4

Ingredients:

2 cups of water

1 cup cooking wine, white

1 lemon, sliced thin

1 small mild onion, sliced thin

1 bay leaf

1 mixed bunch fresh tarragon, dill, and parsley

2.2 pounds salmon fillet, skin on

1 teaspoon salt

1 teaspoon ground black pepper

Directions:

Add all fixings, except salmon and seasoning, to the slow cooker. Cover, cook on low for 1 hour.

Season the salmon, place in the slow cooker skin-side down.

Cover, cook on low for another hour. Serve.

Nutrition:

Calories: 216

Carbs: 1g

Fat: 12g

Protein: 23g

Easy Meatball Crock Pot

Preparation time: 15 minutes

Cooking time: 2 hours

Servings: 3

Ingredients:

For the meatballs:

1 tablespoon tomato paste

1 cup bone broth

Sea salt and pepper

1/2 teaspoon paprika

1/2 tablespoon cumin

1 lb. ground beef

Small handful fresh parsley, diced

For the cauliflower:

Sea salt

2 tablespoons butter or ghee

1/2 large head cauliflower, florets

Pepper

Directions:

Mix the meat, pepper, salt, paprika, and cumin in a bowl.

Form meatballs, then put it inside the slow cooker.

Mix the paste and the broth in a bowl and pour over the meatballs. Cook on high, 2 hours.

Steam the cauliflower florets until well cooked.

Remove the water, then put salt, butter, plus pepper.

Blend the batter using an immersion blender until smooth.

Mash the cauliflower onto a serving plate, top with meatballs, and enough amount of sauce on top. Garnish with parsley and enjoy.

Nutrition:

Calories: 413 Protein: 46.7g

Fat: 17.4g

Carbs: 2.5g

Beef & Broccoli

Preparation time: 15 minutes

Cooking time: 7 hours

Servings: 4

Ingredients:

1 red bell pepper, sliced

1 broccoli, florets

1/2 tsp salt

1/4 tsp red pepper flakes

3 garlic cloves, minced

1 tsp grated ginger

3 tbsp sweetener

1 cup beef broth

2/3 cup liquid amigos

2 lbs. flank steak, chunks

1 tsp sesame seeds, optional

Directions:

Set the slow cooker on low, put the steak, salt, pepper, garlic, sweetener, beef broth, and coconut aminos.

Cook within 5 to 6 hours.

Mix the steak, then put in the red pepper plus the broccoli. Cook within 1 hour, then toss the batter.

Serve with sesame seeds.

Nutrition:

Calories 430 Fat 19g

Carbs 4g Protein 54g

New Mexico Carne Adovada

Preparation time: 30 minutes

Cooking time: 6 hours

Servings: 4

Ingredients:

2 tsp apple cider vinegar

1 tsp kosher salt

1 tsp ground coriander

1 tsp ground cumin

2 tsp dried Mexican oregano

6 garlic, sliced

1 onion, sliced

2 cups chicken stock

6 -8 ounces dried chilies, rinsed

3 pounds pork shoulder, cubes

Directions:

Put all the items in a pot, except the pork. Simmer it within 30-60 minutes, low.

Remove, then cooldown it within a few minutes.

Puree the batter in batches using a blender.

Put now the pork meat in a baking dish, covering it with the sauce. Chill within 1 to 2 days to marinate, stirring frequently.

Cook it in a slow cooker within 4 to 6 hours, low. Serve warm.

Nutrition:

Calories 120.2 Fat 5.3g Carb 11.3g

Protein 8.0g

Beef Chuck Pot Roast

Preparation time: 15 minutes

Cooking time: 5 hours

Servings: 3

Ingredients:

1/4 can cream of celery soup

1/4 packet onion soup dry mix

1 lb. beef for roasting

Directions:

Prick the meat around using a fork or knife, and place in crockpot with the side with the fatty side facing up.

Put the onion soup dry mixture on the meat, followed with the can of mushroom or celery soup over the roast.

Cook within 3 hours on high or 5 hours set on a low heat setting.

Nutrition:

Calories 280

Carbs 2.5g

Fat 13.2g

Proteins 35.5g

Crockpot Turkey Breast

Preparation time: 15 minutes

Cooking time: 8 hours

Servings: 4

Ingredients:

6 tablespoons butter separated

1 cup chicken broth

12-15 baby carrots

2 yellow onions

5 stalks celery

1 (5-6 pounds) bone-in turkey breast, thawed Seasonings

1/4 teaspoon dried sage

1/4 teaspoon dried parsley

1 teaspoon Italian seasoning

1/2 teaspoon pepper

1 teaspoon paprika

1 teaspoon seasoned salt

1 tablespoon dried garlic, minced

1/4 teaspoon dried thyme, optional

Directions:

Thaw the turkey inside the fridge for around 1-2 days. Then coat your slow cooker with non-stick spray.

Add celery to the bottom of the crockpot, cut a yellow onion into large chunks, and add to the cooker. Add in baby carrots along with the chicken broth.

Put the turkey breast on the veggies, breast side down. Then cut the onion in half and put it inside the turkey along with 4 tablespoons butter.

Mix all the seasonings, then put it on the meat. If the breast has skin on, also rub the seasonings under the skin.

Dissolve 2 tablespoons of butter and brush all over the seasoned breast using a pastry brush.

Cook on high for 1 hour. Lower the heat and now cook for 5-7 hours or until the turkey is tender.

Once done, remove the turkey breast from the slow cooker, and break it up. Just remove the wishbone and other bones. Pick the large pieces of the turkey and slice them.

Nutrition:

Calories 330 Carbs 3.7g

Fat 17.9g Protein 38g

Coffee- Braised Brisket

Preparation time: 15 minutes

Cooking time: 10 hours

Servings: 4

Ingredients:

1/2 tablespoon of balsamic vinegar

4 cups of strong brewed coffee

1 large sliced onion

1/2 (3-pound) boneless beef brisket

1/2 teaspoon of salt

1/2 teaspoon of ground black pepper

1/2 teaspoon of garlic powder

1/2 tablespoon of paprika

1/2 tablespoon of ground coffee

1 tablespoon of coconut sugar

Directions:

Mix brown sugar, paprika, garlic powder, pepper, salt, and ground coffee.

Remove the fat from brisket, put the batter all over its surface.

Put the meat in the Crock-Pot, then the onions. Mix in the vinegar plus coffee, then pour inside.

Cover and now cook on low heat for 10 hours or on high heat setting for 5 hours.

Serve the onion mixture with the meat.

Nutrition:

Calories 229 Proteins 32g

Carbs 8g Fat 8g

Keto Slow Cooker Cookbook:

Crockpot Creamy Salsa Chicken

Preparation time: 15 minutes

Cooking time: 4 hours

Servings: 4

Ingredients:

1/2 jar salsa

1/2 can of cream mushroom soup

3 large boneless chicken breasts

Directions:

Lay and settle the chicken breasts inside the slow cooker.

Combine in the salsa plus the mushroom soup. Set it on top of the chicken breasts.

Cook on low within 4 hours, stirring occasionally, and shred once cooked, then serve.

Nutrition:

Calories 254.6

Protein 40.8g

Carbs 5.3g

Fat 6.6g

Slow Cooker Pork Loin

Preparation time: 15 minutes

Cooking time: 6 hours

Servings: 4

Ingredients:

1/4 cup orange juice

1/2 tbsp curry powder

1/2 tsp chicken bouillon granules

1/4 tsp ground ginger

1/8 tsp ground cinnamon

1/4 tsp salt

1/2 onion, diced

1/2 garlic, diced

1/8 cup raisins

1/8 cup flaked coconut

1 tbsp cold water

2 pounds boneless pork loin, diced

1 tbsp arrowroot powder

Directions:

Mix the salt, cinnamon, chicken bouillon, curry powder, and orange in the slow cooker's bottom.

Mix in the coconut, raisins, garlic, onion, and apple, then place the pork cubes into the mixture.

Put the potato starch into water, mix until it dissolved. Then put all inside the slow cooker.

Cook on low within 5 to 6 hours.

Nutrition:

Calories 174

Fat 6g

Carbs 8g

Protein 22g

Flemish Beef Stew

Preparation time: 15 minutes

Cooking time: 8 hours

Servings: 4

Ingredients:

1/2 bay leaf

1/4 teaspoon pepper, freshly ground

Dash teaspoon salt

1/2 teaspoon caraway seeds

3/4 tablespoons Dijon mustard

1/2 clove garlic, minced

1/2 large onion, chopped

2 large carrots or rutabagas, cut into 1-inch pieces

1 cùp white wine1

1/2 tablespoons almond or zucchini flower

6-ounce white button mushrooms, sliced

1-pound bottom round, trimmed of fat and cubed

2 teaspoons canola oil, divided

Directions:

In a skillet, heat 2 teaspoons of oil over medium heat. Put the beef, then cook within 5 minutes, while turning occasionally.

Transfer the meat into a Crockpot, and drain all fat from the pan.

Then add 2 teaspoons of oil and brown the rest of the beef. Move it into the crockpot too.

Return the skillet to heat, add mushrooms and cook over medium heat for about 5-7 minutes while stirring. Remove from heat after the mushrooms give off their liquid.

At this point, sprinkle flour over the cooked mushrooms and cook for 10 seconds, undisturbed. Stir and cook for another 30 seconds.

Pour the beer or ale, bring it to a boil as you whisk continuously. Cook the mushroom mixture within 3 minutes in the crockpot. Add in caraway seeds, mustard, garlic, onion, carrots, salt, bay leaf, and pepper. Stir the ingredients to mix.

Cook on low heat within 8 hours. Once ready, open the lid, discard the bay leaf, then serve.

Nutrition:

Calories 301

Carbs 17g

Fat 10g

Protein 31g

Amazing Spiced Beef Eye Crockpot

Preparation time: 15 minutes

Cooking time: 8 hours

Servings: 4

Ingredients:

3 lb. lean ground beef eye roast

2 T. Worcestershire sauce

4 T. fresh lime juice

1 ½ c. onion, diced

1 c. red bell pepper, diced

3 garlic cloves, minced

3 serrano chilies, seeded, minced

Salt and pepper to taste

½ c. beef broth, non-fat

1 c. canned diced tomatoes

½ t. dried oregano

Directions:

Massage the beef roast with salt plus pepper and put it in the slow cooker. Whisk the rest of the ingredients together and pour over the beef. Cook for 8 hours on LOW. Shred the beef using 2 forks.

Nutrition:

Calories: 247 Fats: 23 g Carbs: 5 g

Fiber: 1 g Protein: 40 g

Garlic Lemon Sauce-less Ribs

Preparation time: 15 minutes

Cooking time: 8 hours

Servings: 4

Ingredients:

4 lb. pork ribs

2 T. garlic powder

2 T. sea salt

2 T. black pepper

1 T. cumin

3 lemons, juiced

Directions:

In a bowl, combine garlic powder, salt, pepper, and cumin. Rub spices over ribs, making sure to coat them thoroughly.

Put the ribs inside the slow cooker, then pour lemon juice over the ribs. Cook on low within 8 hours or on high within 5 hours.

Nutrition:

Calories: 287

Fats: 18 g

Carbs: .5 g

Fiber: 1 g

Protein: 29 g

Garlic Dill Chicken Thighs

Preparation time: 15 minutes

Cooking time: 4 hours

Servings: 4

Ingredients:

2 t. dried parsley

2 t. seasoned salt

1 ½ t. black pepper

1 t. garlic powder

½ t. dried dill

½ t. onion powder

8 boneless, skinless chicken thighs

6 oz pesto

½ c. chicken broth

Directions:

In a small bowl, combine spices. Arrange chicken in a slow cooker. Top with pesto, chicken broth, and spice mixture.

Stir to combine and thoroughly coat each piece of chicken. Cook on high within 3-4 hours.

Nutrition:

Calories: 456

Fats: 30 g

Carbs: 2 g

Fiber: 1 g

Protein: 47 g

Oregano Italian Sausage Meatballs

Preparation time: 15 minutes

Cooking time: 1 hour

Servings: 4

Ingredients:

1 ½ lb. ground beef

2 c. Alfredo sauce

5 pepper jack cheese slices

1 t. oregano

1 t. salt

1 ½ Italian sausage, spicy

1/3 c. pork rinds

2 eggs

1 t. Italian seasoning

Directions:

Combine all ingredients except Alfredo sauce. Form mixture into meatballs. Put the meatballs inside the slow cooker and add Alfredo sauce. Set the slow cooker to LOW and cook for 1 hour.

Serve.

Nutrition:

Calories: 289

Fats: 22.6 g

Carbs: 1.2 g

Fiber: 1 g

Protein: 20.8 g

Tomatoes Mexican Chicken

Preparation time: 15 minutes

Cooking time: 6 hours

Servings: 4

Ingredients:

1 c. sour cream

½ c. chicken stock

1 can (14 oz.) diced tomatoes and green chilies

1 batch homemade taco seasoning

2 lb. chicken breast

Directions:

Mix all the items inside the slow cooker. Cook for 6 hours on LOW.

Nutrition:

Calories: 262

Fats: 10.5 g

Carbs: 10 g

Fiber: 2.5 g

Protein: 32 g

Slow Cooker Shredded Pork

Preparation time: 15 minutes

Cooking time: 6 hours

Servings: 6

Ingredients:

6 lb. pork roast

2 T. butter

1 onion, chopped

2 T. cumin

2 T. thyme

2 T. chili powder

4 T. minced garlic

1 c. water

Salt and black ground pepper, to taste

Directions:

Grease your slow cooker with butter. Place chopped onion and garlic. Slice a crisscross pattern over the top of the pork.

Mix spices, salt, and pepper and rub into meat. Place meat into the slow cooker and add 1 c. water. Cook on high for 6-8 hours. Serve hot.

Nutrition:

Calories: 343

Fats: 22.9 g

Carbs: 2.76 g

Fiber: 0.81 g

Protein: 25.6 g

Chili Ground Beef with Pumpkin

Preparation time: 15 minutes

Cooking time: 6 hours & 30 minutes

Servings: 6

Ingredients:

2 lb. ground beef

1 can pumpkin puree

1 T. pumpkin pie spice

3 c. 100% tomato juice, freshly squeezed if possible

2 tomatoes, diced

1 red bell pepper

1 yellow onion

2 t. each cumin + cayenne pepper

1 T. chili powder

Ghee or coconut oil

Directions:

Grease a large slow cooker with ghee or coconut oil. Place the ground meat and pumpkin puree on the bottom of the slow cooker. Chop all vegetables and place with the rest of ingredients over ground meat and pumpkin puree. Stir slightly.

Cook on low within 4-6 hours. Once ready, season chili with salt and pepper to taste and cook on high another 30 minutes. Serve hot.

Nutrition:

Calories: 35 Fats: 25.24 g Carbs: 9.87 g

Fiber: 2.15 g Protein: 21.7 g

Best Slow Cooker Pizza

Preparation time: 15 minutes

Cooking time: 4 hours

Servings: 6

Ingredients:

¾ lb. ground beef

15 oz. pizza sauce

3 c. spinach

¾ lb. Italian sausage, cooked

3 c. Mozzarella cheese, shredded

16 slices pepperoni

For topping:

1 c. mushrooms, sliced

½ c. sweet onion, diced

¼ c. artichoke hearts, marinated, chopped

2 garlic cloves, diced

1 c. sliced olives

½ bell pepper, chopped

¼ c. tomatoes, chopped

Directions:

Combine hamburger, onions, sausage, and sauce in a bowl.

Add ½ of the mixture to slow cooker then top with spinach and pepperoni along with toppings. Top with Mozzarella cheese and repeat layers ending with cheese.

Set cooker on low and cook for 4 hours. Cool and slice. Serve.

Nutrition:

Calories: 487

Fats: 37 g

Carbs: 11.9 g

Fiber: 1 g

Protein: 30 g

Cumin Chili Steak

Preparation time: 15 minutes

Cooking time: 6 hours

Servings: 6

Ingredients:

3 pounds beef steak, cubed

1 T. paprika

½ t. chili powder

1 t. dried oregano

½ t. ground cumin

Salt and pepper, to taste

4 T. butter

½ c. sliced leeks

2 c. Italian diced tomatoes

1 c. broth, beef

Directions:

Place all the fixing inside the slow cooker by order on the list. Stir together.

Cover, cook on high for 6 hours. Serve with avocado slices topped with sour cream and shredded cheddar cheese.

Nutrition:

Calories: 357

Fats: 26 g

Carbs: 9 g

Fiber: 1.21 g

Protein: 30 g

Spicy Turkey Stew

Preparation time: 15 minutes

Cooking time: 6 hours

Servings: 4

Ingredients:

6 turkey thighs

6 slices of bacon

1 c. coconut water

1 c. coconut milk, unsweetened

3 T. tomato paste

2 T. butter, unsalted

1 c. chopped onion

1 hot pepper, chopped

1 T. thyme, minced, fresh

1 T. basil, minced

2 T. garlic, minced

1 T. coconut flour

3 T. lemon juice

Salt and fresh black pepper, to taste

Directions:

Grease your Slow Cooker with butter. Thinly slice onions and pepper and evenly place them on the bottom of Slow Cooker. Place boneless turkey thighs on top of onions.

Add the sliced bacon. Add seasonings (thyme, basil, salt, pepper, garlic, coconut flour). Pour over the lemon juice, coconut water, coconut milk, and tomato paste.

Cook on low for 6 hours: stir and break up turkey. Serve hot.

Nutrition:

Calories: 409

Fats: 14.3 g

Carbs: 5.56 g

Fiber: 1.17 g

Protein: 42.3 g

Spicy Bacon, Sausages & Red Cabbage

Preparation time: 15 minutes

Cooking time: 6 hours

Servings: 4

Ingredients:

2 lb. red cabbage, shredded

5 oz. bacon, finely diced

4 ½ oz spicy dry-cured sausage, diced

¼ c. extra virgin olive oil

4 cloves garlic, crushed

¼ c. homemade broth or water

Salt

ground black pepper

Directions:

Finely chop the red cabbage. In a greased slow cooker, add in the shredded cabbage followed by the bacon, sausages, and crushed garlic. Pour over the homemade broth and stir.

Cook on low within 4-6 hours. Serve hot.

Nutrition:

Calories: 172

Fats: 11.4 g

Carbs: 11.7 g

Fiber: 4.6 g

Protein: 7.22 g

Cumin Thyme Pork Slow Cooking

Preparation time: 15 minutes

Cooking time: 8 hours

Servings: 8

Ingredients:

2 T. bacon fat or butter

2 T. cumin

2 T. chili powder

1 T. black pepper

1 c. water

8 lb. pork butt

1 onion

2 T. thyme

1 T. salt

4 T. garlic, diced

Directions:

Use butter/fat to coat a slow cooker. Slice the onion and use to line the base of ow cooker and then add garlic. Discard extra fat from meat and use a knife to score meat in a crisscross pattern. Combine spices and use to coat meat all over.

Put the pork over the top of the onions plus garlic and pour in water. Set cooker on HIGH and cook for 8 hours until meat is falling apart. Serve.

Nutrition:

Calories: 265

Fats: 9 g

Carbs: 0 g

Fiber: 1 g

Protein: 8 g

Turmeric Chili Beef Curry

Preparation time: 15 minutes

Cooking time: 6 hours

Servings: 3

Ingredients:

21 oz. stewing beef, cubed

1 c. coconut cream

1 red onion, quartered

1 t. ground cardamom

2 t. ground coriander

1 t. turmeric powder

1 t. Chinese five-spice

½ t. chili powder

1 t. ground cumin

1 t. ground cinnamon

A handful of leafy greens

Directions:

Mix all the fixings inside the slow cooker except the leafy greens and stir well.

Cook for 4-6 hours on high. Three to five minutes before completion of cook time, mix in the leafy greens.

Nutrition:

Calories: 256

Fats: 14.1 g

Carbs: 2 g

Fiber: 0.9 g

Protein: 29.1 g

Alison Jacobs

CHAPTER 9:

Desserts

Tasty Apple and Cranberry Dessert

Preparation time: 15 minutes

Cooking time: 3 hours

Servings: 4

Ingredients:

4 medium-sized sliced apples

1 cup of frozen or fresh cranberries

1 teaspoon of vanilla

8 tablespoons of light brown packed sugar

2 teaspoons of ground cinnamon, divided

1 packet of super moist yellow cake mix, 15 ounces

8 tablespoons of melted butter

Whipped cream

Directions:

Grease the slow cooker. Add 1 teaspoon of cinnamon, brown sugar, apples, and cranberries to the slow cooker and combine them.

Mix the rest of 1 teaspoon of cinnamon with the dry cake mix in a bowl.

Spread the mixture onto the fruits and drizzle the melted butter over the top. Cook within 3 hours, on high. Serve it with whipped cream.

Nutrition:

Calories: 230 Fat: 12 gProtein: 30 g

Carbohydrates: 4.5 g

Caramel Pecan Pudding

Preparation time: 15 minutes

Cooking time: 3 hours

Servings: 4

Ingredients:

1 ½ cups of Bisquick mix

16 tablespoons of sugar, divided

8 tablespoons of unsweetened baking cocoa

8 tablespoons of milk

12 tablespoons of caramel topping, divided

1 2/3 cups of hot water

½ cup of chopped pecans

Directions:

Mix the Bisquick mix, 8 tablespoons of sugar, cocoa, milk, and 6 tablespoons of caramel in a large bowl.

Pour the mixture into a slow cooker. Add the hot water.

Top with the remaining sugar then cooks on low within 3 hours.

Divide into bowls, spread the remaining caramel over the top, sprinkle with pecans, and serve.

Nutrition:

Carbohydrates: 19 g Calories: 544

Fat: 5.6 g Protein: 3.4 g

Mouth-Watering Chocolate Cake

Preparation time: 15 minutes

Cooking time: 3.5 hours

Servings: 4

Ingredients:

1 ½ cups of almond flour

¾ cup of granulated sugar or a sweetener of your preference

2/3 cup of cocoa powder

¼ cup of whey protein powder

2 teaspoons of baking powder

¼ teaspoons of salt

½ cup of melted butter

4 large eggs

¾ cup of unsweetened almond milk

1 teaspoon of vanilla extract

Whipped cream

Directions:

Mix the dry fixing in a large bowl.

Put the wet fixing to it one at a time, stirring as you go along. Whisk together thoroughly.

Grease the slow cooker and add the cake mixture—cover and cook for 3.5 hours on low.

Divide into bowls and serve with whipped cream.

Nutrition:

Calories: 260 Fat: 14 g

Protein: 8 g Carbohydrates: 15 g

Fabulous Peanut Vanilla Chocolate Butter Cake

Preparation time: 15 minutes

Cooking time: 4 hours

Servings: 4

Ingredients:

3/4 cup of melted natural peanut butter

4 large eggs

2 cups of almond flour

½ a cup of water

¼ cup of unflavored whey protein powder

½ cup of melted butter

2 ounces of melted dark chocolate, sugar-free

¾ cup of your preferred sweetener

¼ cup of coconut flour

1 teaspoon of vanilla extract

1 tablespoon of baking powder

¼ teaspoon of salt

1 teaspoon of vanilla extract

Directions:

Deglaze the inside of the slow cooker using a butter.

Combine all the ingredients in a large bowl and whisk together thoroughly.

Spoon 2/3 of the batter onto the base of the slow cooker. Add half of the melted chocolate.

Add the remainder of the batter. Put the remaining chocolate on top.

Cover and cook for 4 hours. Divide onto plates and serve.

Nutrition:

Calories: 335

Carbohydrates: 11.5 g

Fat: 27 g

Fiber: 5.2 g

Protein: 8 g

Poppy Seed Butter Cake

Preparation time: 15 minutes

Cooking time: 3 hours

Servings: 4

Ingredients:

4 large eggs

The zest and juice of 4 lemons

½ cup of melted butter

2 cups of almond flour

3 tablespoons of poppy seeds

2 tablespoons of baking powder

1 tablespoon of vanilla extract

1 teaspoon of salt

½ cup of vanilla protein powder

3 tablespoons of vanilla protein powder

½ cup of xylitol

Directions:

Mix all the items except the eggs in a bowl.

Add the eggs one by one and whisk together thoroughly.

Grease the slow cooker with butter. Pour the batter into the slow cooker.

Cover and cook for 3 hours. Divide onto plates and serve.

Nutrition:

Calories: 143 Carbohydrates: 9 g

Fat: 10 g Fiber: 1 g

Protein: 6 g

Wonderful Raspberry Almond Cake

Preparation time: 15 minutes

Cooking time: 3 hours

Servings: 4

Ingredients:

1 cup of fresh raspberries

1/3 cup of dark chocolate chips, sugar-free

2 cups of almond flour

1 teaspoon of coconut extract

¾ cup of almond milk

4 large eggs

2 teaspoons of baking soda

¼ teaspoon of salt

1 cup of Swerve

½ cup of melted coconut oil

1 cup of shredded coconut unsweetened

¼ cup of powdered egg whites

Directions:

Grease the slow cooker with butter. Mix all the fixing in a bowl.

Pour the batter inside, then cook within 3 hours on low.

Nutrition:

Calories: 362

Carbohydrates: 12.8 g

Fat: 26 g

Protein: 8 g

Scrumptious Chocolate Cocoa Cake

Preparation time: 15 minutes

Cooking time: 4 hours

Servings: 4

Ingredients:

1 ½ cups of ground almonds

½ cup of coconut flakes

6 tablespoons of your preferred sweetener

2 teaspoons of baking powder

A pinch of salt

½ cup of coconut oil

½ cup of cooking cream

2 tablespoons of lemon juice

The zest from 2 lemons

2 large eggs

Espresso and whipped cream for serving

Toppings:

3 tablespoons of sweetener

½ a cup of boiling water

2 tablespoons of lemon juice

2 tablespoons of coconut oil

Directions:

Combine the baking powder, sweetener, coconut, and almonds in a large bowl. Whisk together thoroughly.

In another bowl, combine the eggs, juice, coconut oil, and whisk together thoroughly.

Combine the wet and the dry ingredients and whisk together thoroughly.

Put the aluminum foil inside the bottom of the slow cooker. Pour the batter into the slow cooker.

Mix all the topping fixing in a small bowl, and pour on top of the cake batter.

Cover the slow cooker with paper towels to absorb condensation, then cook within 3 hours on high.

Divide into bowls and serve with espresso and whipped cream.

Nutrition:

Carbs: 5 g Protein: 7 g

Fat: 24 g

Calories: 310

Lemon Cake

Preparation time: 15 minutes

Cooking time: 3 hours

Servings: 8

Ingredients:

1 ½ cup ground almonds

½ cup coconut flakes

6 Tablespoons sweetener like Swerve (Erythritol, or a suitable substitute)

2 teaspoons baking powder

Pinch of salt

½ cup softened coconut oil

½ cup cooking cream

2 Tablespoons lemon juice

Zest from two lemons

2 eggs

Topping:

3 tablespoons Swerve (or a suitable substitute)

½ cup boiling water

2 Tablespoons lemon juice

2 Tablespoons softened coconut oil

Directions:

In a bowl, combine the almonds, coconut, sweetener, baking powder. Whisk until combined.

In a separate bowl, blend coconut oil, cream, juice, and eggs.

Add the egg mixture to the dry fixing, mix.

Line the crockpot with aluminum foil, pour in the batter.

In a bowl, mix the topping. Pour it over the cake batter.

Cover it with paper towels to absorb the water.

Cover, cook on high for 3 hours. Serve warm.

Nutrition:

Calories: 142

Carbs: 0g

Fat: 8g

Protein: 0g

Raspberry & Coconut Cake

Preparation time: 15 minutes

Cooking time: 3 hours

Servings: 10

Ingredients:

2 cups ground almonds

1 cup shredded coconut

¾ cup sweetener, Swerve (or a suitable substitute)

2 teaspoon baking soda

¼ teaspoon salt

4 large eggs

½ cup melted coconut oil

¾ cup of coconut milk

1 cup raspberries, fresh or frozen

½ cup sugarless dark chocolate chips

Directions:

Butter the crockpot.

In a bowl, mix the dry ingredients.

Beat in the eggs, melted coconut oil, and coconut milk. Mix in the raspberries plus chocolate chips.

Combine the cocoa, almonds, and salt in a bowl.

Pour the batter into the buttered crockpot.

Cover the crockpot with a paper towel to absorb the water.

Cover, cook on low for 3 hours. Let the cake cool in the pot.

Nutrition:

Calories: 201

Carbs: 24g Fat: 10g

Protein: 0g

Chocolate Cheesecake

Preparation time: 15 minutes

Cooking time: 2.5 hours

Servings: 8

Ingredients:

3 cups cream cheese

Pinch of salt

3 eggs

1 cup powder sweetener of your choice, Swerve (or a suitable substitute)

1 teaspoon vanilla extract

½ cup sugarless dark chocolate chips

Directions:

Whisk the cream cheese, sweetener, and salt in a bowl.

Add the eggs one at a time. Combine thoroughly.

Spread the cheesecake in a cake pan, which fits in the crockpot you are using.

Dissolved the chocolate chips in a small pot and pour over the batter. Using a knife, swirl the chocolate through the batter.

Put 2 cups of water inside the crockpot and set the cake pan inside. Cover it with a paper towel to absorb the water, then cook on high for 2.5 hours. Remove from the crockpot and let it cool in the pan for 1 hour. Refrigerate.

Nutrition:

Calories: 330 Carbs: 34g

Fat: 19g

Protein: 6g

Crème Brule

Preparation time: 15 minutes

Cooking time: 2 hours

Servings: 6

Ingredients:

5 large egg yolks

6 Tablespoons sweetener, Erythritol

2 cups double cream

1 Bourbon vanilla pod, scraped

Pinch of salt

Directions:

In a bowl, beat the eggs and sweetener together.

Add the cream and vanilla. Whisk together.

Put it in one big dish.

Set it in the crockpot and pour hot water around- so the water reaches halfway up the dish.

Cover, cook on high for 2 hours.

Take the dishes out, let them cool. Refrigerate for 6-8 hours.

Nutrition:

Calories: 120

Carbs: 18g

Fat: 4g

Protein: 3g

Peanut Butter & Chocolate Cake

Preparation time: 15 minutes

Cooking time: 4 hours

Servings: 12

Ingredients:

1 Tablespoon butter for greasing the crockpot

2 cups almond flour

¾ cup sweetener of your choice

¼ cup coconut flakes

¼ cup whey protein powder

1 teaspoon baking powder

¼ teaspoon salt

¾ cup peanut butter, melted

4 large eggs

1 teaspoon vanilla extract

½ cup of water

3 Tablespoons sugarless dark chocolate, melted

Directions:

Grease the crockpot well.

In a bowl, mix the dry ingredients. Stir in the wet ingredients one at a time.

Spread about 2/3 of batter in the crockpot, add half the chocolate. Swirl with a fork. Top up with the remaining batter and chocolate. Swirl again.

Cook on low for 4 hours. Switch off. Let it sit covered for 30 minutes.

Nutrition:

Calories: 270

Carbs: 39g

Fat: 11g

Protein: 5g

Berry & Coconut Cake

Preparation time: 15 minutes

Cooking time: 2 hours

Servings: 8

Ingredients:

1 Tablespoon butter for greasing the crock

1 cup almond flour

¾ cup sweetener of your choice

1 teaspoon baking soda

¼ teaspoon salt

1 large egg, beaten with a fork

¼ cup coconut flour

¼ cup of coconut milk

2 Tablespoons coconut oil

4 cups fresh or frozen blueberries and raspberries

Directions:

Butter the crockpot well.

In a bowl, whisk the egg, coconut milk, and oil together.

Mix the dry ingredients. Slowly stir in the wet ingredients. Do not over mix.

Pour the batter in the crockpot, spread evenly.

Spread the berries on top.

Cover, cook on high for 2 hours. Cool in the crock for 1-2 hours.

Nutrition:

Calories: 263

Carbs: 9g

Fat: 22g

Protein: 5g

Cocoa Pudding Cake

Preparation time: 15 minutes

Cooking time: 3 hours

Servings: 10

Ingredients:

1 Tablespoon butter for greasing the crockpot

1 ½ cups ground almonds

¾ cup sweetener, Swerve (or a suitable substitute)

¾ cup cocoa powder

¼ cup whey protein

2 teaspoons baking powder

¼ teaspoon salt

4 large eggs

½ cup butter, melted

¾ cup full-fat cream

1 teaspoon vanilla extract

Directions:

Butter the crockpot thoroughly.

Whisk the dry fixing in a bowl.

Stir in the melted butter, eggs, cream, and vanilla. Mix well.

Pour the batter into the crockpot and spread evenly.

Cook within 2½ to 3 hours, low. If preferred – more like pudding, cook cake shorter; more dry cake, cook longer.

Cool in the crockpot for 30 minutes. Cut and serve.

Nutrition:

Calories: 250

Carbs: 29g

Fat: 5g

Protein: 22g

Keto Coconut Hot Chocolate

Preparation time: 15 minutes

Cooking time: 4 hours

Servings: 8

Ingredients:

5 cups full-fat coconut milk

2 cups heavy cream

1 tsp vanilla extract

1/3 cup cocoa powder

3 ounces dark chocolate, roughly chopped

½ tsp cinnamon

Few drops of stevia to taste

Directions:

Add the coconut milk, cream, vanilla extract, cocoa powder, chocolate, cinnamon, and stevia to the crockpot and stir to combine.

Cook for 4 hours, high, whisking every 45 minutes.

Taste the hot chocolate and if you prefer more sweetness, add a few more drops of stevia.

Nutrition:

Calories: 135 Carbs: 5g

Fat: 11g

Protein: 5g

Ambrosia

Preparation time: 15 minutes

Cooking time: 3 hours

Servings: 10

Ingredients:

1 cup unsweetened shredded coconut

¾ cup slivered almonds

3 ounces dark chocolate (high cocoa percentage), roughly chopped

1/3 cup pumpkin seeds

2 ounces salted butter

1 tsp cinnamon

2 cups heavy cream

2 cups full-fat Greek yogurt

1 cup fresh berries – strawberries and raspberries are best

Directions:

Place the shredded coconut, slivered almonds, dark chocolate, pumpkin seeds, butter, and cinnamon into the crockpot.

Cook for 3 hours, high, stirring every 45 minutes to combine the chocolate and butter as it melts.

Remove the mixture from the crockpot, place in a bowl, and leave to cool.

In a large bowl, whip the cream until softly whipped.

Stir the yogurt through the cream.

Slice the strawberries into pieces, then put it to the cream mixture, along with the other berries you are using, fold through.

Sprinkle the cooled coconut mixture over the cream mixture.

Nutrition:

Calories: 57

Carbs: 11g

Fat: 1g

Protein: 1g

Dark Chocolate and Peppermint Pots

Preparation time: 15 minutes

Cooking time: 2 hours

Servings: 6

Ingredients:

2 ½ cups heavy cream

3 ounces dark chocolate, melted in the microwave

4 egg yolks, lightly beaten with a fork

Few drops of stevia

Few drops of peppermint essence to taste

Directions:

Mix the beaten egg yolks, cream, stevia, melted chocolate, and peppermint essence in a medium-sized bowl.

Prepare the pots by greasing 6 ramekins with butter.

Pour the chocolate mixture into the pots evenly.

Put the pots inside the slow cooker and put hot water below halfway up.

Cook for 2 hours, high. Take the pots out of the slow cooker and leave to cool and set.

Serve with a fresh mint leaf and whipped cream.

Nutrition:

Calories: 125

Carbs: 15g

Fat: 6g

Protein: 1g

Creamy Vanilla Custard

Preparation time: 15 minutes

Cooking time: 3 hours

Servings: 8

Ingredients:

3 cups full-fat cream

4 egg yolks, lightly beaten

2 tsp vanilla extract

Few drops of stevia

Directions:

Mix the cream, egg yolks, vanilla extract, and stevia in a medium-sized bowl.

Pour the mixture into a heat-proof dish. Place the dish into the slow cooker.

Put hot water into the pot, around the dish, halfway up. Set the temperature to high.

Cook for 3 hours. Serve hot or cold!

Nutrition:

Calories: 206

Carbs: 30g

Fat: 7g

Protein: 6g

Coconut, Chocolate, And Almond Truffle Bake

Preparation time: 15 minutes

Cooking time: 4 hours

Servings: 8

Ingredients:

3 ounces butter, melted

3 ounces dark chocolate, melted

1 cup ground almonds

1 cup desiccated coconut

3 tbsp unsweetened cocoa powder

2 tsp vanilla extract

1 cup heavy cream

A few extra squares of dark chocolate, grated

¼ cup toasted almonds, chopped

Directions:

In a large bowl, mix the melted butter, chocolate, ground almonds, coconut, cocoa powder, and vanilla extract.

Roll the mixture into balls. Grease a heat-proof dish.

Place the balls into the dish—Cook for 4 hours, low setting.

Leave the truffle dish to cool until warm. Mix the cream until soft peak.

Spread the cream over the truffle dish and sprinkle the grated chocolate and chopped toasted almonds over the top. Serve immediately!

Nutrition:

Calories: 115

Carbs: 8g

Fat: 10g

Protein: 2g

Peanut Butter, Chocolate, And Pecan Cupcakes

Preparation time: 15 minutes

Cooking time: 4 hours

Servings: 14

Ingredients:

14 paper cupcake cases

1 cup smooth peanut butter

2 ounces butter

2 tsp vanilla extract

5 ounces dark chocolate

2 tbsp coconut oil

2 eggs, lightly beaten

1 cup ground almonds

1 tsp baking powder

1 tsp cinnamon

10 pecan nuts, toasted and finely chopped

Directions:

Dissolve the dark chocolate plus coconut oil in the microwave, stir to combine, and set aside.

Place the peanut butter and butter into a medium-sized bowl, microwave for 30 seconds at a time until the butter has just melted.

Mix the peanut butter plus butter until combined and smooth.

Stir the vanilla extract into the peanut butter mixture.

Mix the ground almonds, eggs, baking powder, and cinnamon in a small bowl.

Pour the melted chocolate and coconut oil evenly into the 14 paper cases.

Spoon half of the almond/egg mixture evenly into the cases, on top of the chocolate and press down slightly.

Spoon the peanut butter mixture into the cases, on top of the almond/egg mixture.

Spoon the remaining almond/egg mixture into the cases.

Put the pecans on top of each cupcake.

Put the filled cases into the slow cooker—Cook for 4 hours, high setting.

Nutrition:

Calories: 145 Carbs: 20g

Fat: 3g Protein: 4g

Vanilla and Strawberry Cheesecake

Preparation time: 15 minutes

Cooking time: 6 hours

Servings: 8

Ingredients:

Base:

2 ounces butter, melted

1 cup ground hazelnuts

½ cup desiccated coconut

2 tsp vanilla extract

1 tsp cinnamon

Filling:

2 cups cream cheese

2 eggs, lightly beaten

1 cup sour cream

2 tsp vanilla extract

8 large strawberries, chopped

Directions:

Mix the melted butter, hazelnuts, coconut, vanilla, and cinnamon in a medium-sized bowl.

Press the base into a greased heat-proof dish.

Mix the cream cheese, eggs, sour cream, and vanilla extract, beat with electric egg beaters in a large bowl until thick and combined.

Fold the strawberries through the cream cheese mixture.

Put the cream cheese batter into the dish, on top of the base, spread out until smooth.

Put it in the slow cooker and put hot water around the dish until halfway up.

Cook for 6 hours, low setting until just set but slightly wobbly.

Chill before serving.

Nutrition:

Calories: 156

Carbs: 4g

Fat: 7g

Protein: 15g

Coffee Creams with Toasted Seed Crumble Topping

Preparation time: 15 minutes

Cooking time: 4 hours

Servings: 6

Ingredients:

2 cups heavy cream

3 egg yolks, lightly beaten

1 tsp vanilla extract

3 tbsp strong espresso coffee (or 3tsp instant coffee dissolved in 3tbsp boiling water)

½ cup mixed seeds – sesame seeds, pumpkin seeds, chia seeds, sunflower seeds,

1 tsp cinnamon

1 tbsp coconut oil

Directions:

Heat-up the coconut oil in a small frypan until melted.

Add the mixed seeds, cinnamon, and a pinch of salt, toss in the oil and heat until toasted and golden, place into a small bowl and set aside.

Mix the cream, egg yolks, vanilla, and coffee in a medium-sized bowl.

Pour the cream/coffee mixture into the ramekins.

Place the ramekins into the slow cooker. Put hot water inside until halfway.

Cook on low setting for 4 hours.

Remove, then leave to cool slightly on the bench.

Sprinkle the seed mixture over the top of each custard before serving.

Nutrition:

Calories: 35

Carbs: 4g

Fat: 2g

Protein: 1g

Lemon Cheesecake

Preparation time: 15 minutes

Cooking time: 6 hours

Servings: 10

Ingredients:

2 ounces butter, melted

1 cup pecans, finely ground in the food processor

1 tsp cinnamon

2 cups cream cheese

1 cup sour cream

2 eggs, lightly beaten

1 lemon

Few drops of stevia

1 cup heavy cream

Directions:

Mix the melted butter, ground pecans, and cinnamon until it forms a wet, sand-like texture.

Press the butter/pecan mixture into a greased, heat-proof dish and set aside.

Place the cream cheese, eggs, sour cream, stevia, zest, and juice of one lemon into a large bowl, beat with electric egg beaters until combined and smooth.

Put the cream cheese batter into the dish, on top of the base.

Place the dish inside the slow cooker, then put warm water in halfway up.

Cook within 6 hours, low setting.

Set the cheesecake on the bench to cool and set.

Whip the cream until soft peak, and spread over the cheesecake before serving.

Nutrition:

Calories: 271

Carbs: 33g

Fat: 15g

Protein: 2g

Macadamia Fudge Truffles

Preparation time: 15 minutes

Cooking time: 4 hours

Servings: 25

Ingredients:

1 cup roasted macadamia nuts, finely chopped

½ cup ground almonds

2 ounces butter, melted

5 ounces dark chocolate, melted

1 tsp vanilla extract

1 egg, lightly beaten

Directions:

Place the macadamia nuts, almonds, melted butter, melted chocolate, vanilla, and egg into a large bowl, stir until combined.

Grease the bottom of the crockpot by rubbing with butter. Place the mixture into the crockpot and press down.

Set to cook low setting within 4 hours.

Allow the batter to cool until just warm. Take a teaspoon, scoop the mixture out, and roll into balls.

Refrigerate to harden slightly. Store the truffle balls in the fridge.

Nutrition:

Calories: 150

Carbs: 19g

Fat: 6g

Protein: 6g

Chocolate Covered Bacon Cupcakes

Preparation time: 15 minutes

Cooking time: 3 hours

Servings: 10

Ingredients:

10 paper cupcake cases

5 slices streaky bacon, cut into small pieces, fried in a pan until crispy

5 ounces dark chocolate, melted

1 cup ground hazelnuts

1 tsp baking powder

2 eggs, lightly beaten

½ cup full-fat Greek yogurt

1 tsp vanilla extract

Directions:

Mix the fried bacon pieces and melted chocolate in a bowl, set aside.

Mix the ground hazelnuts, baking powder, eggs, yogurt, vanilla, and a pinch of salt in a medium-sized bowl.

Spoon the hazelnut mixture into the cupcake cases.

Spoon the chocolate and bacon mixture on top of the hazelnut mixture.

Place the cupcake cases into the crockpot. Cook for 3 hours, high setting.

Remove the cupcakes from the pot and leave to cool on the bench before storing serving. Serve with whipped cream!

Nutrition:

Calories: 185 Carbs: 27g

Fat: 8g

Protein: 4g

Chocolate, Berry, And Macadamia Layered Jar

Preparation time: 15 minutes

Cooking time: 6 hours

Servings: 6

Ingredients:

5 ounces dark chocolate, melted

½ cup mixed berries, (fresh) – any berries you like

3/4 cup toasted macadamia nuts, chopped

7 ounces cream cheese

½ cup heavy cream

1 tsp vanilla extract

Directions:

Whisk the cream cheese, cream, and vanilla extract in a medium-sized bowl.

Scoop a small amount of melted chocolate, put it into each jar or ramekin.

Place a few berries on top of the chocolate.

Sprinkle some toasted macadamias onto the berries. Scoop the cream cheese mixture into the ramekin.

Place another layer of chocolate, berries, and macadamia nuts on top of the cream cheese mixture.

Put the jars inside the slow cooker and put the hot water until it reaches halfway up.

Set to low, then cook for 6 hours.

Remove the jars and leave them to cool and set on the bench for about 2 hours before serving.

Nutrition:

Calories: 150 Carbs: 25g Fat: 15g Protein: 3g

Salty-Sweet Almond Butter and Chocolate Sauce

Preparation time: 15 minutes

Cooking time: 4 hours

Servings: 1

Ingredients:

1 cup almond butter

2 ounces salted butter

1-ounce dark chocolate

½ tsp sea salt

Few drops of stevia

Directions:

Place the almond butter, butter, dark chocolate, sea salt, and stevia to the crockpot.

Cook for 4 hours, high, stirring every 30 minutes to combine the butter and chocolate as they melt. Serve or store in a fridge.

Nutrition:

Calories: 200 Carbs: 21g Fat: 7g

Protein: 15g

Coconut Squares with Blueberry Glaze

Preparation time: 15 minutes

Cooking time: 3 hours

Servings: 20

Ingredients:

2 cups desiccated coconut

1-ounce butter, melted

3 ounces cream cheese

1 egg, lightly beaten

½ tsp baking powder

2 tsp vanilla extract

1 cup of frozen berries

Directions:

Beat the coconut, butter, cream cheese, egg, baking powder, and vanilla extract, using a wooden spoon in a bowl until combined and smooth.

Grease a heat-proof dish with butter. Spread the coconut mixture into the dish.

Defrost the blueberries in the microwave until they resemble a thick sauce. Spread the blueberries over the coconut mixture.

Put the dish into the slow cooker, then put hot water until it reaches halfway up the dish.

Cook for 3 hours, high. Remove the dish from the pot and leave to cool on the bench before slicing into small squares.

Nutrition:

Calories: 115

Carbs: 20g

Fat: 3g

Protein: 3g

Chocolate and Blackberry Cheesecake Sauce

Preparation time: 15 minutes

Cooking time: 6 hours

Servings: 1

Ingredients:

¾ lb. cream cheese

½ cup heavy cream

1 ½ ounces butter

3 ounces dark chocolate

½ cup fresh blackberries, chopped

1 tsp vanilla extract

Few drops of stevia

Directions:

Place the cream cheese, cream, butter, dark chocolate, blackberries, vanilla, and stevia into the slow cooker.

Place the lid onto the pot and set the temperature to low.

Cook for 6 hours, stirring every 30 minutes to combine the butter and chocolate as it melts. Serve, or store in a fridge.

Nutrition:

Calories: 200

Carbs: 18g

Fat: 13g

Protein: 3g

Hot Fudge Cake

Preparation time: 25 minutes

Cooking time: 3 hours

Servings: 10

Ingredients:

1¼ cup Sukrin Gold, divided

1 cup almond flour

¼ cup plus 3 Tbsp. unsweetened cocoa powder, divided

2 tsp baking powder

½ tsp. salt

½ cup heavy cream

2 Tbsp melted butter

½ tsp. vanilla extract

1¾ cups boiling water

Directions:

Mix ¾ cup Sukrin Gold, almond flour, cocoa, baking powder, and salt. Stir in heavy cream, butter, and vanilla. Put it inside the slow cooker.

Mix ½ cup Sukrin Gold and ¼ cup cocoa, then sprinkle over the mixture in the slow cooker. Pour in boiling water. Do not stir.

Cook 2–3 hours, high. Serve.

Nutrition:

Calories 252

Fat 13 g

Sodium 177 mg

Carbs 28 g

Sugar 25 g

Protein 3 g

Fudgy Secret Brownies

Preparation time: 10 minutes

Cooking time: 2 hours

Servings: 8

Ingredients:

4 oz. unsweetened chocolate

¾ cup of coconut oil

¾ cup frozen diced okra, partially thawed

3 large eggs

36 stevia packets

1 teaspoon pure vanilla extract

¼ tsp. mineral salt

¾ cup coconut flour

½–¾ cup coarsely chopped walnuts or pecans, optional

Directions:

Melt chocolate and coconut oil in a small saucepan. Put okra and eggs in a blender. Blend until smooth.

Measure all other ingredients in the mixing bowl.

Pour melted chocolate and okra over the dry ingredients and stir with a fork just until mixed.

Pour into the greased slow cooker—cover and cook on high for 1½–2 hours.

Nutrition:

Calories 421

Fat 38 g

Sodium 113 mg

Carbs 15 g

Sugar 1 g

Protein 8 g

Black and Blue Cobbler

Preparation time: 20 minutes

Cooking time: 2 hours

Servings: 6

Ingredients:

1 cup almond flour

36 packets stevia, divided

1 tsp baking powder

¼ tsp salt

¼ tsp ground cinnamon

¼ tsp ground nutmeg

2 eggs, beaten

2 Tbsp. whole milk

2 Tbsp. coconut oil, melted

2 cups fresh or frozen blueberries

2 cups fresh or frozen blackberries

¾ cup of water

1 tsp. grated orange peel

Directions:

Combine almond flour, 18 packets stevia, baking powder, salt, cinnamon, and nutmeg.

Combine eggs, milk, and oil. Stir into dry fixing. Put it inside the greased slow cooker.

Mix the berries, water, orange peel, and remaining 18 packets stevia in a saucepan. Bring to boil. Remove from heat and pour over batter. Cook on 2–2½ hours, high. Let it cool within 30 minutes. Serve.

Nutrition:

Calories 224

Fat 16 g

Sodium 174 mg

Carbs 21 g

Sugar 8 g

Protein 7 g

Baked Custard

Preparation time: 15 minutes

Cooking time: 3 hours

Servings: 6

Ingredients:

2 cups whole milk

3 eggs, slightly beaten

2½ Tsp., plus ¼ tsp., erythritol, divided

1 tsp. vanilla extract

¼ tsp. cinnamon

Directions:

Heat milk in a small uncovered saucepan until a skin forms on top. Remove from heat and let cool slightly.

Mix the eggs, 2½ tbsp erythritol, and vanilla in a large bowl. Slowly stir cooled milk into the egg-erythritol mixture.

Pour into a greased 1-qt baking dish which will fit into your slow cooker, or into a baking insert designed for your slow cooker.

Mix cinnamon and 1/2 tsp reserved erythritol in a small bowl. Sprinkle over custard mixture.

Cover baking dish or insert with foil—set the container on a metal rack or trivet in the slow cooker. Pour warm water around the dish to a depth of 1 inch.

Cover cooker. Cook on High 2–3 hours, or until custard is set. Serve warm from baking dish or insert.

Nutrition:

Calories 254

Fat 3 g

Sodium 6 g

Carbs 52 g

Sugar 11 g

Protein 4 g

Maple Pot de Crème

Preparation time: 15 minutes

Cooking time: 3 hours

Servings: 6

Ingredients:

2 egg yolks

2 eggs

1 cup heavy cream

½ cup whole milk

½ cup plus 1 Tbsp. Sukrin Gold

Pinch salt

1 tsp. vanilla extract

¼ tsp. ground nutmeg

Whipped cream, for garnish, optional

Directions:

Whisk the egg yolks plus eggs in al bowl until light and frothy.

Add cream, milk, 1 tbsp Sukrin Gold, salt, vanilla, and nutmeg. Mix well.

Pour mixture in a baking dish and set it in a slow cooker. Carefully pour water around the baking dish until the water comes halfway up the sides.

Cover cooker. Cook on high for 2–3 hours, until Pot de Crème is set but still a little bit jiggly in the middle.

Wearing oven mitts to protect your knuckles, carefully remove the hot dish from the cooker. Set on a wire rack to cool to room temperature.

Chill within 2 hours before you serve. Garnish with whipped cream if you wish.

Nutrition:

Calories 102

Fat 18 g Sodium 46 g

Carbs 12 g

Sugar 2 g

Protein 5 g

Slow-Cooker Pumpkin Pie Pudding

Preparation time: 7 minutes

Cooking time: 7 hours

Servings: 6

Ingredients:

15-oz. can solid pack pumpkin

12-oz. can evaporate milk

¼ cup plus 2 Tbsp. erythritol

½ cup keto-friendly baking mix

2 eggs, beaten

2 Tbsp. melted butter

1 Tbsp. pumpkin pie spice

2 tsp. vanilla extract

Directions:

Mix all ingredients. Pour into the greased slow cooker.

Cook within 6–7 hours, high. Serve.

Nutrition:

Calories 168

Fat 15 g

Sodium 91 g

Carbs 22 g

Sugar 3 g

Protein 9 g

Choco-peanut Cake

Preparation time: 15 minutes

Cooking time: 2 hours

Servings: 10

Ingredients:

15.25 oz. devil's food cake mix

1 cup of water

1/2 cup salted butter, melted

3 eggs

8 oz. pkg. mini Reese's peanut butter cups

For the topping

1 cup creamy peanut butter

3 Tbsp. powdered sugar

Ten bite-size Reese's peanut butter cups

Directions:

Mix the cake mixture, ice, butter, and eggs in a large bowl until smooth. Some lumps are all right, that's all right. Cut the cups of the mini peanut butter.

Cleaner non-stick spray on the slow cooker. Add the butter slowly and spread over an even layer.

Cover and cook on high during the cooking time for 2 hours without opening the lid.

Melt the peanut butter over medium heat in a pan. Stir until melted and smooth; observe as it burns hard. To smooth, add the powdered sugar and whisk.

Pour over the butter of the sweetened peanut in the cake, then serve.

Nutrition:

Calories: 607

Carbohydrates: 57g

Protein: 13g

Fat: 39g

Saturated Fat: 13g

Crockpot Apple Pudding Cake

Preparation time: 15 minutes

Cooking time: 3 hours

Servings: 10

Ingredients:

2 cups all-purpose flour

2/3 plus 1/4 cup sugar, divided

3 tsp baking powder

1 tsp salt

1/2 cup butter cold

1 cup milk

4 apples, diced

1 1& /2 cups orange juice

1/2 cup honey

2 tbsp butter melted

1 tsp cinnamon

Directions:

Mix the flour, 2/3 cup sugar, baking powder, and salt. Slice the butter until you have coarse crumbs in the mixture.

Remove the milk from the crumbs until moistened.

Grease a 4 or 5 qt crockpot's bottom and sides. Spoon the batter into the crockpot's bottom and spread evenly. Place the diced apples evenly over the mixture.

Whisk together the orange juice, honey, butter, remaining sugar, and cinnamon in a medium-sized pan. Garnish the apples.

Place the crockpot opening with a clean kitchen towel, place the lid on, it prevents condensation from reaching the crockpot from the cover.

Place the crockpot on top and cook until apples are tender for 2 to 3 hours. Serve hot.

Nutrition:

Calories 405

Fat 9g

Saturated Fat 3g

Carbohydrates 79g

Fiber 2g

Sugar 63g

Protein 3g

Crockpot Brownie Cookies

Preparation time: 15 minutes

Cooking time: 2 hours

Servings: 10

Ingredients:

One box brownie mix

Two eggs

1/4 c butter melted

1/2 c mini chocolate chips

1/2 c chopped walnuts optional

8 slices cookie dough slices

Directions:

Combine your brownie mixture with butter, eggs, chocolate chips, and nuts.

Sprinkle with non-stick spray the inside of your crockpot. Place eight slices of ready-made cookie dough or pile tbsp of it on the bottom.

In your slow cooker, pour brownie mixture on top and smooth out evenly. Put on the lid and cook on top for 2 hours.

To get both textures in your meal, scoop from the middle out to the edge for each serving. If desired, serve warm for best results, top with ice cream.

Nutrition:

Calories 452 Fat 21g

Saturated Fat 7g Carbohydrates 59g

Sugar 38g

Protein 5g

Crockpot Chocolate Caramel Monkey Bread

Preparation time: 15 minutes

Cooking time: 1 hour & 30 minutes

Servings: 6

Ingredients:

1/2 tbsp sugar

1/4 tsp ground cinnamon

15 oz buttermilk biscuits

20 milk chocolate-covered caramels

caramel sauce for topping (optional)

chocolate sauce for topping (optional)

Directions:

Mix sugar and cinnamon and set aside. Fill a parchment paper crockpot, cover up to the bottom.

Wrap 1 buttermilk biscuit dough around one chocolate candy to cover the candy completely, pinching the seam closed.

Place the biscuit-wrapped candy in the crockpot bottom, start in the middle of the crockpot and work your way to the sides.

Continue to wrap candy and put it in the crockpot, leaving roughly 1/2 inch between each. Repeat these steps with sweets wrapped in the second layer of biscuit.

Sprinkle the remaining cinnamon-sugar mixture on top when using all the dough and confectionery.

Cover the crockpot and cook for 1 1/2 hours on the lower side. Once cooked, remove the lid and let cool slightly.

Use the edges of the parchment paper to lift the monkey bread out of the crockpot. Allow cooling for at least 10-15 minutes.

Cut off any excess parchment paper around the edge when ready to serve. In a shallow bread or bowl, put monkey bread and drizzle with chocolate and caramel sauces.

Nutrition:

Calories: 337

Fat: 16g

Saturated Fat: 4g

Carbohydrates: 44g

Fiber: 1g

Sugar: 12g

Protein: 5g

Slow Cooker Coffee Cake

Preparation time: 15 minutes

Cooking time: 2 hours & 30 minutes

Servings: 12

Ingredients:

2 1/2 cups of all-purpose flour

1 & 1/2 cups of brown sugar

2/3 cup vegetable oil

1 1/3 cups almond milk

Two teaspoons baking powder

1/2 teaspoon baking soda

One teaspoon ground cinnamon

One teaspoon white vinegar

One teaspoon salt

Two eggs

1/2 cup chopped nuts optional

Directions:

In a large bowl, whisk in flour, brown sugar, and salt. Remove the oil until it is crumbly mixed.

In the flour mixture, combine the baking powder, baking soda, and cinnamon with a wooden spoon or spatula. In a measuring cup, place milk, oil, eggs, and vinegar and whisk until the eggs are pounded, then add to the flour mixture and stir until mixed.

Spray a non-stick cooking spray 5-7Qt slow cooker or line with a slow cooker liner. Pour into the crockpot with the batter.

Sprinkle the cake batter's nuts over the end. Put a paper towel over the crockpot insert and place the lid on top of it.

Cook within 1 hour and 30 minutes, high s or 2 hours, and 30 minutes.

Serve warm directly from the crockpot or store for up to 3 days in an airtight container.

Nutrition:

Calories: 411

Carbohydrates: 56g

Protein: 6g

Fat: 19g

Saturated Fat: 3g

Fiber: 2g

Sugar: 33g

Slow Cooker Apple Pear Crisp

Preparation time: 15 minutes

Cooking time: 4 hours

Servings: 8

Ingredients:

Four apples, peeled and cut into 1/2-inch slices

3 Bosc pears, peeled and cut into 1/2-inch slices

1/3 cup light brown sugar

One tablespoon all-purpose flour

One tablespoon lemon juice

1/2 teaspoon ground cinnamon

1/4 teaspoon kosher salt

Pinch of ground nutmeg

For the Topping:

3/4 cup all-purpose flour

3/4 cup old fashioned oats

1/2 cup chopped pecans

1/3 cup light brown sugar

1/2 teaspoon ground cinnamon

1/2 teaspoon kosher salt

Eight tablespoons unsalted butter, cut into cubes

Directions:

Combine flour, oats, pecans, sugar, cinnamon, and salt to make the topping. Press the butter into the dry fixing until it looks like coarse crumbs; set aside.

Coat lightly with a non-stick spray inside a 4-qt slow cooker: put apples and pears in the slow cooker. Add brown sugar, flour, juice of lemon, cinnamon, salt, and nutmeg. Sprinkle with reserved topping, gently pressing the crumbs into the butter using your fingertips.

Layer the slow cooker with a clean dishtowel. Cover and cook for 2-3 hours at low heat or 90 minutes at high temperature, remove the dishtowel and continue to cook, uncovered until the top is browned and apples are tender for about 1 hour. Serve cold.

Nutrition:

Calories: 267 Carbohydrates: 27g

Protein: 3g Fat: 17g

Saturated Fat: 7g

Fiber: 4g

Sugar: 16g.

Key Lime Dump Cake Recipe

Preparation time: 15 minutes

Cooking time: 2 hours

Servings: 8

Ingredients:

15.25 oz. Betty Crocker French Vanilla Cake Mix box

44 oz. Key Lime Pie Filling

8 tbsp. or 1/2 cup butter melted

Directions:

Spray inside the Crock-Pot with a non-stick cooking spray. Empty key lime pie cans filling in the Crock-Pot bottom and then spread evenly.

Mix the dry vanilla cake mix with the dissolved butter in a bowl.

Pour the crumble cake/butter mixture over the crockpot, spread evenly, and cover the crockpot with the lid.

Cook for 2 hours at high or 4 hours at low. serve with ice cream or whip cream.

Nutrition:

Calories: 280 Carbohydrates: 58g

Protein: 2g Fat: 4g

Saturated Fat: 2g

Sugar: 41g

Crockpot Cherry Dump Cake Recipe

Preparation time: 15 minutes

Cooking time: 2 hours

Servings: 8

Ingredients:

15.25 oz. Betty Crocker Devil's Food Cake Mix

42 oz. Cherry Pie Filling

1/2 cup butter melted

Directions:

Spray with a non-stick cooking spray inside the crockpot.

Empty cherry pie filling cans into crockpot's bottom, then evenly spread out.

Combine dry cake mix with butter in a medium bowl.

Pour the crumble cake/butter mixture over the crockpot plus cherries, scatter

evenly, and cover the crockpot with a lid.

Cook for 2 hours at high, or 4 hours at low. Use ice cream or whip cream to serve.

Nutrition:

Calories 566 Fat 17g

Saturated Fat 11g Carbohydrates 98g

Fiber 1g Sugar 37g Protein 3g

Crockpot Pumpkin Spice Cake Recipe

Preparation time: 15 minutes

Cooking time: 2 hours

Servings: 8

Ingredients:

15.25 oz. Betty Crocker Spice Cake Mix

15 oz. Libby's Pure Pumpkin

½ cup Applesauce

Three eggs

1 tsp. Pumpkin Pie Spice

Directions:

Whisk all the fixing with a mixer for 1 minute. Spray with nonstick cooking spray inside the crockpot. Pour over and cover the mixture into the crockpot.

Cook for 1.5 – 2 hours or until finished. Serve.

Nutrition:

Calories: 344 Fat: 30.38g

Carbohydrate: 10.03g Fiber: 5.61g

Protein: 8.26g

Crockpot Blueberry Dump Cake Recipe

Preparation time: 15 minutes

Cooking time: 2 hours

Servings: 8

Ingredients:

15.25 oz. Betty Crocker Lemon Cake Mix

42 oz. Blueberry Pie Filling

1/2 cup butter melted

Directions:

Spray with non-stick cooking spray the crockpot. Put blueberry pie filling evenly into the bottom of the crockpot.

In a mixing bowl, combine dry lemon cake mix with melted butter and stir until crumbly. Break some big chunks into the crumbles of a small spoon. Pour the crumble cake/butter mixture over the blueberry mixture into crockpot, spread evenly, and cover with a lid the crockpot. Cook at high for 2 hours, and at low for 4 hours. Serve.

Nutrition:

Calories: 344 Fat: 30.38g

Carbohydrate: 10.03g Fiber: 5.61g

Protein: 8.26g

Crockpot Strawberry Dump Cake Recipe

Preparation time: 15 minutes

Cooking time: 2 hours

Servings: 8

Ingredients:

15.25 oz. Betty Crocker Strawberry Cake Mix

42 oz. Strawberry Pie Filling

1/2 cup butter melted

Directions:

Spray with a non-stick cooking spray inside the crockpot.

Put the Strawberry Pie Filling into the crockpot's bottom and spread evenly.

Combine strawberry dry cake mixture with the butter in a mixing bowl.

Pour the cake/butter crumbled mixture into crockpot over strawberries and spread evenly, covering the crockpot with a lid.

Cook for 2 hours at high, or 4 hours at low. Serve.

Nutrition:

Calories: 344

Fat: 30.38g

Carbohydrate: 10.03g

Fiber: 5.61g

Protein: 8.26g

Crockpot Baked Apples Recipe

Preparation time: 15 minutes

Cooking time: 4 hours

Servings: 6

Ingredients:

Five medium Gala apples

½ cup Quaker Old Fashioned Oats

½ cup Brown Sugar

3 tsp. Cinnamon

1 tsp. Allspice

1/4 cup butter

Directions:

Pour 1/4 cup of water at crockpot's edge.

Use a sharp knife to carefully core apples.

Mix the oats, cinnamon, brown sugar, and allspice. Fill a single apple with a mixture of oats, sugar, and spice.

Use a butter pat to top each apple. Set in crockpot carefully and put the lid on crockpot.

Cook for 3–4 hours or until finished.

Nutrition:

Calories: 121

Fat 3g

Carbohydrates 48g

Fiber 5g

Sugar 36g

Protein 1g.

Sugar-Free Chocolate Molten Lava Cake

Preparation time: 15 minutes

Cooking time: 3 hours

Servings: 3

Ingredients:

1/2 cup hot water

1-ounce chocolate chips, sugar-free

1/4 teaspoon vanilla liquid stevia

1/4 teaspoon vanilla extract

1 egg yolk

1 whole egg

2 tablespoons butter melted, cooled

1/4 teaspoon baking powder

1/8 teaspoon salt

3 ¾ teaspoons cocoa powder, unsweetened

2 tablespoons almond flour

6 tablespoons Swerve sweetener divided

Directions:

Grease the slow cooker, mix the flour, baking powder, 2 tablespoons cocoa powder, almond flour, and 4 tablespoons of Swerve in a bowl.

In a separate bowl, stir in eggs with melted butter, liquid stevia, vanilla extract, egg yolks, and eggs.

Mix the wet fixing to the dry ones and combine to incorporate fully. Pour the mixture into the slow cooker.

Top the mixture with chocolate chips.

Mix the remaining swerve with cocoa powder and hot water in a separate bowl, and pour this mixture over chocolate chips.

Cook on low within 3 hours. Once done, let cool and then serve.

Nutrition:

Calories 157

Fat 13g

Carbs 10.5g

Protein 3.9g

Blueberry Lemon Custard Cake

Preparation time: 15 minutes

Cooking time: 3 hours

Servings: 3

Ingredients:

2 tablespoons fresh blueberries

1/2 cup light cream

1/8 teaspoon salt

2 tablespoons Swerve sweetener

1/4 teaspoon lemon liquid stevia

1 1/3 tablespoon lemon juice

1/2 teaspoon lemon zest

2 tablespoons coconut flour

1 ½ egg separated

Directions:

Put egg whites into a stand mixture and whip to achieve stiff peaks consistency.

Set the egg whites aside, whisk the yolks and the other ingredients apart from the blueberries.

Mix the egg whites into the batter to thoroughly combine, and then grease the slow cooker.

Put the batter into it, then top with the blueberries—Cook within 3 hours, low.

Let cool when not covered for 1 hour, then keep it chilled for at least 2 hours or overnight.

Serve the cake topped with unsweetened cream if you like.

Nutrition:

Calories 140

Fat 9.2g

Carbs 7.3g

Protein 3.9g

Slow-Cooked Pumpkin Custard

Preparation time: 15 minutes

Cooking time: 2 hours & 45 minutes

Servings: 3

Ingredients:

2 large eggs

2 tablespoons butter or coconut oil

Dash sea salt

1/2 teaspoon pumpkin pie spice

1/4 cup superfine almond flour

1/2 teaspoon vanilla extract

1/2 cup pumpkin puree

1/4 cup granulated stevia

Directions:

Grease a crockpot with butter or coconut oil and set aside. With a mixer, break the eggs into a mixing bowl, and blend until incorporated and thickened.

Gently beat in the stevia, then add in vanilla extract and pumpkin puree. Then blend in pumpkin pie spice, salt, and almond flour.

Once almost incorporated, stream in coconut oil, ghee, and melted butter. Mix until smooth, then move the mixture into a crockpot.

Put a paper towel over the slow cooker to help absorb condensed moisture and prevent it from dripping on your pumpkin custard. Then cover with a lid.

Now cook on low for 2 hours to 2 hours 45 minutes, and check the content after two hours elapse.

Serve the custard with whipped cream sweetened with a little stevia and a sprinkle of nutmeg if you like.

Nutrition:

Calories 147Fat 12g

Carbs 4g

Protein 5g

Almond Flour Mocha Fudge Cake

Preparation time: 15 minutes

Cooking time: 4 hours

Servings: 3

Ingredients:

1/8 teaspoon Celtic sea salt

1/3 teaspoon vanilla or chocolate extract

3 tablespoons hot coffee

1/3 teaspoon baking soda

6 tablespoons blanched almond flour

3 tablespoons sour cream

3/4 oz. unsweetened chocolate, melted

1 egg

1 tablespoon butter or coconut oil

6 tablespoons Swerve

Directions:

Grease the crockpot with oil. Then beat coconut oil and natural sweetener in a bowl until fully incorporated.

Beat in eggs, cream and chocolate. In a bowl, sift baking soda and almond flour and add in the chocolate mixture.

Then beat in coffee, salt, and vanilla until well incorporated. Once done, pour the batter into the cooking pot of the slow cooker.

Cook on low for 2 to 4 hours or until a toothpick inserted in the cake comes out clean.

Nutrition:

Calories 200

Carbs 5.8

Protein 6g

Fat 18g

Slow Cooker Bread Pudding

Preparation time: 15 minutes

Cooking time: 5 hours

Servings: 4

Ingredients:

1 tablespoons raisin

1/2 teaspoon cinnamon

1 1/2 teaspoon vanilla extract

1/4 cup swerve

1 egg white

1 whole egg

1 1/2 cups almond milk

4 slices of pumpkin bread

Directions:

Slice the pumpkin bread into pieces. Then mix all the rest of the fixing in the slow cooker.

Cook within 4 to 5 hours, then serve.

Nutrition:

Calories 182

Fat 2g

Carbs 11g

Protein 8g

Tiramisu Bread Pudding

Preparation time: 15 minutes

Cooking time: 2 hours

Servings: 4

Ingredients:

3/4 teaspoons unsweetened cocoa

1/3 teaspoon vanilla extract

2 tablespoons mascarpone cheese

Cooking spray

3 1/4 cups Keto bread

1 large egg, lightly beaten

6.4 ounces of almond milk, divided

3/4 tablespoons Kahlua (coffee-flavored liqueur)

1 3/4 teaspoons instant espresso granules

2 tablespoons coconut sugar

1.6-ounce water

Directions:

Mix the water, coconut sugar, plus instant espresso granules in a saucepan.

Boil while occasionally stirring for 1 minute, remove, then mix in the Kahlua liqueur.

Whisk the eggs, then the almond milk in a large bowl. Mix in the espresso mixture into it.

Put the Keto friendly bread into a greased casserole. Cook it inside the slow cooker within 2 hours, low.

Mix vanilla, mascarpone cheese plus the remaining almond milk in a bowl.

Garnish with cocoa and serve.

Nutrition:

Calories 199 Fat 9g Protein 6.7gCarbs 9g

Crock Pot Sugar-Free Dairy-Free Fudge

Preparation time: 15 minutes

Cooking time: 2 hours

Servings: 3

Ingredients:

A dash of salt

Dash of pure vanilla extract

½ tablespoon coconut milk

4 tablespoons sugar-free chocolate chips

1/4 teaspoons vanilla liquid stevia

Directions:

Mix in coconut milk, stevia, vanilla, chocolate chips plus salt in a slow cooker.

Cook within 2 hours, then let it sit within 30 minutes.

Mix in within 5 minutes. Put the batter in a casserole dish with parchment paper.

Chill, then serve.

Nutrition:

Calories 65

Fat 5g

Carbs 2g

Protein 1g

Poppy Seed-Lemon Bread

Preparation time: 15 minutes

Cooking time: 2 hours

Servings: 3

Ingredients:

1/2 cups almond flour

1/4 tbsp baking powder

1 tbsp poppy seeds

1 egg

1/4 cup coconut sugar

1/8 tsp salt

2 tbsp vegetable oil

3 tbsp tofu (puree)

1/4 cup almond milk

3/4 cup plain Greek-style yogurt

1/4 cup lemon juice

3/4 tsp shredded lemon peel

1/4 tsp vanilla

Directions:

Grease the slow cooker using a non-stick cooking spray.

Mix the poppy seeds, flour, salt, and baking powder in a bowl, then put it aside.

Mix the tofu puree, sugar, oil, milk, yogurt, lemon juice, lemon peel, and vanilla in a medium bowl.

Put the sugar batter to the flour batter, then mix.

Transfer it in the slow cooker, then cook on high for 1 and 30 minutes to 2 hours, or until set.

Leave for 10-15 minutes to cool., then serve.

Nutrition:

Calories 295.6

Fat 24.3g

Carbs 17.9g

Protein 6.0g

Nutmeg-Infused Pumpkin Bread

Preparation time: 15 minutes

Cooking time: 3 hours

Servings: 4

Ingredients:

0.5 oz. unsalted pecan pieces, toasted

1/4 tablespoon pure vanilla extract

1 tablespoon safflower oil

1 egg white

2 tablespoons plain Greek yogurt

1/4 cup cooked and puréed pumpkin

1/8 teaspoon sea salt

Dash ground allspice

1/4 teaspoon ground nutmeg

Dash teaspoon baking soda

1/2 teaspoon baking powder

2 tablespoons coconut sugar

7 tablespoons almond flour

2 tablespoons dried apple cranberries, unsweetened

3 tablespoons 100% apple juice, plain

Olive oil cooking spray

Directions:

Lightly grease a non-stick loaf pan with cooking spray. Set aside.

Mix cranberries and apple juice in a small saucepan, heat the mixture on high to boil.

Remove, then let cool for around 10 minutes.

Then mix nutmeg, baking soda, allspice, baking powder, salt, maple sugar flakes, and flour in a large bowl. Set aside.

Now mix vanilla, oil, egg whites, yogurt, pumpkin, and the cranberry mixture in a medium bowl.

To the flour mixture, add the pecans and cranberry-pumpkin mixture and stir to incorporate fully.

Spoon the batter into the pan, and use a rubber spatula or back of a spoon to smooth the top.

Arrange a rack inside a crockpot to elevate the pan, and then put the pan on top.

Cook within 3 hours, high.

Cool it down within 10 minutes, before slicing, then serve.

Nutrition:

Calories 159

Carbs 21g

Fat 65g

Protein 4g

CHAPTER 10:

Soups & Stews

Creamy Harvest Pumpkin Bisque

Preparation time: 15 minutes

Cooking time: 5 hours

Servings: 8

Ingredients:

1 Medium pumpkin (butternut, sugar, etc.)

1 medium sweet potato, peeled and diced

2 carrots, chopped

1 medium yellow onion, chopped

2 c. vegetable stock

1 tsp curry powder

½ tsp ground ginger

½ tsp ground nutmeg

½ tsp cumin

1 c. heavy cream

Kosher salt

Freshly ground black pepper

Directions:

Peel pumpkin skin, and remove pulp and seeds. Cube up the pumpkin flesh.

Place pumpkin, potato, carrots, onion, vegetable stock, and spices in the slow cooker.

Cook within 4-5 hours, low or 2-3 hours, high. Make sure vegetables are incredibly tender.

Pulse in a blender, then return it inside the slow cooker and add in the heavy cream, stirring until thoroughly mixed. Season with salt and pepper as desired. Heat back up to desired heat and serve.

Nutrition:

Carbs: 13g

Calories: 125

Fat: 5g

Protein: 2g

Zesty White Chicken Chili

Preparation time: 15 minutes

Cooking time: 8 hours

Servings: 6

Ingredients:

2 lbs. Boneless, skinless chicken breasts or thighs

1 large yellow onion, diced

1 medium green bell pepper, chopped

1 small jalapeno, minced

6 cloves garlic, minced

3 tsp. ground cumin (add more to taste)

1 tsp. dried oregano

2 tsp. chili powder (add more to taste)

1 tsp. kosher salt

¼ tsp. black pepper

6 cups chicken stock

1 lime, juiced

½ cup fresh cilantro, chopped

½ cup chives chopped

Directions:

Throw the peppers, jalapeno, onion, garlic, spices into the slow cooker. Place the chicken on top and fill with all of the broth.

Cook covered on low for 7-8 hours. Check the chicken with a fork to see if it is falling apart.

Add the lime juice and stir, add salt and pepper to taste.

When serving, top off with cilantro and chives.

Nutrition:

Carbs: 6g

Calories: 105

Fat: 0g

Protein: 25 g

Tuscan Zucchini Stew

Preparation time: 20 minutes

Cooking time: 6 hours

Servings: 6

Ingredients:

1 1/2 pounds Italian-seasoned sausage (spicy or sweet, whatever you prefer)

1 cup celery, chopped small

3 cups sliced zucchini, sliced into thin rounds

1 green bell pepper, chopped small

1 red or yellow bell pepper, chopped

1 large onion, diced

3 cloves garlic, minced

½ tsp. fresh ground black pepper

2 teaspoons salt

1 (28 oz) can diced tomatoes

2 (14 oz) cans of fire-roasted diced tomatoes

½ c. water

1 teaspoon brown sugar

2 teaspoon Italian seasoning

1 teaspoon dried basil

¼ c. asiago cheese, grated

Red pepper flakes (optional)

Directions:

Fry the sausage on medium heat on the stove. Break up the meat with a spatula and make sure it's fully cooked (5-8 minutes). Drain off the grease.

Add the celery, onions and peppers continue to cook until the vegetables become soft and translucent (7-8 minutes). Add minced garlic and cook and stir continually until fragrant (2 minutes) Add the salt and pepper, stir and remove from the heat.

Pour sausage mixture into the slow cooker. Put the 3 cans of diced tomatoes, the spices, the sugar, and the water

Cook on low for 4-6 hours. Top with grated asiago, and add a fresh sprig of basil (optional).

Nutrition:

Carbs: 16g

Calories: 280

Fat: 22g

Protein: 23g

Melt-In-Your-Mouth Beef Stew

Preparation time: 15 minutes

Cooking time: 7 hours

Servings: 10

Ingredients:

2 lbs. stewing beef, diced into 1-inch cubes

2 tbsp. extra virgin olive oil

3 large carrots (4-5 medium/small), chopped

2 large yellow onions, diced

2 large stalks of celery, chopped

5 cloves garlic, minced

1 tsp kosher salt

¼ tsp fresh ground black pepper

Salt and pepper

1/4 cup all-purpose flour (can use 1/8c. cornstarch instead)

3 cups beef broth

¼ c. Dijon mustard

2 tbsp. Worcestershire sauce

1 tbsp. brown sugar

3/4 tbsp. dried rosemary

1 tsp. dried thyme

Directions:

Massage the beef with salt plus pepper and coat all sides with the flour.

Heat-up the oil in a large skillet over medium heat, then put the onions and garlic and sauté for 1-2 minutes. Add the flower-coated beef to the skillet and sear on all sides for 2-3 minutes.

Place the beef and onions and garlic into the slow cooker and add the carrots.

Put the skillet with the beef drippings back on the burner and add all of the rest of the ingredients to the hot skillet (beef broth, Dijon, Worcestershire, brown sugar, rosemary, thyme).

Stir the mixture, and make sure to stir up any beef or garlic remnants at the bottom of the pan. Heat-up, then stir until the sugar has dissolved the mixture is well-combined.

Pour the broth mixture over the beef and carrots in the slow cooker—Cook within 7-8 hours, low or high for 4 hours. Keep warm until you're ready to serve it. Garnish with fresh parsley if desired

Nutrition:

Carbs: 11g

Calories: 250

Fat: 12g

Protein: 24g

Mexican Chorizo Enchilada Soup

Preparation time: 15 minutes

Cooking time: 4 hours

Servings: 8

Ingredients:

1 lb. ground beef

1 lb. chorizo sausage

2, (8oz.) packages Neufchâtel (cream) cheese

2 cans of roasted tomatoes, dice

1 medium jalapeno, chopped finely

1 large onion, chopped

1 clove of garlic, minced

1 green bell pepper, chopped

1 (1.25 oz) package taco seasoning (or more to taste)

4 cups of chicken stock

¼ c. fresh cilantro

¼ c. shredded sharp cheddar cheese (optional)

Low-fat Sour cream (optional)

Directions:

Heat-up a large skillet, and brown the beef and chorizo over medium heat. Break the meat up until crumbly with a spatula. Stir in onion, jalapeno, and bell pepper. Cook until onions start to soften (5-7 minutes). Put the garlic and continue to stir and cook for 2 more minutes.

Sprinkle the taco seasoning packet over the meat mixture and stir.

Put the meat batter inside the slow cooker and add the Neufchâtel cheese and canned tomatoes. Stir until the cheese breaks down and mixes in.

Cook within 4 hours, low or high for 2 hours.

Put the cilantro and cook for another 10-15 minutes.

Garnish with cheddar cheese and sour cream, and serve.

Nutrition:

Carbs: 7g Calories: 531 Fat: 42 g Protein: 28g

Hearty Chicken Soup with Veggie Noodles

Preparation time: 15 minutes

Cooking time: 8 hours

Servings: 8

Ingredients:

1 1/2 lbs. boneless chicken breast, cubes

2 C. carrots, sliced into thin rounds

1 large yellow onion, diced

3 stalks celery, chopped

4 cloves garlic, minced

3 tbsp. extra virgin olive oil

1/2 tsp Italian seasoning

¼ tsp dried parsley

6 C. chicken stock

1 C. water

½ tsp kosher salt

¼ tsp. freshly ground black pepper

2 Medium-sized zucchinis

2 c. chopped Napa cabbage

Directions:

Place all ingredients except cabbage and zucchini into the slow cooker. Stir until evenly mixed

Cook on low for 6-8 hrs.

In the last 2 hours of cooking, take the zucchini, and make Zucchini noodles. If you do not have a veggie noodle machine, take a potato peeler and peel the zucchini, then use the peeler to shave off thin strips of zucchini.

Take the zucchini noodles and the chopped cabbage and sauté in a large skillet over medium heat with extra virgin olive oil. Stir occasionally as the vegetables soften, and the cabbage starts to caramelize and brown a little bit (about 7-8 minutes). Put the vegetables inside the slow cooker, then continue to cook for the remaining 1-2 hours, then serve.

Nutrition:

Carbs: 7g Calories: 145

Fat: 6gProtein: 20g

Superb Chicken, Bacon, Garlic Thyme Soup

Preparation time: 15 minutes

Cooking time: 6 hours

Servings: 4

Ingredients:

2 tablespoons of unsalted butter

1 chopped onion

1 chopped pepper

8 chicken thighs

8 slices of bacon

1 tablespoon of thyme

1 teaspoon of salt

1 teaspoon of pepper

1 tablespoon of minced garlic

1 tablespoon of coconut flour

3 tablespoons of lemon juice

1 cup of chicken stock

¼ cup of unsweetened coconut milk

3 tablespoons of tomato paste

Directions:

Spread the butter on the slow cooker base and arrange the peppers and onions on top of it.

Add the chicken thighs and then layer with the bacon. Add the remaining fixing.

Cook within 6 hours, low. Cut the thighs into pieces, arrange in bowls and serve.

Nutrition:

Calories: 396

Fat: 21 grams

Carbs: 7 grams

Fiber: 2 grams

Protein: 41 grams

Delightful Chicken-Chorizo Spicy Soup

Preparation time: 15 minutes

Cooking time: 3.5 hours

Servings: 10

Ingredients:

4 pounds of skinless, boneless chicken

1 pound of chorizo

4 cups of chicken stock

1 cup of heavy cream

1 can of stewed tomatoes

2 tablespoons of minced garlic

2 tablespoons of Worcestershire sauce

2 tablespoons of red sauce

Parmesan and sour cream for garnish

Directions:

Heat a frying pan and brown the sausage.

Place the chicken into the slow cooker and add the remaining ingredients except for the parmesan and sour cream.

Cook within 3 hours, high. Garnish with the parmesan and the sour cream.

Nutrition:

Calories: 659

Fat: 37 grams

Carbs: 6 grams

Fiber: 1 gram

Protein: 52 grams

Delectable Spearmint Liver and Lamb Heart Soup

Preparation time: 15 minutes

Cooking time: 10 hours

Servings: 4

Ingredients:

3 cups of livers and lamb hearts

1 cup of cubed lamb meat

2 cups of broth of your choice

2 cups of hot water

2 bunches of diced spring onions

1 pack of chopped fresh spearmint

2 cups of fresh spinach

1 teaspoon of garlic powder

1 teaspoon of dried basil

1 teaspoon of sweet paprika

1 teaspoon of ground pimento

4 lightly crushed cloves

½ teaspoon of cinnamon

4 tablespoons of olive oil

Salt and pepper

1 large egg

1 cup of Greek yogurt, full fat

Directions:

Put all of the fixings to the slow cooker except the yogurt and the egg.

Cover and cook for 10 hours on low.

Slice the meat into chunks, then put it back to the crockpot.

Mix the yogurt and the egg in a bowl. Add some of the cooked liquid from the slow cooker. Mix thoroughly.

Put the batter inside the slow cooker, then stir to combine. Allow to heat through, and serve.

Nutrition:

Carbs: 12 grams

Protein: 56 grams

Fat: 38 grams

Calories: 560

Lovely Lentil Sausage Soup

Preparation time: 15 minutes

Cooking time: 6 hours

Servings: 4

Ingredients:

1 ½ pound of Italian sausage

2 tablespoons of butter

2 tablespoons of olive oil

5 cups of chicken stock

1 ½ cups of lentils

1 cup of spinach

½ cup of diced carrots

4 minced cloves of garlic

1 trimmed leek

1 diced celery rib

1 cup of heavy cream

½ cup of shredded Parmesan cheese

2 tablespoons of Dijon mustard

2 tablespoons of red wine vinegar

Salt and pepper

Directions:

Place the stock and the lentils into the slow cooker.

In a saucepan, heat the olive oil and the butter and brown the sausage.

In the same saucepan, sauté the celery, pepper, salt, garlic, leek, spinach, onions, and carrots for 10 minutes.

Pour the mixture into the slow cooker. Cook on low for 6-8 hours. Spoon into bowls and serve.

Nutrition:

Calories: 195

Fat: 14 grams

Carbs: 4.9 grams

Protein: 11 grams

Tasty Corned Beef and Heavy Cream Soup

Preparation time: 15 minutes

Cooking time: 5 hours and 30 minutes

Servings: 4

Ingredients:

1 diced onion

2 diced celery ribs

2 cloves of minced garlic

1 pound of chopped corn beef

4 cups of beef stock

1 cup of sauerkraut

1 teaspoon of sea salt

1 teaspoon of caraway seeds

¾ teaspoon of black pepper

2 cups of heavy cream

1 ½ cups of shredded Swiss cheese

Directions:

Heat-up the butter, then sauté the celery, garlic, and onions in a saucepan.

Pour the mixture into the slow cooker.

Put the rest of the items except the cream and the cheese.

Cover and cook on low for 4 hours and 30 minutes.

Add the cream and the cheese and cook for another hour.

Nutrition:

Calories: 225

Fat: 18.5 grams

Carbs: 4 grams

Protein: 11.5 grams

Delicious Beef Meatball and Sour Cream Soup

Preparation time: 15 minutes

Cooking time: 6 hours

Servings: 4

Ingredients:

1 diced red bell pepper

8-10 halved pearl onions

2 cloves of minced garlic

2 tablespoons of olive oil

3 cups of lean ground beef

1 large egg

1 teaspoon of dry savory

Salt and pepper

1 cup of beef broth

2 cups of hot water

1 cup of sour cream

Directions:

Preheat the slow cooker on low. Add the oil and vegetables.

Mix the egg, salt, pepper, dry savory, and meat in a large bowl. Shape into approximately 30 small meatballs.

Cook the broth in a pot, add the meatballs and cook for 2 minutes.

Add the broth and the meatballs to the slow cooker—cover and cook for 6 hours.

Take out a spoonful of the broth, add it to the sour cream, mix, and then put it back inside the slow cooker. Stir gently, spoon into bowls and serve.

Nutrition:

Carbs: 11 grams Protein: 27 grams

Fat: 28 grams Calories: 409

Veggie Soup with Minty Balls

Preparation time: 15 minutes

Cooking time: 6 hours

Servings: 45

Ingredients:

3 cups of beef broth

1 medium zucchini sliced into sticks

2 diced celery sticks

1 diced yellow onion

5 crushed cloves of garlic

1 cubed medium tomato

3 cups of ground veal

½ cup of Parmesan cheese

1 large egg

½ cup of chopped fresh mint

1 teaspoon of dry oregano

1 teaspoon of sweet paprika

Salt and pepper

Directions:

Preheat the slow cooker on low. Add the tomato, onion, celery, zucchini, and broth.

Mix the meat, salt, pepper, seasoning, mint, egg, garlic, and cheese in a large bowl. Shape the meat into small, approximately 45 small meatballs.

Heat-up the olive oil in a pan, then put the meatballs and brown.

Put the meatballs inside the slow cooker, then put one cup of hot water if more liquid is required.

Cook within 6-8 hours, low. Spoon into bowls and serve.

Nutrition:

Carbs: 11 grams

Protein: 32 grams

Fat: 25 grams

Calories: 395 grams

Chicken Cordon Bleu Soup

Preparation time: 15 minutes

Cooking time: 6 hours

Servings: 4

Ingredients:

12 ounces of diced ham

1 pound of chicken breast

4 ounces of diced onion

5 ounces of chopped mushrooms

3 tablespoons of minced garlic

6 cups of chicken broth

2 teaspoons of tarragon

3 tablespoons of salted butter

1 teaspoon of sea salt

1 teaspoon of black pepper

1 ½ cups of heavy cream

½ cup of sour cream

½ cup of grated parmesan cheese

4 ounces of Swiss cheese

Directions:

Place the onion, tarragon, salt, pepper, ham, mushroom, and broth into the slow cooker.

Heat-up the butter in a saucepan, then sauté the garlic. Add the chicken and sear it.

Place the chicken, garlic, and cheese in the slow cooker—cover and cook on low within six hours.

Add cream, and cook for another hour. Serve.

Nutrition:

Calories: 178 Fat: 12 grams

Carbs: 2.75 grams Protein: 16 grams

Ginger Pumpkin Soup

Preparation time: 15 minutes

Cooking time: 4 hours

Servings: 4

Ingredients:

1 diced onion

1 teaspoon of crushed ginger

1 teaspoon of crushed garlic

½ stick of butter

1 pound of pumpkin chunks

2 cups of vegetable stock

1 2/3 cups of coconut cream

Salt and pepper

Directions:

Place all the items inside a slow cooker. Cook on high for 4-6 hours.

Puree the soup using an immersion blender. Spoon into bowls and serve.

Nutrition:

Calories: 234 Fat: 21.7 grams

Carbs: 11.4 grams Fiber: 1.5 grams

Protein: 2.3 grams

Toscana Soup

Preparation time: 15 minutes

Cooking time: 8 hours

Servings: 5

Ingredients:

Italian sausage – ½ lb.

Olive oil 1 tbsp

Onion – ¼ cup, diced

Chicken stock – 18 oz.

Garlic – cloves, minced

Chopped kale – 1 ½ cups

Cauliflower – ½ head, diced florets

Salt – ½ tsp.

Crushed red pepper flakes – ¼ tsp.

Heavy cream – ¼ cup

Pepper – ½ tsp.

Directions:

In a pan, brown the sausage. Transfer the sausage to the Crock-Pot and discard the grease.

Add the oil into the skillet and sauté the onions for 3 to 4 minutes. Add to the Crock-Pot.

Except for the cream, add the rest of the ingredients to the Crock-Pot.

Mix, then cook within 8 hours, low. Add the cream when cooked.

Stir and serve hot.

Nutrition:

Calories: 246

Fat: 19g

Carbs: 7g

Protein: 14g

Rabbit Stew

Preparation time: 15 minutes

Cooking time: 5 hours

Servings: 6

Ingredients:

Rabbit 3 lbs., cut into pieces

Uncured bacon ½ lb., cubed

Butter 2 tbsp.

Dry white wine 2 cups

Large sweet onion 1, chopped

Bay leaves 2

Rosemary 1 large sprig

Salt and pepper to taste

Directions:

Add the cubed bacon and butter in a skillet.

Add the sliced onion and cook for 5 minutes. Then remove the onion and leave the fat in the pan.

Add the rabbit and sauté on high heat until browned. Put in the wine, then simmer for a couple of minutes.

Add everything from the pan to the Crock-Pot. Add bay leaves, rosemary, salt, and pepper.

Cook within 5 hours, low.

Nutrition:

Calories: 517

Fat: 32g

Carbs: 2g

Protein: 36g

Beef Stew

Preparation time: 15 minutes

Cooking time: 5 hours

Servings: 5

Ingredients:

Beef – 2 lbs.

Coconut oil 3 tbsp

Beef broth 3 cups

Medium onion 1, chopped

Apple cider vinegar 2 tbsp.

Fresh thyme 1 tbsp.

Erythritol –2 tsp.

Ground cinnamon – 2 tsp.

Minced garlic – 1 ½ tbsp.

Bay leaves – 2

Black pepper – 1 ½ tsp.

Sage, rosemary, salt, fish sauce, soy sauce – 1 tsp. each

Directions:

Cut up the beef into 1-inch cubes, dice the veggies. Season the meat with salt and pepper.

Add oil in a hot skillet and brown the meat in batches. Once done, add the veggies and cook for a couple of minutes.

Add everything except for thyme, rosemary, and sage in the Crock-Pot.

Cook within 3 hours, high. Put the thyme, rosemary plus sage, then cook 1 to 2 hours in the same setting. Serve.

Nutrition:

Calories: 337.6

Fat: 13.8g

Carbs: 5.5g

Protein: 42.1g

Chicken & Kale Soup

Preparation time: 15 minutes

Cooking time: 6 hours

Servings: 6

Ingredients:

Chicken breast or thigh meat – 2 lbs., without bone or skin

Chicken broth – 14 oz.

Olive oil ½ cup, plus 1 tbsp

Diced onion – 1/3 cup

Chicken stock – 32 oz.

Baby kale leaves – 5 oz.

Salt and pepper to taste

Lemon juice – ¼ cup

Directions:

Heat-up the 1 tbsp of olive oil in a pan over medium heat, then massage the chicken with salt and pepper and place it in the pan.

Lower the heat to medium and cover—Cook within 15 minutes. Shred the meat, then put it in the crockpot.

Mix the rest of the oil, onion, and chicken broth in a bowl. Add it to the crockpot.

Put the rest of the fixing, then cook on low for 6 hours. Stir a couple of times as it cooks.

Nutrition:

Calories: 261 Fat: 21g

Carbs: 2g

Protein: 14.1g

Chicken Chili Soup

Preparation time: 15 minutes

Cooking time: 6 hours

Servings: 4

Ingredients:

Onion – ½, chopped

Unsalted butter – 1 tbsp.

Green pepper – ½, chopped

Chicken thighs – 4, boneless

Bacon – 4 slices

Salt and pepper to taste

Thyme – ½ tbsp.

Minced garlic – ½ tbsp.

Coconut flour – ½ tbsp.

Lemon juice 1 ½ tbsp

Chicken stock – ½ cup

Tomato paste – 1 ½ tbsp.

Unsweetened coconut milk – 2 tbsp.

Directions:

Add the butter into the Crock-Pot. Add the sliced onion and peppers. Then add the chicken on top, and sprinkle with sliced bacon. Put all the dry fixing, then lastly add the liquids.

Cook within 6 hours, low. Mix and break apart the chicken. Serve.

Nutrition:

Calories: 396 Fat: 21g

Carbs: 7g Protein: 41g

Creamy Smoked Salmon Soup

Preparation time: 15 minutes

Cooking time: 3 hours

Servings: 4

Ingredients:

Smoked salmon – ½ lb., roughly chopped

Garlic – 3 cloves, crushed

Small onion – 1, finely chopped

Leek – 1, finely chopped

Heavy cream – 1 ½ cups

Olive oil – 2 tbsp.

Salt and pepper to taste

Fish stock – 1 ½ cups

Directions:

Add oil into the Crock-Pot. Add fish stock, leek, salmon, garlic, and onion into the pot.

Cook within 2 hours, low. Add the cream and stir—Cook for 1 hour more.

Adjust seasoning and serve.

Nutrition:

Calories: 309 Fat: 26.4g

Carbs: 7g Protein: 12.3g

Lamb and Rosemary Stew

Preparation time: 15 minutes

Cooking time: 8 hours

Servings: 4

Ingredients:

Boneless lamb – 1 ½ lbs., cut into cubes

Onion – 1, roughly chopped

Garlic – 3 cloves, finely chopped

Dried rosemary – 1 tsp.

Lamb stock cube – 1

Olive oil – 3 tbsp. divided

Water – 2 cups

Salt and pepper to taste

Directions:

Add olive oil into the Crock-Pot. Brown the lamb in an oiled skillet for 2 minutes.

Add 2 cups of water, stock cube, rosemary, garlic, onion, lamb, salt, and pepper to the pot.

Cook on low within 8 hours. Serve.

Nutrition:

Calories: 427 Fat: 23.3g

Carbs: 3.9g Protein: 48.6g

Lamb and Eggplant Stew

Preparation time: 15 minutes

Cooking time: 8 hours & 30 minutes

Servings: 4

Ingredients:

Minced lamb – 1 ½ lb.

Onion – 1, finely chopped

Garlic – 3 cloves, crushed

Large eggplant ½, cut into small cubes

Tomatoes 1, chopped

Lamb stock cube 1

Dried rosemary 1 tsp

Grated mozzarella ¾ cup

Olive oil 2 tbsp

Water – 2 cups

Salt and pepper to taste

Directions:

Add olive oil into the Crock-Pot. Add water, lamb, onion, garlic, eggplant, stock cube, tomatoes, rosemary, salt, and pepper to the pot. Stir to mix.

Cook within 8 hours, high. Remove the lid and stir the stew.

Sprinkle the mozzarella on top, cover with the lid, and cook 30 minutes more. Serve.

Nutrition:

Calories: 432 Fat: 21g

Carbs: 8.8g Protein: 50.9g

Bacon and Cauliflower Soup

Preparation time: 15 minutes

Cooking time: 4 hours

Servings: 4

Ingredients:

Large cauliflower head – ¾, cut into chunks

Garlic – 3 cloves, crushed

Onion – ¾, finely chopped

Bacon – 4 slices, cut into small pieces

Chicken stock – 2 cups

Smoked paprika – ½ tsp.

Chili powder – ½ tsp.

Heavy cream – ¾ cup

Olive oil 2 tbsp

Salt and pepper to taste

Paprika to taste

Directions:

Add olive oil into the Crock-Pot. Add the garlic, cauliflower, onion, bacon, stock, paprika, chili, salt, and pepper to the pot. Stir to mix.

Cook on high within 4 hours. Open the lid and blend with a hand mixer.

Add the cream and mix. Serve sprinkled with paprika.

Nutrition:

Calories: 265 Fat: 22.3g

Carbs: 6.1g Protein: 10.4g

Vegetable Stew

Preparation time: 15 minutes

Cooking time: 6 hours

Servings: 5

Ingredients:

Olive oil – 1 tbsp.

Onion – 1, chopped

Garlic – 2 cloves, chopped

Cauliflower – ½, cut into florets

Red bell peppers – 1, chopped

Carrot – 1, sliced

Parsnip – 1, cubed

Zucchini – ½, cubed

Cherry tomatoes – ½ cup, halved

Tomato sauce – ¼ cup, no sugar added

Vegetable stock – 1 cup

Bay leaf – 1

Salt and pepper to taste

Butter – 2 tbsp.

Directions:

Heat-up the oil, then put the onion and garlic in a skillet. Cook for 2 minutes to soften, then place in the Crock-Pot.

Add the remaining ingredients, mix, and season with salt and pepper, then cook on low within 6 hours. Serve.

Nutrition:

Calories: 76

Fat: 5.7g

Carbs: 7.1g

Protein: 1.3g

Pot Roast Soup

Preparation Time: 15 minutes

Cooking Time: 5-8 hours

Servings: 4

Ingredients:

1/2 diced medium butternut squash

3/4 cup chicken stock

1 diced big onion

1 (14 ounces) can diced tomatoes

1 1/4 pounds stew meat

3 diced big carrots

7 1/2 ounces mushrooms, diced

dried cumin

dried basil

dried oregano

salt & pepper, as desired

splash apple cider vinegar

Directions:

Arrange the vegetables in layers at the bottom of the crockpot.

Pour in the stew meat, then sprinkle in the spices as desired, then stir to combine.

Cook for 5 hours on low settings and high settings for 8 hours.

Serve and enjoy.

Nutrition:

Calories: 80

Carbs: 10g

Fat: 2g

Protein: 7g

Chicken with Kale Leaves Soup

Preparation Time: 15 minutes

Cooking Time: 6 hours

Servings: 6

Ingredients:

1/4 cup lime juice

1/3 cup onion

1/2 cup olive oil

1 tbsp. olive oil

2 lbs. boneless & skinless chicken breast

5 oz. baby kale leaves

14 oz. chicken broth

32 oz. chicken stock

salt, as desired

Directions:

Using a large skillet, add in a tbsp of oil and heat over medium heat.

Season the chicken with the pepper and salt then place into the hot oil.

Cook the chicken for 15 minutes.

Once done, shred the chicken then transfer it into the crockpot.

Pour the onions, chicken broth, and olive oil into a food processor and blend until well combined.

Pour the broth mix into the crockpot, then add in the rest of the ingredients and stir.

Cover the pot then cook for 6 hours on low settings, occasionally stirring.

Serve and enjoy.

Nutrition:

Calories: 150

Carbs: 12g

Fat: 9g

Protein: 7g

Southern Paleo Crock Pot Chili

Preparation Time: 10 minutes

Cooking time: 8 hours

Servings: 6

Ingredients:

1/2 tsp sea salt

1 tsp paprika

1 diced big onion

1 tsp onion powder

1 tsp garlic powder

1 tbsp. Worcestershire sauce

1 lb. grass-fed organic beef

1 tbsp. fresh parsley, chopped

1 seeded & diced green bell pepper

4 tsp chili powder

4 chopped small big large carrots

26 oz. tomatoes, neatly chopped

a pinch of cumin

diced onions, if desired

sliced Jalapeños, if desired

dairy-free sour cream, if desired

Directions:

Using a medium-sized skillet, add in the ground beef and brown over high heat, occasionally stirring until there is no pink.

Put the browned beef inside the crockpot, including the fat.

Add in the onion, green bell pepper, tomatoes, and carrots into the crockpot.

Mix all the fixing, then put in all the remaining seasonings and spices.

Stir all the ingredients together again, then cover and cook for 8 hours on low settings or 5 on high settings.

Serve then top with sour cream (dairy-free) with extra jalapenos, if desired, and enjoy.

Nutrition:

Calories: 241 Carbs: 24g

Fat: 8g

Protein: 20g

Dairy-Free Chili Chicken Soup

Preparation Time: 30 minutes

Cooking time: 6 hours

Servings: 10

Ingredients:

1/4 teaspoon white pepper

1 cup of coconut milk

1 teaspoon chili powder

1 big diced yellow onion

1 tablespoon minced garlic

1 tablespoon coarse-real salt

2 teaspoons cumin

2 cups chicken broth

2 (8 ounces) cans green chilies, diced

2 & ½-pounds boneless chicken thighs

3 cans Great Northern beans

optional

1/4 cup arrowroot starch

1/2 cup water

for toppings

1/3 cup chopped cilantro

sour cream

tortilla chips

juiced lime

Directions:

Put all the items into the crockpot, then cover and cook for 5-6 hours on high settings.

Remove the chicken from the crockpot, then transfer into a medium-sized bowl, then shred.

Take the chicken back inside the crockpot, then stir until properly distributed, then allow to cook for an extra 30 minutes.

Taste for seasoning as desired.

Serve then garnish with any toppings of your choice and enjoy.

Nutrition:

Calories: 137 Carbs: 9g

Fat: 2g Protein: 0g

Low Carbohydrate Crock Pot Soup

Preparation Time: 15 minutes

Cooking time: 4 hours

Servings: 8

Ingredients:

1/2 cup shredded cheese, to garnish

1-2 tablespoons fresh cilantro

2 pounds ground pork beef

2 tablespoons taco seasonings

2 (10-ounces) diced tomato cans

2 (8-ounces) cream cheese packages

4 cups chicken broth

Directions:

Cook the ground pork beef over medium-high heat in a large skillet.

In the meantime, place the diced tomatoes, cream cheese, and taco seasoning into the crockpot.

Drain the meat of the grease and transfer it into the crockpot.

Mix the ingredients, then add the chicken broth over the meat.

Cover the chicken then cook for 4 hours on low or 2 hours on high settings.

Stir in the cilantro before serving. Serve the garnish with the shredded cheese.

Nutrition:

Calories: 131 Carbs: 11g

Fat: 9g Protein: 5g

Slow Cooker Cheeseburger Soup

Preparation Time: 15 minutes

Cooking time: 3 hours

Servings: 5

Ingredients:

1/2 tsp salt

1/2 tsp pepper

1/2 cup cheese

1/2 cup chopped onions

1/2 chopped red bell pepper

1 tsp garlic powder

1 tsp Worcestershire sauce

1 1/2 tsp parsley

1 1/2 chopped tomatoes

1 1/2 pounds ground beef

2 chopped & cooked bacon slices

3 cups beef broth

3 chopped celery sticks

8 ounces tomato paste

Directions:

Using a large saucepan, add in the ground beef and brown.

Halfway through the browning process, drain off every fat, add in the red pepper, onions, celery, and continue cooking.

Add the remaining ingredients and beef mixture into the crockpot then stir to combine.

If desired, add in more beef broth, cover, and cook for 6-8 hours on low setting or 3-5 hours on a high setting, occasionally stirring.

Serve then top with a full spoon of cheese and bacon slices (if desired), then enjoy.

Nutrition:

Calories: 200 Carbs: 14g

Fat: 13g Protein: 7g

Chicken Thigh & Breast Low Carb Soup

Preparation Time: 5 minutes

Cooking time: 6 hours

Servings: 6

Ingredients:

1/2 tsp fresh ground pepper

1 tsp sea salt

1 chopped medium onion

1 tsp apple cider vinegar

1 tbsp. herbs de Provence

2 organic skin on & bone chicken thighs

2 organic skin on & bone-in chicken breasts

3 diced carrots

3 diced celery stalks

3-4 cups filtered water

Directions:

Place the ingredients in layers inside the crockpot.

Make sure the bone side of the chicken is down on top of the veggies.

Add in surplus water until the veggies are submerged, and the chicken is covered halfway.

Cover the crockpot then cook for 6-8 hours.

Remove the chicken from the crockpot one done and cool, then remove the bones and skin.

Shred the chicken, then return into the crockpot, season to taste, reheat, then serve and enjoy.

Nutrition:

Calories: 97

Carbs: 6g

Fat: 2g

Protein: 14g

Beef & Pumpkin Stew

Preparation Time: 5 minutes

Cooking time: 4 hours

Servings: 4

Ingredients:

1 teaspoon sage

1 teaspoon mixed herbs

2 tablespoons rosemary

2 tablespoons thyme

6 tablespoons coconut oil

200g pumpkin

300g stewing steak

salt & pepper, to taste

Directions:

Trim off every excess fat from the stewing steak then transfer it into the crockpot.

Season the steak with half of the coconut oil then and in the salt & pepper.

Cover the crockpot then cook on high setting for 1 hour.

Remove the steak from the crockpot to a serving platter alongside all the remaining seasoning and coconut oil.

Mix everything, then transfer back into the crockpot with the pumpkin and cook for 3 hours on a low setting. Serve with the fresh mixed herbs and enjoy.

Nutrition:

Calories: 324 Carbs: 37g

Fat: 11g Protein: 23g

Pepper Jalapeno Low Carb Soup

Preparation Time: 10 minutes

Cooking time: 7 hours

Servings: 8

Ingredients:

1/4 tsp paprika

1/2 tsp pepper

1/2 chopped onion

1/2 tsp xanthan gum

1/2 chopped green pepper

1/2 cup heavy whipping cream

1/2 lb. cooked & crumbled bacon

3/4 cup cheddar Cheese

3/4 cup Monterrey Jack Cheese

1 tsp salt

1 tsp cumin

1 & ½-pounds chicken breasts, boneless

2 minced garlic cloves

2 seeded & chopped jalapenos

3 tbsps. butter

3 cups chicken broth

6 oz. cream cheese

Directions:

Dissolve the butter, then cook the green peppers, seasoning, jalapenos, and onions until translucent in a medium-sized pan.

Scoop the mixture into the crockpot, then add in the chicken broth and breast.

Cover the crockpot then cook for 3-4 hours on high or 6-7 hours on a low setting.

Separate the chicken, and shred it, then return it into the crockpot.

Put in the heavy whipping cream, cream cheese, remaining cheeses, bacon then stir until the cheese melts.

Sprinkle the soup with xantham gum to thicken, then allow it to simmer uncovered on low for 10 minutes.

Serve, then top with cheddar cheese, bacon, or jalapenos and enjoy.

Nutrition:

Calories: 240 Carbs: 1g

Fat: 20g Protein: 11g

Lean Beef & Mixed Veggies Soup

Preparation Time: 8 minutes

Cooking time: 6 hours

Servings: 6

Ingredients:

1/2 tsp garlic salt, if desired

1 peeled small onion

1 diced small green pepper

1 tsp garlic & herb seasoning

1 small zucchini, sliced into rounds

1 can rinse & drained cannellini beans

1 small yellow squash, sliced into rounds

1 (14 1/2 ounces) can diced roasted tomatoes

1 & ½-pounds beef stew meat

1-2 tsp ground pepper

1-3 bay leaves

2 cups of frozen mixed vegetables

4 cups low salt beef broth

4 peeled & chopped garlic cloves

Directions:

Add all the ingredients except the zucchini cannellini beans, mixed vegetables, and yellow squash into the crockpot.

Cover the pot then cook on high for 4 hours.

After 4 hours, add in the zucchini, cannellini beans, yellow squash, and mixed vegetables.

Season to taste, and cook for an extra 2 hours on high.

Once done, stir then serve and enjoy.

Nutrition:

Calories: 50 Carbs: 10g

Fat: 0g Protein: 2g

Chicken & Tortilla Soup

Preparation Time: 7 minutes

Cooking time: 2 hours & 10 minutes

Servings: 6

Ingredients:

1 diced sweet onion

1 teaspoon cumin

1 teaspoon chili powder

1 neatly chopped cilantro bunch

1 (28 ounces) can diced tomatoes

1-2 cups water

2 cups celery, chopped

2 cups carrots, shredded

2 tablespoons tomato paste

2 diced & de-seeded jalapenos

2 big skinned chicken breasts, sliced into 1/2" strips

4 minced garlic cloves

32 ounces organic chicken broth

olive oil

sea salt & fresh cracked pepper, as desired

Directions:

Pour a dash of olive oil, 1/4 cup of chicken broth, the garlic, onions, pepper, jalapeno, and sea salt into a Dutch oven and cook over medium-high heat until soft.

Transfer the mixture into the crockpot and ass in the remaining ingredients and cook for 2 hours on low settings.

Shred the chicken, then top with the cilantro, avocado slices and enjoy.

Nutrition:

Calories: 130

Carbs: 16g

Fat: 5g

Protein: 8g

Chicken Chile Verde

Preparation Time: 12 minutes

Cooking time: 6 hours

Servings: 9

Ingredients:

1/4 teaspoon sea salt

2 pounds chopped boneless chicken.

3 tablespoons divided butter

3 tablespoons neatly chopped & divided cilantro

5 minced & divided garlic cloves

1 extra tablespoon cilantro, to garnish

1 1/2 cups salsa Verde

Directions:

Dissolve 2 tablespoons butter in the slow cooker on high.

Add in 4 of the garlic along with 2 tablespoons cilantro then stir.

Use a stovetop, melt 1 tablespoon butter in a big frypan over medium-high heat, and add 1 tablespoon minced garlic and cilantro.

Put in the chopped chicken, then sear until all the sides are browned but not cooked through.

Add the cilantro, garlic, and butter mixture with browned chicken into the crockpot.

Pour in the salsa Verde and stir together.

Cover the crockpot and cook on high settings for 2 hours, then reduce to a low setting for 3-4 extra hours.

Serve the chicken Verde in a lettuce cup or over cauliflower rice.

Nutrition:

Calories: 140

Carbs: 6g

Fat: 4g

Protein: 18g

Cauliflower & Ham Potato Stew

Preparation Time: 5 minutes

Cooking time: 4 hours

Servings: 6

Ingredients:

1/4 tsp salt

1/4 cup heavy cream

1/2 tsp onion powder

1/2 tsp garlic powder

3 cups diced ham

4 garlic cloves

8 oz. grated cheddar cheese

14 1/2 oz. chicken broth

16 oz. bag frozen cauliflower florets

a dash peppers

Directions:

Put all the items except the cauliflower inside the crockpot and mix.

Cover the crockpot then cook for 4 hours on high setting.

Once done, add in the cauliflower and cook for an extra 30 minutes on high. Serve and enjoy.

Nutrition:

Calories: 71

Carbs: 2g

Fat: 4g

Protein: 6g

Minestrone Ground Beef Soup

Preparation Time: 15 minutes

Cooking time: 8 hours

Servings: 1

Ingredients:

1/2 tsp basil, dried

1/2 tsp oregano, dried

1/2 cup vegetable broth

1 diced carrot

1 lb. ground beef

1 diced yellow onion

1 diced celery stalk

1 tbsp. garlic, minced

1 (28 ounces) can diced tomatoes

2 diced small zucchini

Directions:

Using a medium-sized pan on a stovetop, place in the ground beef and brown.

Boil 3 cups of water. Transfer the boiled water and browned beef into the crockpot Put in the remaining fixing into the crockpot.

Cook for 5-8 hours on low settings. Serve and enjoy.

Nutrition:

Calories: 180 Carbs: 24g

Fat: 4g Protein: 13g

Scrumptious Crab Meat Douse

Preparation time: 15 minutes

Cooking time: 5 hours

Servings: 5

Ingredients:

1 package Vegetable recipe mix

1 container sour cream

1 package cream cheese, softened

1 teaspoon lemon juice

1 can crab meat, thawed and drained

Directions:

Put all your fixing into your slow cooker and cook on low heat settings for 4-5 hours. Toss together before serving.

Nutrition:

Calories: 110 Carbs: 1g

Fat: 9g

Protein: 6g

Crock Pot Bay Carrot Garlic Beef Sauce

Preparation time: 20 minutes

Cooking time: 12 hours

Servings: 6

Ingredients:

4 carrots, chopped

1 bay leaf

2 pounds beef stew meat, slice

1 teaspoon paprika

1 stalk celery, diced

1/4 cup all-purpose flour

1 teaspoon Worcestershire sauce

1/2 teaspoon salt

3 potatoes, diced

1 clove garlic, shredded

1 onion, diced

1/2 teaspoon ground black pepper

1 1/2 cups beef broth

Directions:

Mix your salt, flour, and pepper in a small bowl.

Put your beef in the crockpot and pour your flour mixture on it.

Toss together to coat beef.

Put all the other items inside the crockpot and stir together.

Cover and cook on low heat settings for 11-12 hours.

Nutrition:

Calories: 159

Carbs: 20g

Fat: 6g

Protein: 2g

Directions:

Sauté your beef in a skillet until it is brown on all sides and keep aside.

Put your browned beef into your crockpot and add all other ingredients and toss together to blend evenly.

Cook within 8 hours, low.

Nutrition:

Calories: 83

Carbs: 14g

Fat: 3g

Protein: 1g

Delicious Kernel Corn Taco Soup

Preparation time: 10 minutes

Cooking time: 8 hours

Servings: 8

Ingredients:

1 package taco seasoning mix

1-pound ground beef

1 can whole kernel corn, with liquid

1 onion, chopped

1 can dice green chili peppers

1 can tomato sauce

2 cans peeled and diced tomatoes

1 can chili beans, with liquid

2 cups of water

1 can kidney beans with liquid

Sumptuous Ham and Lentil Consommé

Preparation time: 15 minutes

Cooking time: 11 hours

Servings: 6

Ingredients:

8 teaspoons tomato sauce

1 cup onion, diced

1 cup dried lentils

1 cup of water

1 cup celery, chopped

1/2 teaspoon dried basil

32 ounces chicken broth

1 cup carrots, diced

1/4 teaspoon dried thyme

1/4 teaspoon black pepper

2 cloves garlic, minced

1/2 teaspoon dried oregano

1 1/2 cups diced cooked ham

1 bay leaf

Directions:

Put all your fixing into your slow cooker and mix very well to blend well.

Cook within 11 hours, low heat settings. Remove your bay leaf before serving it.

Nutrition:

Calories: 194

Carbs: 21g

Fat: 4g

Protein: 20g

Beef Barley Vegetable Soup

Preparation time: 15 minutes

Cooking time: 8 hours

Servings: 10

Ingredients:

1 package frozen mixed vegetables

Ground black pepper to taste

1 beef chuck roast

1 onion, chopped

salt to taste

1/2 cup barley

4 cups of water

1 can chop stewed tomatoes

1 bay leaf

3 stalks celery, chopped

1/4 teaspoon ground black pepper

3 carrots, chopped

4 cubes beef bouillon cube

2 tablespoons oil

1 tablespoon white sugar

Directions:

Season your beef with salt, adding bay leaf and barley in the last hour; cook your beef in your slow cooker for 8 hours or until tender.

Set your beef aside; keep your broth also aside.

Stir fry your onion, celery, carrots, and frozen vegetable mix until soft.

Add your bouillon cubes, pepper, water, salt, beef mixture, barley mixture, chopped stewed tomatoes, and broth.

Bring to boiling point and simmer at lowered heat for 20 minutes.

Nutrition:

Calories: 69

Carbs: 10g

Fat: 2g

Protein: 5g

Delicious Chicken Soup with Lemongrass

Preparation time: 5 minutes

Cooking time: 8 hours

Servings: 10

Ingredients:

1 stalk of lemongrass, cut into big hunks

1 whole chicken

1 Tablespoon of salt

5 thick slices of fresh ginger

20 fresh basil leaves (10 -slow cooker; 10 - spices)

1 lime

Directions:

Put your lemongrass, ginger, 10 basil leaves, salt, and chicken into the slow cooker.

Fill the slow cooker up with water. Boil the chicken mixture for 480 - 600 minutes.

Scoop the soup into a bowl and adjust your salt to taste. Juice in the lime to taste and spice up with the chopped basil leaves.

Nutrition:

Calories: 105

Carbs: 1g

Fat: 2g

Protein: 15g

Crock Pot Pork Stew with Tapioca

Preparation time: 15 minutes

Cooking time: 10 hours

Servings: 6

Ingredients:

3 tablespoons quick-cooking tapioca

1 tablespoon vegetable oil

1/4 teaspoon pepper

1 large onion, chopped

1 1/2 lb. pork stew meat, cut into bite-size pieces

2 teaspoons Worcestershire sauce

1 stalk celery, chopped

4 carrots, sliced

1 tablespoon beef bouillon granules

3 red potatoes, cubes

3 cups vegetable juice

Directions:

Heat your oil over medium-high heat using a Dutch oven; brown your beef on all sides.

Mix your browned beef with all other ingredients in the crockpot.

Cover and cook on low heat settings for 9-10 hours.

Nutrition:

Calories: 190 Carbs: 0g

Fat: 10g

Protein: 23g

Delicious Bacon Cheese Potato Soup

Preparation time: 15 minutes

Cooking time: 10 hours

Servings: 8

Ingredients:

3 lb. large baking potatoes, peeled, cut into 1/2-inch cubes

1/4 cup chopped fresh chives

8 slices bacon, diced

1 carton fat-free reduced-sodium chicken broth, divided

1/2 cup milk

1 onion, finely chopped

1 pkg. Shredded Triple Cheddar Cheese, divided

1/2 cup Sour Cream

2 tablespoons flour

Directions:

Stir fry bacon over medium heat in a large skillet. Remove bacon with your slotted spoon and leave the drippings in the skillet.

Stir fry your onions in the skillet for few minutes until it is soft and crisp. Add in your flour and cook for 1 minute, stirring it frequently.

Add 1 cup of your chicken broth and cook for 2-3 minutes or until sauce is thick and simmers. Pour the sauce into your slow cooker.

Add your remaining chicken broth and potatoes and cook with slow cooker cover for 8-10 hours on low heat settings.

Transfer 4 cups of your potatoes in a bowl and mash it until smooth, adding 1.5 cups of cheese to the remaining mixture in the slow cooker; stir until melted.

Stir your mashed potatoes into the slow cooker with milk added and cook again within 5 minutes with the lid.

Microwave your bacon in a microwavable plate within 30 seconds or until heated.

Serve your soup with bacon, using sour cream, chives, and remaining cheese as toppings.

Nutrition:

Calories: 100

Carbs: 18g

Fat: 0g

Protein: 2g

Tasty Tomato Soup with Parmesan and Basil

Preparation time: 15 minutes

Cooking time: 3 hours

Servings: 6

Ingredients:

28 oz of tomatoes, chopped

1/2 cup heavy cream

1/2 cup grated Parmesan cheese

10-12 large basil leaves

3 tablespoons chopped garlic

2-3 servings of Erythritol

1/2 tablespoon dried thyme

1/4 teaspoon of red pepper flakes

1 tablespoon onion powder

Directions:

Add all ingredients except your parmesan and heavy cream to your crockpot and cook on high heat for 3 hours.

Add your cheese and cream and stir. Adjust seasoning to taste. Enjoy

Nutrition:

Calories: 110

Carbs: 16g

Fat: 3g

Protein: 5g

Luscious Carrot Beef Stew with Potatoes

Preparation time: 15 minutes

Cooking time: 10 hours

Servings: 8

Ingredients:

32 oz beef broth

One teaspoon oregano

2 cups baby carrots

2 pounds beef stew meat, bite-sized

2 celery ribs, chopped

1 tablespoon dried parsley

¼ cup of water

1 tsp Salt

1 cup of frozen corn

2 Tablespoons Worcestershire sauce

2-3 cloves of garlic, grated

¼ cup flour

6oz can tomato paste

1 tsp pepper

4-5 red potatoes, bite-sized

1 cup frozen pea

1 medium onion, finely chopped

Directions:

Add your tomato paste, beef, beef broth, celery, Worcestershire sauce, carrots, oregano, red onions, parsley, potatoes, garlic, salt, and pepper into your crockpot and mix.

Cook on low heat for 10 hours.

Mix the flour plus water in a small bowl and pour it into your crockpot 30 minutes before serving and mix until well combined.

Stir in your corn and frozen peas and cook for another 30 minutes in the crockpot, covered.

Nutrition:

Calories: 262

Carbs: 9g

Fat: 10g

Protein: 20g

Delicious Lasagna Consommé

Preparation time: 15 minutes

Cooking time: 7 hours

Servings: 8

Ingredients:

2 cups uncooked shell pasta

1 tablespoon dried parsley

1 can of diced tomatoes

1 cup of water

3 cups of beef broth

¼ teaspoon pepper

1 tablespoon dried basil

¼ teaspoon salt

½ cup chopped onion

1 cup V8

4-5 cloves of garlic, grated

1, 6oz can of tomato paste

1 lb. ground beef

Shredded cheese- topping

Directions:

Mix your tomato pastes and can tomatoes in your crockpot.

Add your garlic, salt, broth, V8, pepper, basil, beef, and parsley.

Mix, then cook on low heat for 7 hours.

Precisely 30 minutes left of cooking time, add 1 cup of water and noodles into your crockpot. Stir together and cook with the lid back on for 30 minutes.

Nutrition:

Calories: 68

Carbs: 5g

Fat: 0g

Protein: 12g

Sumptuous Cheese Broccoli Potato Bouillabaisse

Preparation time: 15 minutes

Cooking time: 8 hours

Servings: 8

Ingredients:

1 tablespoon butter

1 1/2 lbs. potatoes, chopped into 3/4 in cubes

2 1/2 cups boiling water

1 cup onion, sliced

1 package frozen broccoli, chopped

1 package cheddar cheese, minced

2 chicken bouillon cubes

Directions:

Butter the saucepan and fry your onions until crisp.

Add your water, bouillon cubes, sautéed onions, and potatoes into a pot and cover it up. Cook under medium heat until potatoes are soft.

Place your cheddar cheese and broccoli in your crockpot while you cook your potatoes.

Melt and defrost your cheese and broccoli on low heat settings.

Blend your soft potatoes contents using a food processor to your desired consistency and pour it into your crockpot.

Heat up on low heat settings until it is warm.

Nutrition:

Calories: 240

Carbs: 5g

Fat: 9g

Protein: 34g

CHAPTER 11:

Meats

Balsamic Beef Pot Roast

Preparation time: 30 minutes

Cooking time: 3 hours

Servings: 10

Ingredients:

1 boneless (3 lb.) chuck roast

1 tbsp. of each:

Kosher salt

Black ground pepper

Garlic powder

¼ c. balsamic vinegar

½ c. chopped onion

2 c. water

¼ t. xanthan gum

For the Garnish: Fresh parsley

Directions:

Massage the chuck roast with garlic powder, pepper, plus salt over the entire surface. Use a large skillet to sear the roast until browned.

Deglaze the bottom of the pot using balsamic vinegar—Cook one minute. Add to the slow cooker.

Mix in the onion, and add the water. Once it starts to boil, secure the lid, and continue cooking on low for three to four hours.

Remove the meat, then chopped it into large chunks. Remove all fat and anything else that may not be healthy such as too much fat.

Mix the xanthan gum into the broth, then put it back to the slow cooker.

Serve and enjoy with a smile!

Nutrition:

Calories: 393

Carbs: 3 g

Protein: 30 g

Fat: 28 g

Beef Bourguignon with Carrot Noodles

Preparation time: 20 minutes

Cooking time: 5 hours

Servings: 6

Ingredients:

5 slices - thick-cut bacon

1 (3 lb.) chuck roast/round roast/your favorite

1 large yellow onion

3 diced celery stalks

1 bay leaf

3 large minced garlic cloves

4 sprigs of fresh thyme

1 lb. sliced white button mushrooms

1 tbsp. tomato paste

1 c. of each:

-Beef/chicken broth (+) more as needed

-Red wine

1 large/2 med. carrots

For the Garnish: Chopped parsley

Salt & Pepper

Optional: Dash of red pepper flakes

Directions:

Prepare the bacon in a frying pan using the medium-high on the stovetop. Drain the grease. Put pepper and salt to taste in the meat cubes. Set the meat in the skillet, cook 1 to 3 minutes, then turn it over and cook for about 2 minutes each side. Put in the slow cooker once the cubes are cooked. Fold in the pancetta, garlic, mushrooms, celery, and onion in the cooker. Push the thyme and bay leaves between the layers.

Empty the porridge and wine to cover the batter within ¾ of the way up the cooker.

Cook for 4 hours on high setting. Make the carrots into a 'noodle' using a peeler. Cook again within an hour.

Trash the bay leaves when the meal is done and mix well. Serve with the parsley and pepper flakes.

Nutrition:

Calories: 548 Carbs: 6 g

Fat: 32 g Protein: 50 g

Beef Brisket

Preparation time: 20 minutes

Cooking time: 8 hours

Servings: 6

Ingredients:

1 (3-4 lb.) brisket

2 t. smoked of each:

Salt

Paprika

1 t. of each:

Onion powder

Black pepper

Garlic powder

Directions:

Towel-dry the brisket and mix the spices with rubbing the meat before placing it in the slow cooker. Put the brisket, then cook about eight hours on the low setting.

Warm up the oven to 150°F.

Put the brisket in a broiler-safe pan, then keep it in the oven while you prepare the gravy. Strain the cooking liquids into a jar.

Place the skimmed cooking juices in a medium saucepan to simmer over medium heat. Whisk until you reach a creamy sauce, usually about 10 minutes.

Transfer the brisket onto a cutting surface and cover loosely with foil to keep it warm. Rest it within 10 minutes, then cut the brisket into slices going against the grain. Put the sauce over the top and serve enjoy.

Nutrition:

Calories: 582 Carbs: 0 g

Fat: 44 g Protein: 42 g

Beef Curry

Preparation time: 35 minutes

Cooking time: 5 hours

Servings: 8

Ingredients:

2 ½ lb. chuck roast

6 tbsp. coconut milk powder

2 c. water

3 tbsp. red curry paste

5 cracked cardamom pods

2 tbsp. of each:

Dried Thai chilis/fresh red chilis

Thai fish sauce

1/8 teaspoon of each:

Cloves

Nutmeg

1 tbsp. of each:

Dried onion flakes

Ground coriander

Ground ginger

ground cumin

Granulated sugar substitute

Serving Ingredients:

2 tbsp. of each:

Coconut milk powder

Granulated sugar substitute

1 tbsp. red curry paste

¼ c. chopped of each:

Fresh cilantro

Cashews (can omit)

Optional: ¼ t. xanthan gum

Directions:

Arrange the chuck roast in the cooker. Empty the milk, water, fish sauce, curry paste, ginger, cloves, nutmeg, coriander, cumin, your chosen sweetener, the onion flakes, chilis, and cardamom pods. Secure the top of the pot.

Use the low setting for eight hours or high for five hours.

Right before serving, arrange the meat on a plate.

Whisk the sauce with two tablespoons of the milk powder, the xanthan gum, sugar substitute sweetener, and curry paste. Tear the meat to shreds, and stir into the sauce. Garnish with some cilantro, and serve.

Nutrition:

Calories: 351 Protein: 26.0 g

Carbs: 5 g Fat: 22 g

Beef Dijon

Preparation time: 15 minutes

Cooking time: 5 hours

Servings: 4

Ingredients:

4 (6 oz.) small round steaks

2 tbsp. of each:

Steak seasoning - to taste

Avocado oil

Peanut oil

Balsamic vinegar/dry sherry

4 tbsp. large chopped green onions/small chopped onions for the garnish - extra

1/4 c. whipping cream

1 c. fresh crimini mushrooms - sliced

1 tbsp. Dijon mustard

Directions:

Warm up the oils using the high heat setting on the stovetop. Flavor each of the steaks with pepper and arrange to a skillet. Cook two to three minutes per side until done.

Place into the slow cooker. Pour in the skillet drippings, half of the mushrooms, and the onions.

Cook within 4 hours, low.

When the cooking time is done, scoop out the onions, mushrooms, and steaks to a serving platter.

Whisk the mustard, balsamic vinegar, whipping cream, and the steak drippings from the slow cooker.

Empty the gravy into a gravy server and pour over the steaks. Enjoy with some brown rice, riced cauliflower, or potatoes.

Nutrition:

Calories: 535

Carbs: 5.0 g

Fat: 40 g

Protein: 39 g

Beef Ribs

Preparation time: 30 minutes

Cooking time: 6 hours

Servings: 4

Ingredients:

3 lb. beef back ribs

1 tbsp. of each:

-Sesame oil

- Rice vinegar

- Hot sauce

- Honey

- Garlic powder

- Kosher salt

½ t. black pepper

1 tbsp. potato starch/ cornstarch

¼ c. light soy sauce/ coconut aminos

Directions:

Arrange the ribs in your slow cooker. Cut them in half if it doesn't fit well in your cooker.

Whisk the rest of the ingredients together, but omit the cornstarch for now.

Put the sauce batter over the ribs, set to low, then cook within 6 hours. It will be fall off the bone tender.

Prepare the oven to 200°F.

Transfer the ribs to a baking pan, and cover with foil to keep warm.

Strain the liquid into a saucepan, then set to high setting, then mix in the cornstarch with cold water.

Continue cooking within five to ten minutes. Put the glaze sauce over the ribs, then serve.

Nutrition:

Calories: 342 Carbs: 7 g

Fat: 27 g

Protein: 23 g

Beef Stroganoff

Preparation time: 10 minutes

Cooking time: 6 hours

Servings: 10

Ingredients:

4 minced garlic cloves

1 c. white mushrooms (approx. 10)

1 large chopped onion

3 tbsp. chopped parsley

2 c. bone broth – homemade or Kettle & Fire (ex.)

2 lbs. beef roast into small strips

Pepper & salt to taste

Ingredients for Serving:

1 cucumber – peeled into long wide strips

½ c. coconut milk/cream

3 tbsp. Dijon mustard

Garnish with parsley

Salt to taste

Directions:

Arrange the strips of roast in the cooker. Stir in the salt, pepper, beef broth, mushrooms, garlic, and onion.

Cook for six to eight hours using the low-temperature setting.

When done, stir in the coconut cream, mustard, and salt.

Cover a serving bowl with the cucumber noodles.

Top it off with the stroganoff. Garnish with the parsley if desired.

Nutrition:

Calories: 462

Carbs: 4.0 g

Fat: 36 g

Protein: 26.0 g

Cabbage & Corned Beef

Preparation time: 10 minutes

Cooking time: 8 hours

Servings: 10

Ingredients:

6 lb. corned beef

1 large head of cabbage

4 c. water

1 celery bunch

1 small onion

4 carrots

½ t. of each:

Ground mustard

Ground coriander

Ground marjoram

Black pepper

Salt

Ground thyme

Allspice

Directions:

Dice the carrots, onions, and celery and toss them into the cooker. Pour in the water.

Combine the spices, rub the beef, and arrange in the cooker. Cook on low within seven hours.

Remove the top layer of cabbage. Wash and cut it into quarters it until ready to cook. When the beef is done, add the cabbage, and cook for one hour on the low setting. Serve and enjoy.

Nutrition:

Calories: 583

Carbs: 13 g

Fat: 40 g

Protein: 42 g

Chipotle Barbacoa – Mexican Barbecue

Preparation time: 10 minutes

Cooking time: 4 hours

Servings: 9

Ingredients:

½ c. beef/chicken broth

2 med. chilis in adobo (with the sauce, it's about 4 teaspoons)

3 lb. chuck roast/beef brisket

5 minced garlic cloves

2 tbsp. of each:

Lime juice

Apple cider vinegar

2 t. of each:

Sea salt

Cumin

1 tbsp. dried oregano

1 t. black pepper

2 whole bay leaves

Optional: ½ t. ground cloves

Directions:

Mix the chilis in the sauce, and add the broth, garlic, ground cloves, pepper, cumin, salt, vinegar, and lime juice in a blender, mixing until smooth.

Chop the beef into two-inch chunks, and toss it in the slow cooker. Empty the puree on top. Toss in the two bay leaves.

Cook four to six hours on the high setting or eight to ten using the low set.

Dispose of the bay leaves when the meat is done.

Shred the meat, then mix into the juices to simmer for five to ten minutes.

Nutrition:

Calories: 242

Carbs: 2 g

Fat: 11 g

Protein: 32 g

Corned Beef Cabbage Rolls

Preparation time: 25 minutes

Cooking time: 6 hours

Servings: 5

Ingredients:

3 ½ lb. corned beef

15 large savoy cabbage leaves

¼ c. of each:

White wine

Coffee

1 large lemon

1 med. sliced onion

1 tbsp. of each:

Rendered bacon fat

Erythritol

Yellow mustard

2 t. of each:

Kosher salt

Worcestershire sauce

¼ t. of each:

Cloves

Allspice

1 large bay leaf

1 t. of each:

Mustard seeds

Whole peppercorns

½ t. red pepper flakes

Directions:

Add the liquids, spices, and corned beef into the cooker. Cook six hours on the low setting.

Prepare a pot of boiling water. When the time is up, add the leaves and the sliced onion to the water for two to three minutes. Transfer the leaves to a cold-water bath - blanching them for three to four minutes. Continue boiling the onion.

Pat-dry the leaves. Put the onions plus beef, then roll up the cabbage leaves.

Drizzle with freshly squeezed lemon juice.

Nutrition:

Calories: 481.4

Carbs: 4.2 g

Protein: 34.87 g

Fat: 25.38 g

Cube Steak

Preparation time: 15 minutes

Cooking time: 8 hours

Servings: 8

Ingredients:

8 cubed steaks (28 oz.)

1 ¾ t. adobo seasoning/garlic salt

1 can (8 oz.) tomato sauce

1 c. water

Black pepper to taste

½ med. onion

1 small red pepper

1/3 c. green pitted olives (+) 2 tbsp. brine

Directions:

Slice the peppers and onions into ¼-inch strips.

Sprinkle the steaks with the pepper and garlic salt as needed and place it in the cooker.

Fold in the peppers, onion, water, sauce, and olives with the liquid/brine from the jar.

Close the lid. Prepare using the low-temperature setting for eight hours.

Nutrition:

Calories: 154

Carbs: 4 g

Protein: 23.5 g

Fat: 5.5 g

Eggplant & Ground Beef Casserole

Preparation time: 15 minutes

Cooking time: 4 hours

Servings: 12

Ingredients:

2 c. cubed eggplant

2 lb. ground beef

½ t. pepper

1 tbsp. olive oil

2 t. of each:

Salt

Mustard

Worcestershire sauce

1 can of each:

28 oz. drained diced tomatoes

16 oz. canned tomato sauce

1 t. oregano

2 c. grated mozzarella cheese

2 tbsp. parsley

Needed for the Slow Cooker: 9x13 pan

Directions:

Dust the salt over the cubed eggplant. Let it rest for 30 minutes. Add to a container and cover with the oil.

Mix the beef, salt, pepper, mustard, and Worcestershire sauce, then mash the mixture into the pan's bottom. Top it off with the eggplant, then spread out the tomatoes and sauce. Add in along with the rest of the fixings. Prepare using the high setting for two to three hours or low for three to four hours.

Nutrition:

Calories: 209 Protein: 15.9 g

Fat: 12.8 g Carbs: 5.7 g

Italian Meatballs & Zoodles

Preparation time: 35 minutes

Cooking time: 6 hours

Servings: 12

Ingredients:

1 medium spiraled zucchini

32. oz. beef stock

1 small diced onion

2 chopped celery ribs

1 chopped carrot

1 med. diced tomato

6 minced garlic cloves

1 ½ lb. ground beef

1 ½ t. garlic salt

½ c. shredded parmesan cheese

1 large egg

½ t. black pepper

4 tbsp. freshly chopped parsley

1 ½ t. of each:

Onion powder

Sea salt

1 t. of each:

Italian seasoning

Dried oregano

Directions:

Warm up the slow cooker with the low setting function.

Add the zucchini, beef stock, onion, celery, tomato, garlic salt, and carrot to the cooker. Cover with the lid.

Combine the beef, egg, parmesan, parsley, Italian seasonings, pepper, sea salt, oregano, garlic, and onion powder in a mixing container. Mix and shape into 30 meatballs.

Warm up the oil using med-high heat in a frying pan. When it's hot, add the meatballs—Brown and toss it into the cooker.

Prepare with the lid on for six hours on the low setting.

Nutrition:

Calories: 129

Carbs: 3 g

Fats: 6 g

Protein: 15 g

London Broil

Preparation time: 20 minutes

Cooking time: 4 hours

Servings: 4

Ingredients:

2 LB. London broil

1 tbsp. Dijon mustard

2 tbsp. of each:

Reduced sugar ketchup

Coconut Aminos or soy sauce

½ c. of each:

Coffee

Chicken broth

¼ c. white wine

2 t. of each:

Onion powder

Minced garlic

Directions:

Arrange the beef in the slow cooker. Cover both sides with the mustard, soy sauce, ketchup, and minced garlic.

Pour the liquids into the cooker and give it a sprinkle of the onion powder.

Cook for four to six hours. When it's ready, shred the meat. Combine with the juices.

Serve and enjoy.

Nutrition:

Calories: 409

Carbs: 2.6 g

Fat: 18.3 g

Protein: 47.3 g

Machaca - Mexican Pot Roast

Preparation time: 20 minutes

Cooking time: 7 hours

Servings: 10

Ingredients:

3 ½ LB. beef chuck roast

2 t. granulated garlic

½ t. ground coriander

1 t. ground cumin

3 tbsp. bacon grease

1 t. freshly ground black pepper

Kosher salt

2 tbsp. of each:

Organic tomato paste

Worcestershire sauce

1 c. low-sodium beef/bone broth

2 c. fresh salsa

Directions:

Combine the garlic, cumin, salt, pepper, coriander, and cumin. Rub the beef all over.

Render the bacon grease in a large skillet using the med-high setting. Brown the meat (2 min. each side). Arrange in the slow cooker and add the salsa, Worcestershire, tomato paste, and broth over the roast. Add the juices from the bacon and cover the slow cooker.

Cook one hour on the high setting. Lower the heat and cook until tender on the low power setting – about six to eight hours.

When ready, shred, and remove any fat.

Place the meat back into the juices of the slow cooker. Stir to coat and serve.

Nutrition:

Calories: 365

Carbs: 3 g

Fat: 26 g

Protein: 27 g

Parmesan Garlic Nut Chicken Wings

Preparation time: 15 minutes

Cooking time: 4 hours

Servings: 4

Ingredients:

½ cup chicken wings

1/2 tablespoon chopped garlic

1 tablespoon olive oil

2 tablespoons ghee

1 tablespoon mayonnaise

1 tablespoon Stevia

1 tablespoon grated Parmesan cheese

1 teaspoon lemon juice

1 teaspoon apple cider vinegar

1 pinch of dry oregano

1 pinch of dried basil

Salt, pepper, and chili pepper to taste

Fresh basil or parsley (to embellish)

1 pinch xanthan gum optional thickener

Directions:

Mix all the items except for the chicken to make the sauce in a large bowl.

Smear the Slow Cooker with a little butter or a non-sticking spray, then pour half the sauce on the bottom. Add the chicken wings and cover.

Cook at HIGH temperature for 4 hours.

Take the chicken wings on a baking tray covering with aluminum foil.

Pour the left-over sauce on the wings and bake in the oven on grill mode for another 15 minutes at about 200 degrees C to get a crunchy crust.

Serve the chicken wings topped with garlic and parmesan while it's still hot.

Nutrition:

Calories: 180 Carbs: 1g

Fat: 16g Protein: 8g

Tikka Masala Chicken

Preparation time: 15 minutes

Cooking time: 4 hours

Servings: 4

Ingredients:

½ cup of chicken breast

2 tablespoons tomato sauce

2 tablespoons coconut milk

1 teaspoon fresh ginger

1 pinch of onion powder

1 clove garlic

1 teaspoon thickener Xanatum gum

2 tablespoons olive oil

1 tablespoon cocoa butter

1 tablespoon of garam masala

1 pinch of cumin powder

1 pinch of salt

1 pinch of Curcuma

1 pinch of ground black pepper

1 pinch of paprika

1 pinch of fresh coriander

1 dash of lemon juice

Directions:

Rinse the chicken breast leaving the skin and cut it into cubes of about 3 cm

With your hands, grease the chicken cubes all around in the cocoa butter so to soften the meat uniformly

Clean and chop the garlic and ginger. Regarding the ginger, you can also leave it in bigger pieces and remove it at the end of the cooking if you do not wish to eat it, otherwise chop it finely

Combine all spices and salt

At this point, combine all the ingredients into the Slow Cooker, with the chicken and cover with tomato sauce, coconut milk, olive oil, and lemon juice. Stir well for the whole to season the meat evenly. Cook in the slow cooker within 4 hours, high.

Put a tablespoon of thickener, 1 hour before it's done, to thicken the cooking broth, and stir well to avoid lumps.

Garnish it all with crushed fresh coriander.

Nutrition:

Calories: 180 Carbs: 4g

Fat: 7g Protein: 25g

Hot Spicy Chicken

Preparation time: 15 minutes

Cooking time: 3 hours

Servings: 5

Ingredients:

½ cup chicken, skinless

2 tablespoons olive oil

1 tablespoon fresh ginger root

1 tablespoon white onion, sliced

1 tablespoon cocoa butter

1 teaspoon rosemary needles

1 pinch of salt

Directions:

Cut the onion in slices, and roll it with your hands into the cocoa butter to soften.

Clean and divide the ginger into 2 parts. Put all the items in the slow cooker, adding salt and rosemary.

Cover it with oil, and mix the ingredients well.

Cook in the slow cooker within 3 hours, high. After half of the cooking time, turn the chicken over.

After cooking, pour over the chicken a bit of the stew liquid. The chicken will be uniquely soft.

Nutrition:

Calories: 140

Carbs: 10g Fat: 5g

Protein: 16g

Savory Duck Breast

Preparation time: 15 minutes

Cooking time: 5 hours

Servings: 6

Ingredients:

½ cup duck breast

2 tablespoons pine nuts

1 tablespoon fresh plums, diced

2 tablespoons carrot, diced

1 pinch of onion powder

2 tablespoons celery stalk, diced

2 tablespoons ghee

1 pinch of fresh basil, chopped

1 pinch of chili powder

1 pinch of salt

For the dip:

2 tablespoons / 28 gr of mayonnaise

1 pinch of chili powder

Directions:

Open the duck breast by placing the inside upward, season with salt and pepper and a dash of oil

Chop all the vegetables together and mix with the pine nuts, ghee, and plums, then put it on the Slow Cooker.

If you have a grid, put it in the pot over the vegetables and lay on it the duck.

Cook within 5 hours, high.

When finished cooking, remove the chest from the pot and place it on a plate, remove the skin that should be easily removable at this point

At this point, you can use the seasoning and pour it over the meat. Garnish with some basil leaves

Nutrition:

Calories: 180 Carbs: 0g

Fat: 6g Protein: 29g

Lemon Scented Chicken

Preparation time: 15 minutes

Cooking time: 4 hours

Servings: 3

Ingredients:

½ cup of chicken breast

2 tablespoons lemon juice

2 tablespoons of olive oil

1 pinch of rosemary, fresh

1 pinch of sage, fresh

1 pinch of garlic powder

1 oz of white wine (Pinot Grigio)

For the dip:

1 pinch of chili

1 tablespoon / 14 gr of eggplant, diced

2 tablespoons / 28 gr of mayonnaise

1 pinch of fresh parsley, chopped

1 pinch of garlic powder

1 dash of lemon juice

1 pinch of salt

Directions:

Put the chicken legs in a pan and sauté them with olive oil until each side becomes golden, sprinkling with white wine at the end.

Put the chicken into your Slow Cooker, add the lemon juice and a half lemon.

Add crushed herbs with garlic powder.

Add salt and cook on HIGH temperature for 4 hours.

In the meantime, prepare the dip. Preheat the oven to 480°F, then bake the eggplant for half an hour on a baking pan. Then remove and mix all of the dip ingredients in a small bowl. Chill for a few hours to give the flavors time to develop

Nutrition:

Calories: 287 Carbs: 0g

Fat: 0g Protein: 0g

Autumn Sweet Chicken

Preparation time: 15 minutes

Cooking time: 5 hours

Servings: 6

Ingredients:

3 tablespoons Stevia powder

2 tablespoons walnuts, roasted

1 pinch of ground cinnamon

1 pinch of ground nutmeg

1 pinch of ground turmeric

A pinch of salt

1 boneless and skinless chicken leg

2 tablespoons olive oil

2 tablespoons ghee

1 pinch of onion powder

1 dash of lemon juice

1 oz of chicken broth

1 pinch of rosemary

½ cinnamon stick

Directions:

Roast the walnuts in a frying pan. Put it aside to cool.

Divide in half and use a blender to crumble half of them.

Mix the stevia, ground cinnamon, turmeric, nutmeg, and salt in a large bowl. Add the skinless chicken and roll it, so it is covered evenly.

Heat a frying pan and sauté the chicken until golden.

Dissolve the butter in the same pan on medium heat.

Put the onions powder, chopped nuts, lemon juice, and broth into your Slow Cooker pot with a spoon. Add the spicy chicken and the remaining spice mixture.

Add by mixing the garlic clove, rosemary, and cinnamon stick.

Cook within 5 hours, low.

Nutrition:

Calories: 454 Carbs: 53g

Fat: 15g

Protein: 30g

Coconut & Basil Chicken

Preparation time: 15 minutes

Cooking time: 4 hours

Servings: 4

Ingredients:

½ cup skinless and boneless chicken

1 oz of coconut milk

2 tablespoons ghee

1 tablespoon fresh basil leaves

1 teaspoon chopped ginger

1 clove garlic

1 dash of lime juice

1 pinch of cumin

For the dip:

2 tablespoons of olive oil

1 tablespoon grated coconut, dehydrated

1 pinch of curry

1 pinch of salt

1 pinch of fresh basil, chopped

Directions:

Prepare the chicken sauce combining the coconut milk, basil, ginger, garlic, lime juice, cumin, curry, salt, pepper, and cinnamon in a mixer. Mix until it's well combined.

Meanwhile, mix all the dip ingredients mixing well. Put aside to chill for a few hours, so the flavors enrich.

Lay the skinless and boneless chicken in the slow cooker. Pour the sauce over the chicken and cook for 4 hours on high.

When the chicken is tender and well-cooked, separate it from the sauce.

Pour the sauce into a saucepan and heat it on the stove for a few minutes to make it denser, before pouring over the chicken on a plate.

Nutrition:

Calories: 240 Carbs: 30g

Fat: 5g Protein: 178g

BBQ Dip Hot Chicken Wings

Preparation time: 15 minutes

Cooking time: 6 hours

Servings: 5

Ingredients:

Ingredients for the chicken:

¼ cup skinless and boneless chicken

2 tablespoons of butter

1 tablespoon BBQ sauce

1 pinch of parsley

1 pinch of salt and black pepper

Ingredients for the BBQ dip:

For the BBQ dip sauce:

1 tablespoon ketchup

2 tablespoons olive oil

1 tablespoon liquid Stevia

1 teaspoon apple cider vinegar

1 pinch of pepper

1 pinch of onion powder

1 dash of Worcestershire sauce

Directions:

Lay the chicken breast in your Slow cooker.

Pour the BBQ sauce over the chicken, cover and cook on low for 6 hours.

Cut the butter in small pieces and smear all the chicken with it, leave it to cook again in an hour on low, removing the lid.

Serve hot with the dip as a side dish.

Nutrition:

Calories: 180 Carbs: 7g Fat: 10g

Protein: 18g

Cheesy Chicken Pot

Preparation time: 15 minutes

Cooking time: 8 hours

Servings: 4

Ingredients:

¼ cup skinless and boneless chicken

2 tablespoons white onion, chopped

2 tablespoons carrots, finely chopped

1 tablespoon Cheddar cheese, diced

2 tablespoons ghee

1 pinch of oregano

1 pinch of time

1 tablespoon cocoa butter

¼ cup sour cream

Directions:

Pour all of your ingredients in the Slow Cooker pot, except for the sour cream, cocoa butter, and cheddar and ghee. Cook within 8 hours, low, and pour the sour cream, cheddar, and ghee.

Cook for another half an hour without the lid.

Nutrition:

Calories: 242 Carbs: 8g Fat: 10g Protein: 27g

Beijing Chicken Soup

Preparation time: 15 minutes

Cooking time: 4 hours

Servings: 3

Ingredients:

¼ cup finely chopped chicken scallops

1 oz chicken broth

2 tablespoons shitake mushrooms, minced

1 tablespoon fresh grated ginger

2 tablespoons carrots, julienne cut

2 tablespoons ghee

2 tablespoons olive oil

1 pinch of garlic powder

1 heart of lemongrass stem, crushed

1 tablespoon spicy soy sauce

1 pinch of freshly chopped coriander

1 oz of water

1 pinch of salt

Directions:

Pour in your Slow Cooker the vegetables, chicken, minced mushrooms, ginger, and garlic. Add the water, broth, lemongrass, soy sauce, and coriander. Cook within 4 hours, low.

Nutrition:

Calories: 125 Carbs: 4g Fat: 8g Protein: 10g

Lamb Curry

Preparation time: 15 minutes

Cooking time: 3 hours

Servings: 4

Ingredients:

1 lb. diced lamb

6 oz fresh baby spinach

5 teaspoons curry powder

15-ounces marinara sauce, sugar-free

1/2 cup water

Directions:

Place a medium-sized skillet over medium heat, grease with oil, and add the diced lamb.

Stir in the curry powder and a pinch of salt, cook gently for 7 to 10 minutes, or golden brown.

Transfer the meat into a 4-quart slow-cooker.

Stir in the marinara sauce and the water, ensuring the meat is fully immersed in the liquid.

Cover and seal the slow-cooker, allowing the food to cook for 3 hours at a high heat setting.

Mix in the spinach leaves, then continue cooking for another half hour, or until the spinach is tender.

Serve warm with cauliflower rice.

Nutrition:

Calories: 310 Carbohydrates: 5 g

Fats: 17 g Protein: 33 g

Lamb and Green Beans

Preparation time: 15 minutes

Cooking time: 6 hours

Servings: 4

Ingredients:

3 lb. lamb leg, on the bone

6 cups fresh green beans, trimmed

4 cloves of garlic, peeled and sliced

2 tablespoons dried mint

2 cups of chicken broth or water

Directions:

Massage the lamb on all sides with salt and black pepper.

Place a large skillet over medium heat, allow 2 tablespoons of butter to melt, then add the seasoned lamb.

Allow to brown, frequently turning; to make it is golden brown on all sides. It should take 10 – 15 minutes.

Transfer the lamb to the slow-cooker, sprinkle with the garlic and mint, and add the water.

Cover the slow-cooker with the lid, and allow the lamb to cook for 6 hours at a high heat setting.

Check occasionally and if the lamb gets dry, pour in an additional 1/2 cup of water.

Place the beans into the slow-cooker, and allow to continue cooking for another hour. The beans should be tender-crisp.

Serve hot.

Nutrition:

Calories: 525

Carbohydrates: 12 g

Fats: 36.4 g

Protein: 37.3 g

Lamb Shoulder

Preparation time: 15 minutes

Cooking time: 7 hours

Servings: 4

Ingredients:

1 lamb shoulder, on the bone

2 tablespoons mixed herbs

1/4 teaspoon xanthan gum

2 cups chicken stock, warmed

Directions:

Grease a 4-quarts slow-cooker with a non-stick cooking spray.

Season the lamb with the mixed herbs and a pinch of salt and pepper, and place it in the slow-cooker.

Pour over the stock, and seal the slow-cooker with its lid. Cook within 7 to 8 hours, allow the meat to cook on a low heat setting, or until the meat is tender.

Transfer the lamb meat to a plate and keep warm.

Transfer the cooking liquid into a saucepan, stir in the xanthan gum and allow to cook gently until the gravy has reduced to the desired thickness.

Carve the meat into slices, and serve with a jug of gravy alongside.

Nutrition:

Calories: 488 Carbohydrates: 1 g

Fats: 36 g

Protein: 39 g

Cinnamon Lamb

Preparation time: 15 minutes

Cooking time: 5 hours & 20 minutes

Servings: 4

Ingredients:

2 lb. lamb shoulder, diced

4 tomatoes, chopped

2 cloves of garlic, minced

1 tablespoon ground cinnamon

1 large bunch of coriander

Directions:

Place the lamb in a 4-quart slow-cooker.

Add the tomatoes, garlic, cinnamon, a pinch of salt and pepper, and pour in 1/2 cup water.

Cut off the stalks from the coriander bunch and add these.

Cover the slow-cooker with the lid, and set the cooking time for 5 hours at a low heat setting.

After this time, roughly chop the coriander leaves, and add them to the slow-cooker, allowing a further 20 minutes of cooking time at a high heat setting.

Serve with cauliflower rice.

Nutrition:

Calories: 352

Carbohydrates: 4 g

Fats: 27 g

Protein: 39 g

Lamb Stew

Preparation time: 15 minutes

Cooking time: 6 hours

Servings: 4

Ingredients:

8 lamb shoulder chops, trimmed and cut into bite-sized pieces

8 oz turnips or carrots, peeled and chopped

8 oz mushrooms, sliced

2 garlic cloves, minced

2 cups beef broth, warmed

Directions:

Grease the slow-cooker with a non-stick cooking spray, put all of the items inside, and add a pinch of salt and pepper.

Cover and seal the slow-cooker with its lid and cook for 6 hours on a low heat setting.

Transfer the stew to a serving platter, with all cooking juices, garnish with mint leaves, and serve.

Nutrition:

Calories: 405

Carbohydrates: 13 g

Fats: 18.9 g Protein: 53 g

Lamb with Onions and Thyme

Preparation time: 25 minutes

Cooking time: 4 hours

Servings: 4

Ingredients:

6 lb. leg of lamb

4 large white onions, peeled and diced

small bunch thyme sprigs

1/2 cup parsley leaves

10 oz red wine

Directions:

Season the leg of lamb with a pinch of salt and black pepper.

Place a large skillet over medium heat, and add 2 tablespoons of oil.

Allow the lamb to turn golden-brown on all sides, frequently turning for about 15 minutes.

Transfer the lamb onto a plate and add the onions into the pan.

Allow to cook gently for 10 minutes, until the onions are soft and lightly browned.

Spoon onion mixture into a 4-quart slow-cooker, then add the lamb, the wine, and the herbs.

Seal the slow-cooker with its lid, and allow to cook on high heat for 4 hours.

Garnish with thyme sprigs to serve.

Nutrition:

Calories: 183

Carbohydrates: 3 g

Fats: 12 g

Protein: 19 g

Lamb with Edamame Beans and Tomatoes

Preparation time: 15 minutes

Cooking time: 5 hours

Servings: 8

Ingredients:

12 oz ground lamb

1 cup frozen edamame beans, thawed

3 cups diced tomatoes,

1 tablespoon minced garlic

2 teaspoons curry powder,

Directions:

Grease a 4-quarts slow-cooker with a non-stick cooking spray and place all of the ingredients inside.

Put salt to taste, then mix in 1 1/2 cups of water.

Cover the slow-cooker with its lid, and allow the food to cook for 5 to 6 hours at a low heat setting.

Pour into warmed bowls, and serve immediately.

Nutrition:

Calories: 243.4

Carbohydrates: 13.8 g

Fats: 15.4 g

Protein: 38.4 g

Mustard Lamb

Preparation time: 15 minutes

Cooking time: 4 hours

Servings: 6

Ingredients:

12 lamb shoulder chops, trimmed

1/4 cup Dijon mustard

1 cup raw honey

1/2 cup chicken stock

Directions:

Grease a 4-quarts slow-cooker with a non-stick cooking spray and place the lamb chops inside. Mix the rest of the fixing in a bowl until mixed well, and pour it over the lamb chops. Cover the slow-cooker with its lid, and set the cooking timer for 4 to 5 hours, allowing to cook at a high heat setting. Serve immediately.

Nutrition:

Calories: 153 Carbohydrates: 2 g

Fats: 4 g Protein: 26 g

Sweet and Spicy Lamb

Preparation time: 15 minutes

Cooking time: 4 hours & 15 minutes

Servings: 6

Ingredients:

12 lamb shoulder chops, trimmed and cut into bite-sized pieces

1 medium-sized white onion, peeled and chopped

2 garlic cloves, minced

1/8 teaspoon xanthan gum

1 cup sweet and sour sauce, low-carb and sugar-free

3/4 cup hot barbecue sauce, low-carb and sugar-free

Directions:

Grease a 4-quart slow-cooker with a non-stick cooking spray. Place the meat pieces, onion, garlic, and sauces into the slow-cooker, and cover it with the lid.

Cook within 4 to 5 hours at a high heat setting.

Stir in xanthan gum, and continue cooking for 10 to 15 minutes, until the sauce thickens to the desired consistency.

Serve warm with cooked cauliflower rice.

Nutrition:

Calories: 166.1 Carbohydrates: 0.9 g

Fats: 6.3 g Protein: 23.9 g

Chinese Style Lamb Shoulder

Preparation time: 15 minutes

Cooking time: 4 hours

Servings: 4

Ingredients:

3 lb. lamb shoulder

5 carrots, peeled and cut into chunks

1 large white onion, peeled and chopped

1/4 cup minced ginger

2 teaspoons Chinese five-spice powder

2 tablespoons soy sauce

Directions:

Place the onion, ginger, and carrots in a 4-quart slow-cooker. Mix the soy sauce and the Chinese five-spice powder, then rub this mixture over the lamb shoulder. Put the lamb over the vegetables in the slow-cooker, and place the lid on the slow-cooker. Cook within 3 to 4 hours at a high heat setting.

Serve the cooked vegetables alongside the lamb.

Nutrition:

Calories: 412.8 Carbohydrates: 5 g

Fats: 20.9 g Protein: 44 g

Oriental Braised Pork

Preparation time: 15 minutes

Cooking time: 8 hours

Servings: 8

Ingredients:

3 lb. pork loin, pastured

2 Tbsp red pepper flakes

4 cloves garlic, minced

2 small onions, minced

2 tsp ground garlic

2 tsp ground ginger

1 tsp cinnamon

1 tsp ground star anise

2 Tbsp rice vinegar

6 Tbsp tamari soy sauce or coconut aminos

2 tsp sesame oil

Directions:

Put a non-stick skillet over medium flame and brown the pork loin all over. Drain well and transfer into the slow cooker.

Put the remaining fixings into the slow cooker.

Cook within 8 hours on low.

Nutrition:

Calories: 120 Carbs: 5g

Fat: 8g Protein: 11g

Pork Adobo

Preparation time: 15 minutes

Cooking time: 6 hours

Servings: 12

Ingredients:

5 lb. pork loin, pastured

1 1/2 tsp canola oil

2 small onions, diced

8 cloves garlic, minced

2 1/4 cups water

1/3 cup freshly squeezed lime juice

2/3 cup apple cider vinegar

5 Tbsp low-calorie sweetener

1 1/2 Tbsp ground Anaheim chili

1 1/2 Tbsp ground cumin

1 1/2 tsp ground cayenne pepper

Directions:

Put a skillet over medium flame, then heat the canola oil. Brown the pork all over, then transfer into the slow cooker.

Place the onion, garlic, water, lime juice, vinegar, sweetener, chili, cumin, and cayenne into the slow cooker. Mix well—Cook within 6 hours on low. Transfer the pork into a deep dish. Put the sauce into a saucepan, and place over medium flame. Simmer until thickened, then pour all over the pork.

Nutrition:

Calories: 251 Carbs: 2g Fat: 18g Protein: 18g

Country-Style Pork Ribs

Preparation time: 15 minutes

Cooking time: 8 hours

Servings: 6

Ingredients:

4 1/2 lb. country pork ribs, pastured

1 large sweet onion, diced

2/3 cup low-calorie sweetener

3 Tbsp coconut aminos

2/3 tsp ground cinnamon

2/3 tsp ground ginger

2/3 tsp ground allspice

5 cloves garlic, minced

1/3 tsp freshly ground black pepper

Cayenne pepper or dried red pepper flakes

Directions:

Separate the ribs, then place the pieces into the slow cooker together with the onions.

In a bowl, mix the rest of the ingredients very well. Pour into the slow cooker. Turn the ribs several times to coat. Cook within 8 hours on low.

Nutrition:

Calories: 240 Carbs: 0g

Fat: 18g Protein: 18g

Italian Meatloaf

Preparation time: 15 minutes

Cooking time: 6 hours

Servings: 10

Ingredients:

2 lbs. extra lean sirloin, ground

½ teaspoon black pepper, ground

2 large eggs

½ teaspoon of sea salt

1 cup zucchini, drained and grated

2 tablespoons onion powder

½ cup parmesan cheese, grated

1 tablespoon dried oregano

½ cup parsley, chopped fine

3 tablespoons balsamic vinegar

4 cloves garlic, minced

¼ cup mozzarella cheese, shredded

¼ cup tomato sauce

Non-stick cooking spray

Directions:

Place strips of aluminum foil at the bottom of the slow cooker. Use non-stick cooking spray to grease the foil.

Mix all items in a large mixing bowl. You should get a wet and loose mixture.

Pour the mixture on top of the aluminum strips in the slow cooker and mold it into an oblong.

Cook within 6 hours, low or on high for about 3 hours.

Turn the slow cooker off once there are only 15 minutes left in your cooking time.

Place ketchup on top of the meatloaf, then sprinkle with cheese. Put the cover back in place and allow the meatloaf to sit in the slow cooker for about 10 minutes more.

Nutrition:

Calories: 230 Carbs: 18g

Fat: 9g Protein: 21g

Shredded Taco Pork

Preparation time: 15 minutes

Cooking time: 10 hours

Servings: 10

Ingredients:

2 cups chicken stock

¼ cup butter, grass-fed

4 lb. pork roast

2 tablespoons chili powder

½ teaspoon garlic salt

2 tablespoons cumin

2 teaspoons celery salt

½ teaspoon black pepper

2 teaspoons onion powder

½ teaspoon cayenne pepper

2 teaspoons garlic powder

Directions:

Mix all of the flavorings in a small bowl.

Put the flavoring mixture in the slow cooker along with the remaining ingredients.

Cook inside the slow cooker within 8-10 hours, low.

Nutrition:

Calories: 83

Carbs: 1g

Fat: 3g

Protein: 13g

Crock Pot Fajitas

Preparation time: 15 minutes

Cooking time: 8 hours

Servings: 6

Ingredients:

3 lb. chuck roast, cubed

1 teaspoon salt

½ cup onion, diced

1 tablespoon olive oil

4 cloves garlic, chopped

1 beef bouillon cube

2 medium green peppers, sliced

1 teaspoon oregano

2 medium red peppers, sliced

2 tablespoons chili powder

6 oz. tomato paste

Black pepper

Directions:

Mix all of the items in a slow cooker and set on low.

Cook for about 8 hours. Once done, drain excess liquid from the vegetables and meat. Adjust seasoning if needed.

Nutrition:

Calories: 121

Carbs: 12g

Fat: 2g

Protein: 15g

Sausage-Stuffed Peppers

Preparation time: 15 minutes

Cooking time: 6 hours

Servings: 5

Ingredients:

1 lb. Italian sausage, ground

2 teaspoons dried thyme

4-5 assorted bell peppers

2 teaspoons dried oregano

½ head of cauliflower, grated

2 teaspoons dried basil

8 oz. tomato paste

½ clove garlic, minced

1 small white onion, diced

Directions:

Remove the top of the bell peppers and set it aside, then discard the seeds. Combine garlic, cauliflower, basil, onions, and dried herbs in a bowl. Cook the sausage in a pan until slightly brown. Add it into the bowl containing cauliflower mixture along with tomato paste.

Mix everything by hand. Fill the hollowed-out bell peppers with the meat mixture.

Place the stuffed bell peppers in the slow cooker and arrange the sliced tops back on.

Cook in the slow cooker within 6 hours, low.

Nutrition:

Calories: 130 Carbs: 0g

Fat: 10g Protein: 8g

Paprika Pork Tenderloin

Preparation time: 15 minutes

Cooking time: 4 hours & 20 minutes

Servings: 4

Ingredients:

1 ½ lb. lean pork tenderloin

½ teaspoon salt

2 tablespoons paprika, smoked

1 cup chicken broth

1 tablespoon oregano

½ cup of salsa

Black pepper

Directions:

Pour chicken stock in a small mixing bowl.

Add salsa, pepper, paprika, salt, and oregano. Mix well.

Remove the fat from the pork before placing it in the slow cooker. Add the liquid mixture.

Cook within 4 hours on high.

Shred the pork, then cook for another 20 minutes without cover.

Nutrition:

Calories: 160

Carbs: 2g

Fat: 8g

Protein: 22g

Pork Carnitas

Preparation time: 15 minutes

Cooking time: 8 hours

Servings: 16

Ingredients:

8 lb. Boston pork butt

1 cup of water

2 tablespoons butter

2 tablespoons chili powder

4 tablespoons garlic, minced

1 large onion, sliced thin

1 tablespoon pepper

2 tablespoons cumin

1 tablespoon salt

2 tablespoons thyme

Directions:

Grease the slow cooker using butter. Distribute onion and garlic evenly in the bottom of the slow cooker.

Remove the fat from the meat and lightly slice the top with a crisscross pattern. Mix the spices in a bowl, then coat the meat with it.

Put meat in the slow cooker with water—Cook for about 8 hours, high.

Nutrition:

Calories: 200

Carbs: 0g

Fat: 14g

Protein: 20g

Lemongrass Coconut Pulled Pork

Preparation time: 15 minutes

Cooking time: 8 hours

Servings: 8

Ingredients:

3 lb. butt roast or pork loin

½ cup of coconut milk

2-inch ginger, sliced

3 tablespoons lemongrass, minced

1 onion, sliced

3 cloves garlic, minced

1 teaspoon ground pepper

2 teaspoons kosher salt

1 tablespoon apple cider vinegar

3 tablespoons olive oil

Directions:

Remove fat from the roast and cut a crisscross pattern into it. Distribute onion and ginger slices evenly at the bottom of a slow cooker.

Mix olive oil, pepper, salt, apple cider vinegar, lemongrass, and garlic in a bowl until a loose paste is formed. Coat the pork with the mixture and put it in the slow cooker.

Cover and leave it overnight. Once done, pour coconut milk into the slow cooker and set it on low—Cook for 8 hours. Shred the meat using forks.

Nutrition:

Calories: 120 Carbs: 0g

Fat: 3g Protein: 23g

Pork Loin Roast with Onion Gravy

Preparation time: 15 minutes

Cooking time: 6 hours

Servings: 6

Ingredients:

4 lb. pork loin roast

2 tablespoons coconut aminos

1 tablespoon of sea salt

¼ cup of water

2 teaspoon black pepper

2 medium onions, sliced

2 cloves garlic, minced

Directions:

Put pepper, salt, and garlic in a bowl and mix well. Use it to coat all sides of the roast.

Distribute onion slices in the slow cooker. Pour in coconut aminos and water.

Put the roast in the slow cooker.

Cook within 4-6 hours, low.

Transfer the cooking juices and onions into a blender. Process until smooth.

Pour mixture over pork roast.

Nutrition:

Calories: 190

Carbs: 5g

Fat: 10g

Protein: 18g

Lime Pork Chops

Preparation time: 15 minutes

Cooking time: 4 hours

Servings: 8

Ingredients:

3.32 lb. pork sirloin

¾ teaspoon black pepper

3 tablespoons butter

½ ground cumin

¾ teaspoon salt

½ cup of salsa

¾ teaspoon garlic powder

5 tablespoons lime juice

Directions:

Mix all of the flavorings in a small bowl. Cover the meat all over with the flavoring mixture.

Using a pan, sear the meat in butter over medium-high heat until brown on both sides.

Combine lime juice and salsa in a separate bowl. Mix well.

Put the pork chops inside the slow cooker and pour the salsa mixture on top.

Cook within 3-4 hours, low.

Nutrition:

Calories: 170

Carbs: 8g

Fat: 6g

Protein: 18g

Carne Asada

Preparation time: 15 minutes

Cooking time: 5 hours

Servings: 4

Ingredients:

2 lb. chuck roast

1 large shallot, chopped

¼ cup olive oil

2 teaspoon of sea salt

¼ cup cilantro, minced

¼ teaspoon cumin

1 teaspoon red pepper flakes

2 teaspoons oregano

4 cloves garlic, minced

½ teaspoon coriander

1 teaspoon coconut sugar

¼ cup of water

Lime juice

Orange juice

Directions:

Except for meat and water, combine all of the ingredients in a food processor. Process until mixed thoroughly.

Put roast inside the slow cooker, then put the liquid mixture over it. Add water.

Cook within 5 hours, low, turning the meat occasionally.

Set aside for 20 minutes. Pour leftover juices on the meat.

Nutrition:

Calories: 56

Carbs: 0g

Fat: 4g

Protein: 5g

Lemongrass and Coconut Chicken Drumsticks

Preparation time: 15 minutes

Cooking time: 5 hours

Servings: 3

Ingredients:

10 organic chicken drumsticks

1 thick stalk fresh lemongrass, trimmed

4 cloves garlic, minced

1 thumb-size piece of ginger, thinly sliced

1 cup (235ml) coconut milk (+¼ cup optional at the end)

2 tablespoons fish sauce

3 tablespoons coconut aminos

1 teaspoon five-spice powder

1 large onion, thinly sliced

¼ cup fresh scallions, chopped

Salt and pepper to taste.

Directions:

Grab yourself a nice big bowl and place your drumsticks inside.

Remove the skins, and season with salt plus pepper to taste.

Place the ginger, garlic, lemongrass, fish sauce, coconut milk, coconut aminos, and five-spice powder into a high-speed blender and blitz until you form a smooth sauce.

Pour this into the bowl over the chicken and mix well.

Open up your slow cooker and layer the sliced onion over the bottom, followed by the drumsticks and marinade.

Turn onto low and cook for 4-5 hours.

Serve and enjoy!

Nutrition:

Calories: 126 Carbs: 3g

Fat: 2g

Protein: 24g

Best Jerk Chicken

Preparation time: 15 minutes

Cooking time: 6 hours

Servings: 5

Ingredients:

5 drumsticks and 5 wings

4 teaspoons salt

4 teaspoons paprika

1 teaspoon cayenne pepper

2 teaspoons onion powder

2 teaspoons thyme

2 teaspoons white pepper

2 teaspoons garlic powder

1 teaspoon black pepper

Directions:

Toss all the spices and mix them in a large bowl. If you're not a spicy fan, leave out the cayenne and paprika, then add more onion powder instead.

Now place the chicken into the bowl, rub the spices into it, and then put it into the slow cooker.

Cook within 5-6 hours, low. Cook until the chicken is perfect, then serve and enjoy!

Nutrition:

Calories: 100

Carbs: 0g

Fat: 7g

Protein: 10g

Mexican Crock Pot Fajita Chicken

Preparation time: 15 minutes

Cooking time: 8 hours

Servings: 6

Ingredients:

2lbs (907g) chicken breast, sliced thin

4 cloves garlic, minced

2 cups bell peppers, sliced

1 teaspoon kosher salt

1 teaspoon ground coriander

1 teaspoon dried oregano

1/2 teaspoon ground cumin

1/2 teaspoon chipotle chili powder

14oz (400g) can diced tomatoes

Directions:

Put the chicken inside the slow cooker's bottom, cover with the sliced onion, pepper, and garlic and sprinkle the spices over the top.

Finally, pour over the diced tomatoes, then cover with the lid and cook on low for 6-8 hours until cooked.

Serve and enjoy!

Nutrition:

Calories: 135

Carbs: 3g

Fat: 2g

Protein: 26g

Slow-Cooker Roasted Chicken with Lemon Parsley Butter

Preparation time: 15 minutes

Cooking time: 3 hours

Servings: 6

Ingredients:

1 whole chicken

1 cup of water

1/2 teaspoon salt

1/4 teaspoon ground black pepper

1 whole lemon, sliced thinly

4 tablespoons butter

2 tablespoons chopped fresh parsley

Directions:

Rub the chicken with salt and pepper.

Open up the slow cooker, place the chicken inside, and pour the water over. If the water doesn't cover the bottom, add more.

Coo within 3 hours, high, until cooked.

Then add the butter, parsley, and lemon into the pot and return to the heat for 10 minutes.

Serve and enjoy!

Nutrition:

Calories: 176

Carbs: 2g

Fat: 8g

Protein: 23g

Greek Chicken

Preparation time: 15 minutes

Cooking time: 8 hours

Servings: 4

Ingredients:

3-4 boneless, skinless chicken breasts

2 tablespoons fresh garlic, minced

Butter or lard, to greas

3 tablespoons lemon juice

1½ cups (350ml) hot water

2 chicken bouillon cubes

1 teaspoon dried oregano

½ teaspoon dried thyme

½ teaspoon dried mint

½ teaspoon dried basil

¼ teaspoon dried marjoram

½ teaspoon onion powder

¼ teaspoon garlic powder

Salt and pepper to taste

Directions:

Start by greasing your slow cooker pan generously with butter or lard.

Place the spices into a large bowl and stir well to combine.

Take the chicken breasts, place onto a clean plate, and rub each piece generously with the fresh garlic.

Put the chicken into the spice mixture, then rub the spices into the flesh and ensure it all gets covered.

Put the chicken breasts inside the bottom of the slow cooker, followed by the lemon juice.

Dissolve the chicken bouillon cubes into the hot water, and then pour over the chicken. Cook within 6-8 hours, low, until cooked and tender.

Serve and enjoy!

Nutrition:

Calories: 251

Carbs: 5g

Fat: 15g

Protein: 24g

Sesame- Orange Chicken

Preparation time: 15 minutes

Cooking time: 8 hours

Servings: 4

Ingredients:

For the chicken:

¼ cup melted coconut oil

¼ cup of coconut milk

2 tablespoons butter or lard

2 tablespoons erythritol

1 teaspoon toasted sesame oil

1 teaspoon soy sauce

½ teaspoon fresh ginger, grated

½ teaspoon toasted sesame seeds

½ teaspoon orange extract

¼ teaspoon fish sauce

1½ lbs. chicken legs or thighs

For the garnish:

1 tablespoon black sesame seeds

4 green onions, sliced

Directions:

First, take a small bowl, add all the ingredients except the chicken, and stir well until combined.

Then place the butter into your slow cooker's bottom, followed by the chicken pieces, then the sauce, and replace the lid.

Cook within 6-8 hours, low, or overnight until tender. Serve and enjoy!

Nutrition:

Calories: 235 Carbs: 25g Fat: 8g

Protein: 12g

Chinese 5-Spice Pork Ribs

Preparation time: 15 minutes

Cooking time: 8 hours

Servings: 6

Ingredients:

3 lbs. (1.36kg) baby back pork ribs

Salt and pepper to taste

2 teaspoons Chinese five-spice powder

3/4 teaspoon coarse garlic powder

1 fresh jalapeño, cut into rings

2 tablespoons rice vinegar

2 tablespoons coconut aminos (or soy sauce)

1 tablespoon tomato paste

Directions:

Start by cutting the ribs in the pieces so they'll fit into the slow cooker. Massage with salt and pepper.

Mix the Chinese 5-spice mixture and garlic and massage into the meat in a small bowl.

Place the jalapeño rings into the bottom of your slow cooker, followed by the rice vinegar, the coconut aminos, and the tomato paste and stir it all together until combined.

Add the ribs but stand them up, pop the lid back on and cook for 6-8 hours on high.

Cook until the ribs almost fall apart.

Nutrition:

Calories: 164 Carbs: 6g Fat: 7g

Protein: 19g

Pork Stew with Oyster Mushrooms

Preparation time: 15 minutes

Cooking time: 8 hours

Servings: 4

Ingredients:

2 tablespoons butter or lard

1 medium onion, chopped

1 clove garlic, chopped

2lbs (900g) pork loin, cut into 1" cubes and patted dry

½ teaspoon salt

½ teaspoon freshly cracked black pepper

2 tablespoons dried oregano

2 tablespoons dried mustard

½ teaspoon ground nutmeg

1½ cups (355ml) bone broth or stock

2 tablespoons white wine vinegar

2 lbs. (900g) oyster mushrooms

¼ cup (60ml) full-fat coconut milk

¼ cup (60ml) ghee

3 tablespoons capers

Directions:

Turn your slow cooker onto a high heat and melt the butter or lard. Add the meat and cook well until brown on both sides. Remove the meat but keep the juices at the bottom.

Add some more fat and add the onions and garlic and cook for around 5 minutes until soft.

Add the oregano, mustard, nutmeg, broth, and vinegar and stir well to combine. Return the meat into the slow cooker, then cover with the lid and cook for 6 hours on low.

Remove the lid, throw in the mushrooms and an extra cup of water and cook for a further 1-2 hours.

Whisk in the coconut milk, ghee, and capers, then serve and enjoy!

Nutrition:

Calories: 190

Carbs: 0g

Fat: 10g

Protein: 23g

Chili Pulled Pork

Preparation time: 15 minutes

Cooking time: 10 hours

Servings: 10

Ingredients:

4 1/2 lb. (2kg) pork butt / shoulder

2 tablespoons chili powder

1 tablespoon salt

1 ½ teaspoon ground cumin

½ teaspoon ground oregano

¼ teaspoon crushed red pepper flakes

Pinch ground cloves

½ cup (120ml) stock or bone broth

1 bay leaf

Directions:

Start by grabbing a bowl and throwing in the chili, salt, cumin, oregano, red pepper flakes, and a pinch of cloves then stir well to combine.

Lay the pork out on a clean plate, remove the skin if applicable, then rub the spice mixture into the pork. Put into the fridge within 1-2 hours.

When you're ready to cook, pop the pork in the bottom of the slow cooker, add the bay leaf and the stock or broth, replace the lid and switch on. Cook on low for 8-10 hours (or overnight) until tender.

Remove the lid, lift the pork from the slow cooker, and place onto a cutting board then shred with two forks.

Serve and enjoy!

Nutrition:

Calories: 210 Carbs: 0g

Fat: 15g

Protein: 0g

Pork Chili Verde

Preparation time: 15 minutes

Cooking time: 8 hours

Servings: 6

Ingredients:

For the pork:

2 lbs. (900g) boneless, pork stewing meat, chopped

3 tablespoons butter

3 tablespoons cilantro, chopped finely

1½ cups (390g) salsa Verde

5 cloves garlic, minced and divided.

¼ teaspoon of sea salt

To serve:

1 tablespoon extra cilantro

Directions:

Place the butter into the bottom of your slow cooker and allow it to melt on high heat. Add the minced garlic and the cilantro and stir well.

Add the cubed pork into the bottom of the pan of your slow cooker and stir well. Cook until just browned.

Put the salsa Verde into the slow cooker, give it a good stir, and then cook on low for 6-8 hours.

Serve, sprinkle with extra cilantro and enjoy! Easy!

Nutrition:

Calories: 130

Carbs: 6g

Fat: 8g

Protein: 9g

Beef, Bacon & Cabbage Stew

Preparation time: 15 minutes

Cooking time: 8 hours

Servings: 8

Ingredients:

½ lb. (225g) uncured bacon, cut into strips

3 lbs. (1.3kg) beef, cut into medium- pieces

2 large red onions, sliced

1 tablespoon butter

1 clove garlic, minced

1 small green or Savoy cabbage

Salt and pepper to taste

1 sprig fresh thyme

1 cup beef bone broth or water

Directions:

Open your slow cooker (but don't turn on yet) and add the butter, followed by the bacon, the onion slices, and the garlic

Add the beef and surround it with the cabbage slices.

Sprinkle everything with the thyme, pour over the broth, season with salt and pepper, and pop that lid back on.

Cook within 7-8 hours, low, until the meat is beautifully tender.

Nutrition:

Calories: 190 Carbs: 11g

Fat: 9g Protein: 15g

Sweet Pepper Beef Tongue

Preparation time: 15 minutes

Cooking time: 6 hours

Servings: 8

Ingredients:

3lb (1.3kg) beef tongue

1 onion, quartered

1 onion, diced

1 green bell pepper, diced

1 yellow pepper, diced

2 Jalapeno Pepper, diced

6 cloves garlic, minced

2 teaspoons salt, divided

1 teaspoon pepper

1 teaspoon Cajun spice

8 oz. (225g) can tomato sauce

2 cups chicken stock or water)

1 ¾ stick (200g) butter

1 bunch green onions

Directions:

First, we'll be cooking the tongue to perfect. Simply place into a large stockpot, cover with water, add a quartered onion, 1 teaspoon salt, and simmer for about 3 hours until cooked.

Remove from the pan and cool until you can handle it. Remove the skin, then cut into cubes. Pop to one side.

Open up your slow cooker and add approximately half of the butter. Melt over high heat.

Add the onion, peppers, garlic and cook for about five minutes until they begin to soften. Put the rest of the spices, then cook for a further 1-2 minutes. Add the chicken stock and the tomato sauce, followed by the tongue's chunks, replace the lid, adjust to low, and cook for around 6 hours.

Once you're ready to serve, open the lid, and melt over the rest of the butter. Serve and enjoy!

Nutrition:

Calories: 190 Carbs: 4g

Fat: 14g Protein: 0g

Easy Slow Cooker Beef Chili

Preparation time: 15 minutes

Cooking time: 8 hours

Servings: 6

Ingredients:

2 ½ lbs. (1.1kg) ground beef

1 medium red onion, chopped and divided

4 tablespoons garlic, minced

3 large ribs of celery, diced

2 tablespoons butter, lard, or oil

¼ cup (25g) pickled jalapeno slices

6 oz. (170g) can tomato paste

14oz (400g) can tomatoes and green chilies

14oz (400g) can stewed tomatoes with Mexican seasoning

2 tablespoons Worcestershire sauce

4 tablespoons chili powder

2 tablespoons cumin

2 teaspoons sea salt

1/2 teaspoon cayenne

1 teaspoon garlic powder

1 teaspoon onion powder

1 teaspoon oregano

1 teaspoon black pepper

1 bay leaf

Directions:

Firstly, add the butter, oil, or lard to your slow cooker and turn onto a high heat. Put half of the onions, then cook for 5 minutes. Put the garlic, then cook for a further minute.

Put the beef to the onion mixture, and cook until browned, stirring often—heat in the slow cooker on a low setting.

Toss in the rest of the fixing, stir it all to make sure it's well combined, and replace the lid.

Cook within 6-8 hours, low. Serve and enjoy!

Nutrition:

Calories: 174

Carbs: 2g

Fat: 6g

Protein: 26g

Coconut & Broccoli Chicken Curry

Preparation time: 15 minutes

Cooking time: 6 hours

Servings: 4

Ingredients:

13 oz. (370ml) can coconut milk

1 lb. (450g) chicken thighs, chopped into bite-sized chunks

2 tablespoons curry paste

12 oz. (340g) broccoli florets

1 medium carrot, shredded (optional)

1 bell pepper, sliced in strips

1 handful fresh cilantro, chopped

Salt and pepper, to taste

Directions:

Start by pouring the coconut milk into your slow cooker, followed by the curry paste. Stir to combine well, then add the chopped chicken, pop on the lid, and cook on low for 4 hours.

Open up that lid and add the broccoli, carrots (if using), and pepper and cook for another hour with the cover.

Remove the lid and check the consistency.

Put salt plus pepper, top with cilantro, and enjoy!

Nutrition:

Calories: 190

 Carbs: 3g

Fat: 13g

Protein: 17g

Spiced Oxtail Stew

Preparation time: 15 minutes

Cooking time: 6 hours

Servings: 4

Ingredients:

4.4lb (2 kg) oxtail or beef suitable for slow cooking (bones included)

1 tablespoon ghee, butter or lard

2 cups (480ml) beef stock

1 red onion, peeled and halved

1 garlic head

1 carrot

2 celery stalks

Juice and peel from an orange

1 cinnamon stick

1/4 teaspoon nutmeg

5-8 cloves

1 x star anise

2 bay leaves

Salt and pepper

4 heads small lettuce

Directions:

Start by opening up your slow cooker and placing the butter, ghee, or lard inside.

Switch on the heat, add the oxtail and brown over high heat.

Now add the red onion, the spices, the stock, the orange juice, the carrot, and garlic heads, replace the heat and cook on high for a few minutes, then turn down the heat and cook for 4-6 hours until the meat is beautifully soft.

Remove from oven and allow to cool. Serve and enjoy!

Nutrition:

Calories: 121

Carbs: 24g

Fat: 1g

Protein: 6g

Kalua Pork

Preparation time: 15 minutes

Cooking time: 8 hours

Servings: 8

Ingredients:

4 lbs. pork shoulder roast

1 tbsp liquid smoke

2 tsp sea salt

Directions:

Place pork roast into the slow cooker. Pour liquid smoke and sea salt all over the pork roast.

Cook within 8 hours, low. Shred the meat, then serve.

Nutrition:

Calories 582

Fat 46.2 g

Carbohydrates 0 g

Sugar 0 g

Protein 38.1 g

Cholesterol 161 mg

Fiber 0 g

Tasty Cuban Mojo Pork

Preparation time: 15 minutes

Cooking time: 8 hours

Servings: 6

Ingredients:

2 lbs. pork shoulder, boneless and cut into 2 pieces

2 bay leaves

1/2 tsp paprika

1/2 tsp cumin

1 1/2 tsp dried oregano

1/2 tsp pepper

3 garlic cloves, minced

1 jalapeno pepper, halved

1 small onion, chopped

1 lime zest

1/4 cup lime juice

1/2 cup orange juice

1/4 cup vinegar

3/4 cup chicken broth

1 tsp salt

Directions:

Place pork roast into the slow cooker. Add remaining ingredients into the slow cooker.

Cook within 8 hours, low setting. Discard bay leaves and shred the meat using a fork. Serve and enjoy.

Nutrition:

Calories 468

Fat 32.7 g

Carbohydrates 4.6 g

Sugar 2.5 g

Protein 36.3 g

Cholesterol 136 mg

Fiber 0.7 g

Net carbs 4.6 g

Green Chili Pork

Preparation time: 15 minutes

Cooking time: 8 hours

Servings: 8

Ingredients:

3 lbs. boneless pork, cubed

2 garlic cloves, minced

16 oz stewed tomatoes

4 oz green chilies, chopped

1 cup chicken broth

1 tsp oregano

1 tsp cumin

1 small onion, chopped

1 tbsp olive oil

Pepper

Salt

Directions:

Heat-up the olive oil in a pan medium-high heat. Brown the pork in hot oil. Transfer pork into the slow cooker.

Add remaining ingredients and stir well— Cook within 8 hours, low. Serve and enjoy.

Nutrition:

Calories 284

Fat 8.1 g

Carbohydrates 4.6 g

Sugar 2.5 g

Protein 45.9 g

Cholesterol 124 mg

Fiber 1 g

Net carbs 3.6 g

Thai Curried Pork

Preparation time: 15 minutes

Cooking time: 8 hours

Servings: 6

Ingredients:

4 pork chops, boneless

1/2 cup chicken broth

1 tsp red pepper flakes

2 tsp cardamom

2 tsp cumin

1 tbsp curry powder

1 tbsp turmeric

8 oz baby carrots, peeled and chopped

1 tbsp fresh ginger, grated

4 garlic cloves, minced

1 small onion, chopped

Pepper

Sea salt

Directions:

Spray slow cooker from inside with cooking spray. Put all the items into the slow cooker, and stir well.

Cook within 8 hours, low. Shred the pork chops using a fork. Serve and enjoy.

Nutrition:

Calories 211 Fat 14 g

Carbohydrates 7.9 g Sugar 2.5 g

Protein 13.4 g Cholesterol 46 mg

Fiber 2.4 g Net carbs 5.5 g

Ranch Pork Chops

Preparation time: 15 minutes

Cooking time: 6 hours

Servings: 8

Ingredients:

3 lbs. pork chops

1 tsp garlic powder

1 oz ranch dressing mix

1 oz onion soup mix

22.5 oz cream of mushroom soup

1/2 tsp black pepper

Directions:

Spray slow cooker form inside with cooking spray. Put all listed items into the slow cooker, then mix well.

Cook within 6 hours on low. Serve and enjoy.

Nutrition:

Calories 591

Fat 44.6 g

Carbohydrates 5.4 g

Sugar 0.9 g

Protein 39.2 g

Cholesterol 146 mg

Fiber 0.3 g

Net carbs 5.1 g

Delicious Coconut Pork

Preparation time: 15 minutes

Cooking time: 8 hours

Servings: 6

Ingredients:

3 lbs. pork shoulder, boneless and cut into chunks

1/2 cup fresh cilantro, chopped

1 1/2 cups coconut water

1/4 cup fish sauce

2 tbsp olive oil

5 scallions, chopped

Directions:

Heat-up olive oil in a pan over medium heat. Brown the meat in hot oil. Transfer meat into the slow cooker.

Add the rest of the items into the slow cooker and mix well. Cook on low within 8 hours. Serve and enjoy.

Nutrition:

Calories 722

Fat 53.3 g

Carbohydrates 3.6 g

Sugar 2.3 g

Protein 54.1 g

Cholesterol 204 mg

Fiber 1 g

Net carbs 2.6 g

Spicy Adobo Pulled Pork

Preparation time: 15 minutes

Cooking time: 8 hours

Servings: 4

Ingredients:

2 lbs. pork

1 tbsp ground cumin

1 tbsp garlic, minced

7 oz chipotle peppers in adobo sauce

1 can chicken broth

Directions:

Put all listed items into the slow cooker and stir well. Cook within 8 hours on low.

Shred the meat using a fork. Stir well and serve.

Nutrition:

Calories 391

Fat 9.9 g

Carbohydrates 10.1 g

Sugar 3.3 g

Protein 62.7 g

Cholesterol 166 mg

Fiber 5.9 g Net carbs 4.2 g

Tasty Lamb Shoulders

Preparation time: 15 minutes

Cooking time: 4 hours

Servings: 4

Ingredients:

2 lbs. lamb shoulder

1/4 cup beef broth

1/4 cup fresh mint

1/4 cup onion, chopped

1/4 lb. carrots

2 tbsp spice rub

Directions:

Pour beef broth into the slow cooker. Rub spice on all over the lamb shoulder and place lamb shoulder into the slow cooker.

Add remaining ingredients into the slow cooker—Cook within 4 hours on high.

Shred the meat using a fork. Serve and enjoy.

Nutrition:

Calories 441

Fat 16.8 g Carbohydrates 4 g

Sugar 1.7 g

Protein 64.5 g

Cholesterol 204 mg

Fiber 1.2 g

Net carbs 2.8 g

Thyme Lamb Chops

Preparation time: 15 minutes

Cooking time: 6 hours

Servings: 2

Ingredients:

2 lamb shoulder chops, bone-in

1/4 cup fresh thyme

1 tsp garlic paste

1/2 cup red wine

1 cup beef broth

Pepper

Salt

Directions:

Put all fixing into the slow cooker, and mix well. Cook within 6 hours, low setting. Serve and enjoy.

Nutrition:

Calories 257

Fat 10.1 g

Carbohydrates 6.4 g

Sugar 0.9 g

Protein 25.1 g

Cholesterol 75 mg

Fiber 2.3 g

Garlic Herbed Lamb Chops

Preparation time: 15 minutes

Cooking time: 4 hours

Servings: 4

Ingredients:

8 lamb loin chops

2 garlic cloves, minced

1/8 tsp black pepper

1/2 tsp garlic powder

1/2 tsp dried thyme

1 tsp dried oregano

1 medium onion, sliced

1/4 tsp salt

Directions:

Mix oregano, garlic powder, thyme, pepper, and salt in a small bowl.

Rub herb mixture over the lamb chops.

Place lamb chops into the slow cooker—top lamb chops with garlic and sliced onion.

Cook within 4 hours, low. Serve and enjoy.

Nutrition:

Calories 656

Fat 52.1 g

Carbohydrates 3.7 g

Sugar 1.3 g Protein 38.5 g

Cholesterol 160 mg

Fiber 0.9 g

Tasty Pork Tacos

Preparation time: 15 minutes

Cooking time: 8 hours

Servings: 8

Ingredients:

2 lbs. pork tenderloin

2 tsp cayenne pepper

24 oz salsa

3 tsp garlic powder

2 tbsp ground cumin

2 tbsp chili powder

1 1/2 tsp salt

Directions:

Place pork tenderloin into the slow cooker.

Mix all rest of the ingredients except salsa in a small bowl.

Rub spice mixture over pork tenderloin. Pour salsa on top of pork tenderloin.

Cook within 8 hours, low. Transfer the pork from slow cooker, and shred using a fork.

Return shredded pork into the slow cooker and stir well with salsa. Serve and enjoy.

Nutrition:

Calories 202

Fat 4.9 g

Carbohydrates 8 g

Sugar 3.1 g

Protein 31.7 g

Cholesterol 83 mg

Fiber 2.4 g

Onion Pork Chops

Preparation time: 15 minutes

Cooking time: 6 hours

Servings: 6

Ingredients:

2 lbs. pork chops, boneless

1/4 tsp garlic powder

1 tbsp apple cider vinegar

2 tbsp Worcestershire sauce

1/3 cup butter, sliced

1 large onion, sliced

1/8 tsp red pepper flakes

1 tbsp olive oil

1/4 tsp pepper

1/4 tsp salt

Directions:

Heat-up the olive oil in a pan over medium-high heat. Brown pork chops in hot oil from both sides.

Add remaining ingredients except for onion and butter into the slow cooker and stir well.

Place brown pork chops into the slow cooker and top with butter and onion.

Cook within 6 hours, low. Serve and enjoy.

Nutrition:

Calories 611 Fat 50.2 g

Carbohydrates 3.5 g Sugar 2.1 g

Protein 34.4 g Cholesterol 157 mg

Fiber 0.6 g Net carbs 2.9 g

Creamy Pork Chops

Preparation time: 15 minutes

Cooking time: 4 hours

Servings: 4

Ingredients:

4 pork chops, boneless

1 cup chicken stock

1/2 cup sour cream

1 can onion soup

Directions:

Pour chicken broth into the slow cooker. Place pork chops into the slow cooker.

Cook within 3 1/2 hours, low. Once it is done, then open the slow cooker and drain juices from the slow cooker.

Mix the sour cream plus onion soup in a small bowl, and pour over pork chops.

Cook again within 30 minutes, low. Serve and enjoy.

Nutrition:

Calories 354

Fat 27.1 g

Carbohydrates 6.4 g

Sugar 2.3 g

Protein 21.3 g

Cholesterol 81 mg

Fiber 0.5 g

Delicious Balsamic Lamb Chops

Preparation time: 15 minutes

Cooking time: 6 hours

Servings: 6

Ingredients:

3.4 lbs. lamb chops, trimmed off

1/2 tsp ground black pepper

2 tbsp rosemary

2 tbsp balsamic vinegar

4 garlic cloves, minced

1 large onion, sliced

1/2 tsp salt

Directions:

Put the onion to the bottom of the slow cooker.

Place lamb chops on top of onions, add rosemary, vinegar, garlic, pepper, and salt.

Cook within 6 hours on low. Serve and enjoy.

Nutrition:

Calories 496

Fat 19.1 g

Carbohydrates 3.9 g

Sugar 1.1 g

Protein 72.7 g

Cholesterol 231 mg

Fiber 1.1 g

Barbacoa Lamb

Preparation time: 25 minutes

Cooking time: 6 hours

Servings: 12

Ingredients:

¼ c. dried mustard

5 ½ lbs. leg of lamb - boneless

2 tbsp. of each:

Smoked paprika

Himalayan salt

1 tbsp. of each:

Chipotle powder

Dried oregano

ground cumin

1 c. water

Directions:

Combine the paprika, oregano, chipotle powder, cumin, and salt.

Cover the roast with the dried mustard, and sprinkle with the prepared spices. Arrange the lamb in the slow cooker, cover, and let it marinate in the refrigerator overnight.

In the morning, let the pot come to room temperature. Once you're ready to cook, just add the water to the slow cooker on the high heat setting—Cook for six hours.

When done, remove all except for one cup of the cooking juices, and shred the lamb.

Using the rest of the cooking juices, adjust the seasoning as you desire, and serve.

Nutrition:

Calories 492

Carbs 1.2 g

Fat 35.8 g

Protein 37.5 g

Lamb with Mint & Green Beans

Preparation time: 15 minutes

Cooking time: 10 hours

Servings: 4

Ingredients:

½ t. salt – Himalayan pink

Freshly cracked black pepper

1 lamb leg – bone-in

2 tbsp. lard/ghee/tallow

4 garlic cloves

6 c. trimmed green beans

¼ freshly chopped mint/1-2 tbsp. dried mint

Directions:

Heat-up the slow cooker with a high setting.

Dry the lamb with some paper towels. Sprinkle with the pepper and salt. Grease a Dutch oven or similar large pot with the ghee/lard.

Sear the lamb until golden brown and set aside.

Remove the peels from the garlic and mince—dice up the mint. Arrange the seared meat into the slow cooker and give it a shake of the garlic and mint.

Secure the lid and program the cooker on the low-heat function (10 hrs.) or the high-function (6 hrs.).

After about four hours, switch the lamb out of the cooker. Toss in the green beans and return the lamb into the pot.

Let the flavors mingle for about two more hours. The meat should be tender and the beans crispy. Serve and enjoy!

Nutrition:

Calories 525

Carbs 7.6 g

Protein 37.3 g

Fat 36.4 g

Succulent Lamb

Preparation time: 20 minutes

Cooking time: 8 hours

Servings: 6

Ingredients:

¼ c. olive oil

1 (2 lb.) leg of lamb

1 tbsp. maple syrup

2 tbsp. whole grain mustard

4 thyme sprigs

6-7 mint leaves

¾ t. of each:

Dried rosemary

Garlic

Pepper & salt to taste

Directions:

Cut the string off of the lamb, then slice three slits over the top.

Cover the meat with the oil and the rub (mustard, pepper, salt, and maple syrup). Put the rosemary plus garlic into the slits.

Prepare on the low setting for seven hours. Garnish with the mint and thyme—Cook one more hour. Place on a platter and serve.

Nutrition:

Calories 414

Carbs 0.3 g

Fat 35.2 g

Protein 26.7 g

Tarragon Lamb & Beans

Preparation time: 15 minutes

Cooking time: 9 hours

Servings: 12

Ingredients:

4 (1 ½ lb.) lamb shanks

1 can (19 0z.) white beans/cannellini- for example

1 ½ c. peeled - diced carrot

2 thinly sliced garlic cloves

1 c. onion

¾ c. celery

2 t. dried tarragon

¼ t. freshly cracked black pepper

2 t. dried tarragon

1 can (28 oz.) diced tomatoes - not drained

Recommended: 7-quart slow cooker

Directions:

Discard all the fat from the lamb shanks. Pour the beans, cloves of garlic, chopped carrots, chopped celery, and onion in the cooker.

Put the shanks over the beans, and sprinkle with the salt, pepper, and tarragon. Empty the tomatoes over the lamb - including the juices—Cook, the lamb in the slow cooker on high for approximately one hour.

Reduce the temperature to the low setting and cook for nine hours or until the lamb is tender.

Remove, and set it aside. Empty the bean mixture through a colander over a bowl to reserve the liquid. Let the juices stand for five minutes and skim off the fat from the surface.

Return the bean mixture to the liquid in the slow cooker. Strip the lamb bones and throw the bones away. Serve with the bean mixture and enjoy.

Nutrition:

Calories 353

Carbs 12.9 g

Fat 16.3 g

Protein 50.3 g

BBQ Beef Burritos

Preparation time: 15 minutes

Cooking time: 8 hours

Servings: 4

Ingredients:

2 lb. top sirloin steak

½ t. black pepper

1 t. of each:

Ground chipotle pepper – optional

Cinnamon

2 t. of each:

Sea salt

Garlic powder

4 minced garlic cloves

½ white onion

2 bay leaves

1 c. of each:

Chicken broth

BBQ sauce – your favorite

Assembly Ingredients:

1 ½ c. coleslaw mix

8 low-carb wraps

½ c. mayonnaise

Directions:

Pat the steak dry using some paper towels. Slice using a sharp knife along the sides. Combine the seasonings and sprinkle on the meat. Chop the onion, then the garlic, and put to the crockpot. Pour in the broth. Add the steak and bay leaf. Secure the lid and cook eight hours on the low setting. When done, remove the steak and drain the juices. Arrange the beef, garlic, and onion back into the cooker and shred. Put in the barbecue sauce, then stir well.

Assemble the burritos using the beef fixings, a bit of slaw, and a dab of mayo.

Nutrition:

Calories 750 Carbs 14 g

Fat 48 g Protein 58 g

Cheeseburger & Bacon Pie

Preparation time: 15 minutes

Cooking time: 4 hours

Servings: 8

Ingredients:

6 bacon slices – chopped

1 lb. ground beef

2 minced garlic cloves

¼ t. hot pepper flakes

Pepper & Salt

6 large eggs

4 oz. softened cream cheese

1 ½ c. Mexican shredded cheese/shredded cheese

Suggested to Use: 6-quart slow cooker

Directions:

Grease the slow cooker insert about 1/3 of the way up the sides.

Prepare the bacon until crispy in a skillet and drain on paper towels. Save the drippings and add the ground beef - cooking (med. heat) until browned.

Stir in the pepper flakes, garlic, pepper, and salt, then cook one minute and spread over the cooker's bottom. Add ¾ of the bacon pieces and one cup of the cheese.

Whisk the eggs and cream cheese together until smooth. Scrape over the beef.

Prepare 3 ½ to 4 hours using the low-heat setting. The center should be just set. Garnish with the rest of the cheese and secure the lid. Give it ten minutes to melt the cheese and sprinkle with the rest of the bacon. Serve and enjoy!

Nutrition:

Calories 376 Fat 25.93 g

Carbs 1.48 g

Protein 28.21 g

Italian Meatloaf

Preparation time: 15 minutes

Cooking time: 3 hours

Servings: 8

Ingredients:

2 lb. ground sirloin - extra-lean

Non-stick cooking spray/spritzer bottle with olive oil

2 large eggs

1 c. grated zucchini

4 minced garlic cloves

1 tbsp dried oregano

½ c. fresh each of:

Finely chopped parsley (+) more for topping

Grated parmesan cheese

3 tbsp. balsamic vinegar

2 tbsp. onion powder/minced dry onion

½ t. of each: Sea salt & ground black pepper

Topping Ingredients:

2 tbsp. freshly chopped parsley

¼ c. of each:

Shredded mozzarella cheese – approx. 2-3 slices

Tomato sauce/ketchup

Suggested for Use: 6-quart oval slow cooker

Directions:

Line the cooker with aluminum foil strips, and spray with the cooking spray.

Combine all the fixings leave out the topping ingredients.

Shape the mixture into an oblong loaf and arrange on a sling. Make the sling using aluminum foil strips long enough to wrap around the dish to remove it from the slow cooker.

Secure the lid. Program the cooker on high (3 hrs.) or low (6 hrs.). Let the meal rest for another five to ten minutes, then remove it from the pot using the aluminum strips. Add to a serving platter and sprinkle with some parsley.

Nutrition:

Calories 292

Carbs 5 g

Fat 17 g

Protein 29 g

Beef Bourguignon with Carrot Noodles

Preparation time: 15 minutes

Cooking time: 5 hours

Servings: 6

Ingredients:

5 slices - thick-cut bacon

1 (3 lb.) chuck roast/round roast/your favorite

1 large yellow onion

3 diced celery stalks

3 large minced garlic cloves

1 bay leaf

4 sprigs of fresh thyme

1 lb. white button mushrooms - sliced

1 tbsp. tomato paste

1 c. of each:

Beef/chicken broth (+) more as needed

Red wine

1 large/2 med. carrots

For the Garnish: Chopped parsley

Salt & Pepper

Optional: Dash of red pepper flakes

Directions:

Cook the bacon over medium-high. Drain the excess oil and set aside.

Put pepper and spice to taste in the beef cubes. Arrange the meat in the skillet, and cook for about 1 to 3 minutes. Turn it over and cook again within 2 to 3 minutes. Place it in the slow cooker once the cubes are cooked.

Place in the bacon, garlic, mushrooms, celery, and onion inside the slow cooker. Put the thyme and bay leaves in the middle of the layers.

Put the puree and wine to cover the mixture.

Set to cook within 4 hours on high setting. Grate the carrots to form a 'noodle' using a peeler. Cook again within an hour or until the beef falls from the bone.

Trash the bay leaves when the meal is done and mix well.

Serve with the parsley and pepper flakes.

Nutrition:

Calories 548

Carbs 6 g

Fat 32 g

Protein 50 g

Beef Ribs

Preparation time: 30 minutes

Cooking time: 6 hours

Servings: 4

Ingredients:

3 lb. beef back ribs

1 tbsp. of each:

Sesame oil

Rice vinegar

Hot sauce

Garlic powder

Kosher salt

½ t. black pepper

1 tbsp. potato starch/ cornstarch

¼ c. light soy sauce or 1/8 c. coconut aminos

Directions:

Cut and add the ribs to fit in the slow cooker. Whisk the rest of the ingredients together but omit the cornstarch for now. Put the mixture over the ribs, making sure the sauce covers all sides.

Use the low setting and cook for six hours. It will be fall off the bone tender.

Prepare the oven to 200ºF. Transfer the prepared ribs to a baking pan, and cover.

Strain the liquid into a saucepan. Prepare on the high setting and whisk in the cornstarch with a little bit of cold water.

Continue cooking - whisking often - just until the sauce has thickened into a glaze - usually about five to ten minutes.

Brush the sauce glaze over the ribs and serve.

Nutrition:

Calories 342 Fat 27 g

Carbs 7 g Protein 23 g

Braised Oxtails

Preparation time: 20 minutes

Cooking time: 7 hours

Servings: 3

Ingredients:

2 c. beef broth

2 lbs. (bone-in) oxtails

1 tbsp. fish sauce

1/3 c. butter

2 tbsp. soy sauce

1 t of each:

Minced garlic

Onion powder

Dried thyme

3 tbsp. tomato paste

Pepper & salt to taste

½ t. guar gum

½ t. ground ginger

Directions:

On the stovetop, warm up the broth and combine with the fish sauce, soy sauce, butter, and tomato paste. Pour into the cooker along with the meat and flavor with the spices.

Prepare for six to seven hours on the low setting. Remove the oxtail and set aside on towels to drain.

Add the guar gum to the rest of the liquids and blend to thicken using an immersion blender.

Enjoy with your favorite side dish.

Nutrition:

Calories 433

Carbs 3.2 g

Fat 29.7 g

Protein 28.3 g

Brisket & Onions

Preparation time: 30 minutes

Cooking time: 8 hours

Servings: 6

Ingredients:

1 ½ lb. red/yellow onions -2 larges

1 tbsp. olive oil

3 ½ lb. beef brisket

6 minced garlic cloves

Coarse kosher salt

Freshly cracked black pepper

1 tbsp. soy sauce

2 c. beef broth

2 tbsp. Worcestershire sauce – homemade

Directions:

Prepare a cast iron skillet with the oil (med heat). Slice the onions into half-moons and add them to the pan. Sauté about 20 minutes until they are lightly caramelized.

Pat the brisket dry and season with the pepper and salt. Sear until it's crusty brown. Add to the cooker with the fat side up.

Add the garlic over the meat along with the lightly browned onions.

Prepare the broth (soy, Worcestershire, and broth). Pour it into the slow cooker. Secure the lid and prepare for six to eight hours on the low heat function.

Set the cooker to warm when done and let it rest at least 20 minutes or place it in a warm oven in a baking dish. Slice and serve.

Nutrition:

Calories 127

Fat 61.3 g

Carbs 4.7 g

Protein 48 g

Italian Ragu

Preparation time: 15 minutes

Cooking time: 8 hours

Servings: 2

Ingredients:

¼ of each - diced:

Carrot

Rib of celery

Onion

1 minced garlic clove

½ lb. top-round lean beef

6 tbsp. (3 oz.) of each:

Diced tomatoes

Crushed tomatoes

2 ½ t. beef broth (+) ¼ c.

1 ¼ t. of each:

Chopped fresh thyme

Minced fresh rosemary

1 bay leaf

Pepper & salt to taste

Directions:

Arrange the prepared celery, onion, garlic, and carrots into the slow cooker. Trim away the fat, and toss in the meat. Sprinkle with the salt and pepper Stir in the rest of the fixings. Prepare on the low setting for six to eight hours. Enjoy any way you choose.

Nutrition: Calories 224 Carbs 6 g

Protein 27 g Fat 9 g

CHAPTER 12:

Fish & Seafood

Butterfly Tilapia

Preparation time: 15 minutes

Cooking time: 2 hours

Servings: 4

Ingredients:

4 tilapia fillets

For the garlic-butter compound:

8 tbsp. butter

8 chopped garlic cloves

8 tsp chopped parsley

Directions:

Mix all of the garlic-butter compound ingredients in a mixing bowl.

Place each tilapia fillet in the middle of a large sheet of aluminum foil. Generously season fillets with salt and pepper.

Divide the garlic butter compound into each fillet, then seal all the fish's sides using a foil. Place into the slow cooker. Cover with lid— Cook for 2 hours on high.

Nutrition:

Calories: 309 Fat: 24.1 g

Protein: 21.9 g Carbs: 2.5 g

Tuna and Olive-Orange Tapenade

Preparation time: 15 minutes

Cooking time: 1 hour

Servings: 4

Ingredients:

12 oz. tuna

5oz. pitted brine-cured black olives

5oz. pitted mild green olives

5 tbsps. extra-virgin olive oil, and extra for the spinach

6oz. fresh baby spinach

3 fresh bay leaves

2 thinly sliced garlic cloves

¼ c. fish stock or vegetable broth

¼ c. dry white or rose wine

½ tsp. kosher salt

½ medium finely chopped onion

1 tsp. red or white wine vinegar

1 orange zest

Black pepper

Directions:

In the slow cooker, combine the broth, wine, the 4 tablespoons olive oil, bay leaves, and salt. Season with pepper to taste. Stir to combine. Cover the slow cooker with lid. Cook for 30 minutes on low.

Add in the tuna. Turn to coat each piece evenly with the cooked broth wine mix. Cover and cook for 25-35 minutes on low or until the fish is opaque. When the fish is opaque, remove with a slotted spoon and transfer to a serving platter. Shred the fish into large flakes. Cover with foil to keep warm. Discard the cooking liquid.

While the fish is cooking, put the orange zest, garlic, olives, vinegar, and the remaining 1 tablespoon olive oil in a food processor. Pulse until the mix is a thick puree.

When ready to serve, put the spinach in a mixing bowl. Toss with a little olive oil—season with salt and pepper. Divide into the number of servings indicated, creating a bed for the tuna. Evenly distribute the tuna flakes into the number of servings. Top with the tapenade. Serve at room temperature.

Nutrition:

Calories: 414 Fat: 31 g

Protein: 25.1 g

Carbs: 9 g

Heart and Tuna Stuffed Mushroom

Preparation time: 15 minutes

Cooking time: 5 hours

Servings: 15

Ingredients:

8 oz. shredded Italian cheese blend

3 tbsp. mayonnaise

3 sliced scallions

3 oz. softened cream cheese

2 lbs. cleaned mushrooms

¼ c. minced fresh parsley

½ tsp. pepper

7 oz. drained tuna

14 oz drained chopped artichoke hearts

¼ tsp. hot sauce

Directions:

Place artichoke hearts, scallions, and the tuna in a mixing bowl and heat until well combined.

Then add in the Italian cheese, cream cheese, pepper, hot sauce, mayo, and parsley. Mash all your ingredients until well blended.

Stuff the tuna-artichoke mix into the mushroom caps.

Place a basket-type steamer in the slow cooker. Arrange a layer of the stuffed mushrooms on the basket steamer.

Take a piece of aluminum foil, then make holes in the foil using a fork. Fit the holed aluminum foil down the first layer of the stuffed mushrooms. Make a hole in the middle.

Arrange another layer of stuffed mushrooms on the foil. Do the process again to ensure that the mushrooms are well arranged. Close the lid—Cook for about 4-5 hours on low.

When cooked, serve in the slow cooker to keep warm or transfer them into a serving platter.

Nutrition:

Calories: 142

Fat: 9 g

Protein: 10.7 g

Carbs: 6.2 g

Etouffee

Preparation time: 15 minutes

Cooking time: 7 hours

Servings: 9

Ingredients:

1½ lbs. peeled and deveined raw shrimp

1½ lbs. quartered scallops

4 tbsp. olive oil

2 medium onions diced

9 scallions, chopped

3 celery stalks, diced

2 diced small green bell peppers

2 diced small jalapeno peppers

3 minced garlic cloves

20oz. diced tomatoes

5 tbsp tomato paste

¾ tsp dried basil

¾ tsp dried thyme

¾ tsp dried oregano

1/3 tsp cayenne pepper

3 tsp almond meal

1½ tbsp. cold water

Hot sauce

Sea salt

Directions:

Combine the olive oil and onion in the slow cooker. Add the scallions, bell pepper, jalapeno, and celery. Mix well.

Cook within 30 minutes, high.

Add the tomato paste and garlic—cover and cook for 15 minutes on high.

Add the tomatoes, cayenne, thyme, oregano, basil, and salt—Cook within 6 hours on low.

Add the shrimp and scallops. Set heat to high, cover, and cook for 15 minutes.

Combine the almond meal and water. Add the mixture in your slow cooker for about 6 minutes to thicken. Add a few drops of hot sauce and stir.

Nutrition:

Calories: 247

Protein: 19 g

Fat: 1.3 g

Carbs: 6.2 g

Poached Salmon

Preparation time: 15 minutes

Cooking time: 1 hour

Servings: 8

Ingredients:

2 tbsps. butter

1 sliced large sweet onion

3 c. water

2 tbsps. lemon juice

2 sprigs fresh dill

8 salmon fillets

Sea salt

2 quartered lemons

Directions:

Butter the inside of the slow cooker. Place the onion rings on the bottom in a single layer.

Slowly pour the water into the slow cooker—Cook within a half an hour on high.

On top of the onion slices, place salmon fillets—season with the fresh dill, salt, and some lemon juice.

Cover the cooker and cook for 30 mins on high or until the salmon is no longer pink on the outside.

Drain the fillets very well and serve with the lemon wedges.

Nutrition:

Calories: 100 Protein: 40.1 g

Fat: 3.4 g Carbs: 3.75 g

Tuscan Fish Soup

Preparation time: 15 minutes

Cooking time: 4 hours

Servings: 3

Ingredients:

½ qt chicken broth

¼ c. dry red wine or chicken broth

1½ lb. chopped tomatoes

1 chopped medium onion

1½ minced garlic cloves garlic

½ tsp dried oregano

½ tsp dried sage

½ tsp. dried rosemary leaves

1/8 tsp. red pepper, crushed

¾ lb. assorted skinless fish fillets

3 oz. peeled and deveined shrimp

Salt

Pepper

3 slices Italian bread, toasted

1 halved clove garlic

Directions:

In a slow cooker, mix all of the ingredients except the seafood, salt, pepper, bread, and halved garlic cloves. Cook on high for 4 hours.

In the last 15 minutes, add the seafood—season with salt and pepper.

In the meantime, rub the garlic cloves on the bread. Place bread into soup bowls and ladle the soup on top. Serve piping hot.

Nutrition:

Calories: 132.2 Fat: 3.3 g

Carbs: 18.9 g

Protein: 7.6 g

Chili Shrimps

Preparation time: 15 minutes

Cooking time: 2 hours

Servings: 6

Ingredients:

1½ pounds peeled and deveined raw shrimps

1-pound tomatoes, fire-roasted

2 tablespoons spicy salsa

½ c. chopped bell pepper

Sea salt

Black pepper

½ teaspoon cumin

½ teaspoon cayenne pepper

½ teaspoon minced garlic

4 tablespoons chopped cilantro

2 tablespoons olive oil

Directions:

Drizzle the slow cooker with a generous amount of olive oil. Place the shrimps at the bottom of it.

Put the rest of the fixing into the slow cooker. Cook on high for 2 hours.

Nutrition:

Calories: 185 Fat: 6.7 g

Carbs: 5.2 g Protein: 28.4 g

Fennel Scented Fish Stew

Preparation time: 15 minutes

Cooking time: 6 hours

Servings: 4

Ingredients:

½ qt clam juice

¼ c. dry white wine

2½ peeled and chopped medium tomatoes

½ c. carrots, chopped

½ c. onion, chopped

1½ minced garlic cloves

½ tbsp minced orange zest

½ tsp. lightly crushed fennel seeds

1 lb. firm fish fillets, chopped

1/8 c. parsley chopped

Salt

Pepper

Directions:

In a slow cooker, mix all the ingredients, except the fish fillets, parsley, salt, and pepper. Cook on low for 6 hours. Add the fish within the last 15 minutes. Add the parsley and stir to distribute—season with salt and pepper before serving.

Nutrition:

Calories: 342 Fat: 8.2 g

Carbs: 21 g Protein: 36 g

Chinese Oyster Soup

Preparation time: 15 minutes

Cooking time: 6 hours

Servings: 2

Ingredients:

1¼ c. chicken broth

1 tbsp. soy sauce

1 c. sliced Napa cabbage

4 o sliced mushrooms

½ tbsp. ginger root, minced

½ pint fresh oysters

Salt

Pepper

Directions:

In a slow cooker, mix the broth, soy sauce, cabbage, mushrooms, bean sprouts, green onions, and ginger root. Cook for 6 hours on low. In the last 15 minutes, put the oysters and liquid—season with salt and pepper before serving.

Nutrition:

Calories: 206.89 Fat: 5.93 g

Carbs: 5.1 g Protein: 30.98 g

Hearty White Fish Stew

Preparation time: 15 minutes

Cooking time: 6 hours

Servings: 3

Ingredients:

1½ pounds sliced white fish

2 tbsps. butter

1-pound diced tomatoes

2 small sliced zucchinis

1 minced clove garlic

1 chopped large onion

1 chopped green bell pepper

½ teaspoon basil, dried

½ teaspoon oregano, dried

Salt

Black pepper

¼ c. fish stock

Directions:

Stir in everything together in the slow cooker pot. Put and secure the lid. Cook the dish on high for 5-6 hours. Serve.

Nutrition:

Calories: 168

Fat: 6.8 g

Carbs: 4.5 g

Protein: 16.4 g

Catfish Creole

Preparation time: 15 minutes

Cooking time: 4 hours

Servings: 3

Ingredients:

8 oz. diced tomatoes

¼ c. clam juice or chicken broth

1½ tbsp tomato paste

¼ c. medium onion, chopped

¼ c. green bell pepper, chopped

2 sliced green onions

½ thinly sliced rib celery

2 minced garlic cloves

¼ tsp dried marjoram and thyme leaves

½ tsp celery seeds

½ tsp. ground cumin

¾ lb. catfish fillets

Salt

Hot pepper sauce

Red Pepper Rice:

¾ c. uncooked long-grain rice

1/8tsp. ground turmeric

¼ tsp. paprika

½ coarsely chopped roasted red pepper

Directions:

Mix all of the catfish creole ingredients, except the catfish fillets, salt, and red pepper sauce, in the slow cooker. Cook on high for 4 hours.

Add the fish within the last 15 minutes—season with salt and hot pepper sauce. Serve with Red Pepper Rice.

To make Red Pepper Rice, cook the long grain rice-based on package instructions. Add the turmeric into the cooking water.

After the rice is cooked, add the paprika and roasted red pepper and stir gently to distribute.

Nutrition:

Calories: 580

Fat: 5 g

Carbs: 26 g

Protein: 20 g

Mexican Corn and Shrimp Soup

Preparation time: 15 minutes

Cooking time: 4 hours & 10 minutes

Servings: 2

Ingredients:

1 c. reduced-sodium vegetable broth

2½ c. whole kernel corn

1/3 c. onion, chopped

1 small jalapeno chili, minced

1 minced garlic clove

1 tbsp. chopped epazote leaves

6 oz. peeled and deveined shrimp

Salt

Cayenne pepper

Roasted Red Pepper Sauce:

1 halved large red bell pepper

½ tsp. sugar

Directions:

In a slow cooker, mix all the ingredients, except the epazote, shrimp, salt, and cayenne pepper. Cook on high for 4 hours.

Blend the soup into a food processor or blender and add the epazote leaves. Blend until smooth and pour back into a slow cooker. Add the shrimp. Cook within 10 minutes on high. Season with salt and pepper.

To make the Roasted Red Pepper Sauce, put the pepper with the skin side up on a broiler pan. Broil until the skin becomes blackened and blistered.

Transfer the roasted pepper into a plastic bag and set aside for 5 minutes. Then, peel off the skin. Blend with the sugar in a food processor or blender until smooth.

Soup can be served warm or chilled. Add 3 tablespoons of Roasted Red Pepper Sauce into each serving bowl.

Nutrition:

Calories: 194.9

Carbs: 24.2 g

Fat: 6.3 g

Protein: 13.6 g

Cod with Fennel and Tomatoes

Preparation time: 15 minutes

Cooking time: 7 hours & 45 minutes

Servings: 8

Ingredients:

4 medium fennel bulbs, stalks discarded

½ c. olive oil

2 large sliced onions

4 minced cloves garlic

48 ounces diced tomatoes

1 c. white wine, dry

2 tablespoons lemon zest, grated

1 c. lemon juice

2 tablespoons fennel seeds, crushed

4 pounds cod fillets

Sea salt

Black pepper

Directions:

Rinse the fennel, then remove the core and outermost flesh. Slice thinly and set aside.

Place a skillet over a medium-high flame and heat the oil. Sauté the onion and garlic until onion becomes translucent. Stir in the fennel and cook for 2 minutes. Transfer into the slow cooker.

Stir the tomatoes, lemon zest and juice, wine, and fennel seeds into the slow cooker—Cook within 7 hours on low. Season the fish with salt and pepper.

Increase heat to high and add the fish into the slow cooker. Cook within 45 minutes or until the fish is cooked through.

Nutrition:

Calories: 217

Carbs: 12.9 g

Protein: 41.4 g

Fat: 29.1 g

Mahi-Mahi Taco Wraps

Preparation time: 5 minutes

Cooking time: 2 hours

Servings: 6

Ingredients:

1-pound Mahi-Mahi, wild-caught

½ cup cherry tomatoes

1 green bell pepper

1/4 medium red onion

½ teaspoon garlic powder

1 teaspoon of sea salt

½ teaspoon ground black pepper

1 teaspoon chipotle pepper

½ teaspoon dried oregano

1 teaspoon cumin

2 tablespoons avocado oil

1/4 cup chicken stock

1 medium avocado, diced

1 cup sour cream

6 large lettuce leaves

Directions:

Grease a 6-quarts slow cooker with oil, place fish in it and then pour in chicken stock.

Stir together garlic powder, salt, black pepper, chipotle pepper, oregano, and cumin and then season fish with half of this mixture.

Layer fish with tomatoes, pepper, and onion, season with remaining spice mixture, and shut with lid.

Plugin the slow cooker, then cook fish for 2 hours at a high heat setting or until cooked.

When done, evenly spoon fish among lettuce, top with avocado and sour cream, and serve.

Nutrition:

Calories: 193.6

Fat: 12g

Protein: 17g

Carbs: 5g

Fiber: 3g

Sugar: 2.5g

Shrimp Scampi

Preparation time: 5 minutes

Cooking time: 2 hours & 30 minutes

Servings: 4

Ingredients:

1 pound wild-caught shrimps, peeled & deveined

1 tablespoon minced garlic

1 teaspoon salt

½ teaspoon ground black pepper

1/2 teaspoon red pepper flakes

2 tablespoons chopped parsley

2 tablespoons avocado oil

2 tablespoons unsalted butter

1/2 cup white wine

1 tablespoon lemon juice

1/4 cup chicken broth

½ cup grated parmesan cheese

Directions:

Place all the ingredients except for shrimps and cheese in a 6-quart slow cooker and whisk until combined. Add shrimps and stir until evenly coated and shut with lid. Cook in the slow cooker for 1 hour and 30 minutes to 2 hours and 30 minutes at low heat setting or until cooked. Then top with parmesan cheese and serve.

Nutrition:

Calories: 234 Total Fat: 14.7g Protein: 23.3g

Carbs: 2.1g Fiber: 0.1g Sugar: 2g

Shrimp Tacos

Preparation time: 5 minutes

Cooking time: 3 hours

Servings: 6

Ingredients:

1 pound medium wild-caught shrimp, peeled and tails off

12-ounce fire-roasted tomatoes, diced

1 small green bell pepper, chopped

½ cup chopped white onion

1 teaspoon minced garlic

½ teaspoon of sea salt

½ teaspoon ground black pepper

½ teaspoon red chili powder

½ teaspoon cumin

¼ teaspoon cayenne pepper

2 tablespoons avocado oil

1/2 cup salsa

4 tablespoons chopped cilantro

1 ½ cup sour cream

2 medium avocados, diced

Directions:

Rinse shrimps, layer into a 6-quarts slow cooker, and drizzle with oil.

Add tomatoes, stir until mixed, then add peppers and remaining ingredients except for sour cream and avocado and stir until combined.

Plugin the slow cooker, shut with lid, and cook for 2 to 3 hours at low heat setting or 1 hour and 30 minutes to 2 hours at high heat setting or until shrimps turn pink.

When done, serve shrimps with avocado and sour cream.

Nutrition:

Calories: 369

Fat: 27.5g

Protein: 21.2g

Carbs: 9.2g

Fiber: 5g

Sugar: 5g

Fish Curry

Preparation time: 5 minutes

Cooking time: 4 hours 7 30 minutes

Servings: 6

Ingredients:

2.2 pounds wild-caught white fish fillet, cubed

18-ounce spinach leaves

4 tablespoons red curry paste, organic

14-ounce coconut cream, unsweetened and full-fat

14-ounce water

Directions:

Plug in a 6-quart slow cooker and let preheat at high heat setting.

In the meantime, whisk together coconut cream and water until smooth.

Place fish into the slow cooker, spread with curry paste, and then pour in coconut cream mixture.

Cook within 2 hours at a high setting or 4 hours at low heat setting until tender.

Then add spinach and continue cooking for 20 to 30 minutes or until spinach leaves wilt.

Serve straight away.

Nutrition:

Calories: 323

Fat: 51.5g

Protein: 41.3g

Carbs: 7g

Fiber: 2.2g

Sugar: 2.3g

Salmon with Creamy Lemon Sauce

Preparation time: 5 minutes

Cooking time: 2 hours & 15 minutes

Servings: 6

Ingredients:

For the Salmon:

2 pounds wild-caught salmon fillet, skin-on

1 teaspoon garlic powder

1 ½ teaspoon salt

1 teaspoon ground black pepper

1/2 teaspoon red chili powder

1 teaspoon Italian Seasoning

1 lemon, sliced

1 lemon, juiced

2 tablespoons avocado oil

1 cup chicken broth

For the Creamy Lemon Sauce:

Chopped parsley, for garnish

1/8 teaspoon lemon zest

1/4 cup heavy cream

1/4 cup grated parmesan cheese

Directions:

Line a 6-quart slow cooker with parchment sheet spread its bottom with lemon slices, top with salmon and drizzle with oil.

Stir together garlic powder, salt, black pepper, red chili powder, Italian seasoning, and oil until combined and rub this mixture all over salmon.

Pour lemon juice and broth around the fish and shut with lid.

Cook in the slow cooker within 2 hours at a low heat setting.

In the meantime, set the oven at 400 degrees F and let preheat.

When fish is done, lift out an inner pot of slow cooker, place into the oven, then cook within 5 to 8 minutes or until the top is nicely browned.

Lift out the fish using a parchment sheet and keep it warm.

Remove, transfer juices to a medium skillet pan, place it over medium-high heat, and then bring to boil and cook for 1 minute.

Turn heat to a low level, whisk the cream into the sauce, and lemon zest and parmesan cheese and cook for 2 to 3 minutes or until thickened.

Cut salmon in pieces, then top each portion with lemon sauce and serve.

Nutrition:

Calories: 340

Fat: 20g

Protein: 32g

Carbs: 8g

Fiber: 2g

Sugar: 2g

Salmon with Lemon-Caper Sauce

Preparation time: 5 minutes

Cooking time: 1 hour & 30 minutes

Servings: 6

Ingredients:

1 pound wild-caught salmon fillet

2 teaspoon capers, rinsed and mashed

1 teaspoon minced garlic

1 teaspoon salt

½ teaspoon ground black pepper

1/2 teaspoon dried oregano

1 teaspoon lemon zest

2 tablespoons lemon juice

4 tablespoons unsalted butter

Directions:

Cut salmon into 4 pieces, then season with salt and black pepper and sprinkle lemon zest on top.

Arrange a 6-quart slow cooker with parchment paper, place seasoned salmon pieces on it, and shut with lid.

Set to cook in the slow cooker within 1 hour and 30 minutes or until salmon is cooked through. Prepare lemon-caper sauce and for this, place a small saucepan over low heat, add butter and let it melt. Then add capers, garlic, lemon juice, stir until mixed and simmer for 1 minute.

Remove saucepan from heat and stir in oregano. When salmon is cooked, spoon lemon-caper sauce on it and serve.

Nutrition:

Calories: 368.5 Fat: 26.6g

Protein: 19.5g Carbs: 2.7g

Fiber: 0.3g Sugar: 2g

Spicy Barbecue Shrimp

Preparation time: 5 minutes

Cooking time: 1 hour & 30 minutes

Servings: 6

Ingredients:

1 1/2 pounds large wild-caught shrimp, unpeeled

1 green onion, chopped

1 teaspoon minced garlic

1 ½ teaspoon salt

¾ teaspoon ground black pepper

1 teaspoon Cajun seasoning

1 tablespoon hot pepper sauce

¼ cup Worcestershire Sauce

1 lemon, juiced

2 tablespoons avocado oil

1/2 cup unsalted butter, chopped

Directions:

Place all the ingredients except for shrimps in a 6-quart slow cooker and whisk until mixed.

Plugin the slow cooker, then shut with lid and cook for 1 hour and 30 minutes at a high heat setting.

Then take out ½ cup of this sauce and reserve.

Add shrimps to slow cooker.

Nutrition:

Calories: 321

Fat: 21.4g

Protein: 27.3g

Carbs: 4.8g

Fiber: 2.4g

Sugar: 1.2g

Lemon Dill Halibut

Preparation time: 15 minutes

Cooking time: 2 hours

Servings: 2

Ingredients:

12-ounce wild-caught halibut fillet

1 teaspoon salt

½ teaspoon ground black pepper

1 1/2 teaspoon dried dill

1 tablespoon fresh lemon juice

3 tablespoons avocado oil

Directions:

Cut an 18-inch piece of aluminum foil, halibut fillet in the middle, and then season with salt and black pepper.

Whisk the remaining ingredients, drizzle this mixture over halibut, then crimp foil's edges and place it into a 6-quart slow cooker.

Cook within 1 hour and 30 minutes or 2 hours at high heat setting or until cooked.

When done, carefully open the crimped edges and check the fish; it should be tender and flaky.

Serve straight away.

Nutrition:

Calories: 321.5 Fat: 21.4g

Protein: 32.1g Carbs: 0g

Fiber: 0g

Sugar: 0.6g

Coconut Cilantro Curry Shrimp

Preparation time: 15 minutes

Cooking time: 2 hours & 30 minutes

Servings: 4

Ingredients:

1 pound wild-caught shrimp, peeled and deveined

2 ½ teaspoon lemon garlic seasoning

2 tablespoons red curry paste

4 tablespoons chopped cilantro

30 ounces coconut milk, unsweetened

16 ounces of water

Directions:

Whisk together all the ingredients except for shrimps and 2 tablespoons cilantro and add to a 4-quart slow cooker.

Plugin the slow cooker, shut with lid, and cook for 2 hours at high heat setting or 4 hours at low heat setting.

Then add shrimps, toss until evenly coated and cook for 20 to 30 minutes at high heat settings or until shrimps are pink.

Garnish shrimps with remaining cilantro and serve.

Nutrition:

Calories: 160.7 Total Fat: 8.2g

Protein: 19.3g

Carbs: 2.4g

Fiber: 0.5g

Sugar: 1.4g

Shrimp in Marinara Sauce

Preparation time: 15 minutes

Cooking time:5

hours & 10 minutes

Servings: 5

Ingredients:

1 pound cooked wild-caught shrimps, peeled and deveined

14.5-ounce crushed tomatoes

½ teaspoon minced garlic

1 teaspoon salt

1/2 teaspoon seasoned salt

¼ teaspoon ground black pepper

½ teaspoon crushed red pepper flakes

1/2 teaspoon dried basil

1/2 teaspoon dried oregano

½ tablespoons avocado oil

6-ounce chicken broth

2 tablespoon minced parsley

1/2 cup grated Parmesan cheese

Directions:

Place all the ingredients except for shrimps, parsley, and cheese in a 4-quart slow cooker and stir well.

Then plug in the slow cooker, shut with lid, and cook for 4 to 5 hours at a low heat setting.

Then add shrimps and parsley, stir until mixed and cook for 10 minutes at high heat setting.

Garnish shrimps with cheese and serve.

Nutrition:

Calories: 358.8

Fat: 25.1g

Protein: 26g

Carbs: 7.2g

Fiber: 1.5g

Sugar: 3.6g

Garlic Shrimp

Preparation time: 5 minutes

Cooking time: 1 hour

Servings: 5

Ingredients:

For the Garlic Shrimp:

1 1/2 pounds large wild-caught shrimp, peeled and deveined

1/4 teaspoon ground black pepper

1/8 teaspoon ground cayenne pepper

2 ½ teaspoons minced garlic

1/4 cup avocado oil

4 tablespoons unsalted butter

For the Seasoning:

1 teaspoon onion powder

1 tablespoon garlic powder

1 tablespoon salt

2 teaspoons ground black pepper

1 tablespoon paprika

1 teaspoon cayenne pepper

1 teaspoon dried oregano

1 teaspoon dried thyme

Directions:

Stir together all the ingredients for seasoning, garlic, oil, and butter and add to a 4-quart slow cooker.

Plugin the slow cooker, shut with lid, and cook for 25 to 30 minutes at high heat setting or until cooked.

Then add shrimps, toss until evenly coated, and continue cooking for 20 to 30 minutes at high heat setting or until shrimps are pink.

When done, transfer shrimps to a serving plate, top with sauce, and serve.

Nutrition:

Calories: 233.6

Fat: 11.7g

Protein: 30.9g

Carbs: 1.2g

Fiber: 0g

Sugar: 0g

Lemon Pepper Tilapia

Preparation time: 5 minutes

Cooking time: 3 hours

Servings: 6

Ingredients:

6 wild-caught Tilapia fillets

4 teaspoons lemon-pepper seasoning, divided

6 tablespoons unsalted butter, divided

1/2 cup lemon juice, fresh

Directions:

Put each fillet in the center of the foil, then season with lemon-pepper seasoning, drizzle with lemon juice, and top with 1 tablespoon butter.

Gently crimp the edges of foil to form a packet and place it into a 6-quart slow cooker.

Plugin the slow cooker, shut with lid, and cook for 3 hours at high heat or until cooked.

Serve straight away.

Nutrition:

Calories: 201.2

Fat: 12.9g

Protein: 19.6g

Carbs: 1.5g

Fiber: 0.3g

Sugar: 0.7g

Clam Chowder

Preparation time: 15 minutes

Cooking time: 6 hours

Servings: 6

Ingredients:

20-ounce wild-caught baby clams, with juice

½ cup chopped scallion

½ cup chopped celery

1 teaspoon salt

1 teaspoon ground black pepper

1 teaspoon dried thyme

1 tablespoon avocado oil

2 cups coconut cream, full-fat

2 cups chicken broth

Directions:

Grease a 6-quart slow cooker with oil, then add ingredients and stir until mixed.

Plugin the slow cooker, shut with lid, and cook for 4 to 6 hours at low heat setting or until cooked.

Serve straight away.

Nutrition:

Calories: 357 Fat: 28.9g

Protein: 15.2g Carbs: 8.9g

Fiber: 2.1g Sugar: 3.9g

Soy-Ginger Steamed Pompano

Preparation time: 5 minutes

Cooking time: 1 hour

Servings: 4

Ingredients:

1 wild-caught whole pompano, gutted and scaled

1 bunch scallion, diced

1 bunch cilantro, chopped

3 teaspoons minced garlic

1 tablespoon grated ginger

1 tablespoon swerve sweetener

¼ cup of soy sauce

¼ cup white wine

¼ cup sesame oil

Directions:

Place scallions in a 6-quart slow cooker and top with fish.

Whisk together remaining ingredients, except for cilantro, and pour the mixture all over the fish.

Plugin the slow cooker, shut with lid, and cook for 1 hour at high heat or until cooked.

Garnish with cilantro and serve.

Nutrition:

Calories: 202.5 Fat: 24.2g

Protein: 22.7g Carbs: 4g

Fiber: 0.5g Sugar: 1.1g

Vietnamese Braised Catfish

Preparation time: 5 minutes

Cooking time: 6 hours

Servings: 3

Ingredients:

1 fillet of wild-caught catfish, cut into bite-size pieces

1 scallion, chopped

3 red chilies, chopped

1 tablespoon grated ginger

1/2 cup swerve sweetener

2 tablespoons avocado oil

1/4 cup fish sauce, unsweetened

Directions:

Put a small saucepan over medium heat, put the sweetener, and cook until it melts.

Then add scallion, chilies, ginger, and fish sauce and stir until mixed.

Transfer this mixture in a 4-quart slow cooker, add fish and toss until coated.

Plugin the slow cooker, shut with lid, and cook for 6 hours at low heat setting until cooked.

Drizzle with avocado oil and serve straight away.

Nutrition:

Calories: 110.7 Fat: 8g Protein: 9.4g

Carbs: 0.3g Fiber: 0.2g

Poached Salmon in Court-Bouillon Recipe

Preparation time: 5 minutes

Cooking Time: 2 hours 30 minutes

Servings: 2

Ingredients:

2 whole black peppercorns

1/2 medium carrot, thinly sliced

1/2 celery rib, thinly sliced

2 salmon steaks in 1-inch-thick slices

1 1/2 tbsp white wine vinegar

Directions:

Put all the items in the crockpot except for the salmon. You can also add parsley and bay leaf for extra flavor. Rub salmon slices with salt and pepper to taste. Cook within 2 hours on high.

Put some of the liquid over the top. Cook again within 30 minutes, high.

Nutrition:

Calories: 197 Fat: 7.7g Carbs: 4.8g

Protein: 18.3g Cholesterol: 95mg

Sodium: 366mg

Braised Squid with Tomatoes and Fennel

Preparation time: 20 minutes

Cooking Time: 4 hours

Servings: 2

Ingredients:

1 1/2 cups clam juice

1 can plum tomatoes

1/2 fennel bulb, minced

3 tbsp all-purpose flour

1 lb. squid in 1-inch pieces

Directions:

Add chopped onions, fennel, and garlic to the flameproof insert of a crockpot and cook on a stove in medium heat for about 5 minutes.

Whisk in flour and tomato paste until thoroughly mixed, then add the clam juice, tomatoes, 1 tsp salt, and pepper. Boil for about 2 minutes.

Transfer to the crockpot, cover, and cook for 3 hours on low.

Uncover, add the squid and mix well—Cook for another 1 hour.

Nutrition:

Calories: 210

Fat: 25g

Carbs: 6g

Protein: 29g

Seafood Stir-Fry Soup

Preparation time: 30 minutes

Cooking Time: 3 hours & 10 minutes

Servings: 2

Ingredients:

7.25 oz low-carb Udon noodle, beef flavor

1/2 lb. shrimp

1/4 lb. scallops

3 cups low-sodium broth

1 carrot, shredded

Directions:

Add all ingredients except noodles, shrimp, and scallops to the crockpot. Include seasonings such as garlic, ginger, salt, and pepper to taste. Add vinegar, soy sauce, and fish sauce, 1/2 tbsp each. Stir to mix well.

Cook on high for 2-3 hours. Add udon noodles, shrimp, and scallops. Cook on high for additional 10-15 minutes.

Nutrition:

Calories: 266

Fat: 19g

Carbs: 8g

Protein: 27.5g

Cholesterol: 173mg

Sodium: 489mg

Shrimp Fajita Soup

Preparation time: 20 minutes

Cooking Time: 2 hours

Servings: 2

Ingredients:

1/2 lb. shrimp

32 oz chicken broth

1 tbsp fajita seasoning

1/2 bell pepper, sliced or diced

Directions:

Put all the listed items except the shrimp in the crockpot. Add onion slices to taste and stir to mix well.

Cook on high for 2 hours. Add the shrimp, and cook for additional 5-15 minutes.

Nutrition:

Calories: 165

Fat: 7.3g

Carbs: 3.7g

Protein: 15.9g

Cholesterol: 87mg

Sodium: 215mg

Fish and Tomatoes

Preparation time: 7 minutes

Cooking Time: 3 hours

Servings: 2

Ingredients:

1/2 bell pepper, sliced

1/8 cup low-sodium broth

8 oz diced tomatoes

1/2 tbsp rosemary

1/2 lb. cod

Directions:

Put all the listed fixing except the fish in the crockpot. Add garlic, salt, and pepper to taste.

Season fish with your favorite seasoning and place other ingredients in the pot. Cook for 3 hours on low.

Nutrition:

Calories: 204 Fat: 16.8g

Carbs: 5g Protein: 25.3g

Cholesterol: 75mg Sodium: 296mg

Hot Crab Dip

Preparation time: 10 minutes

Cooking Time: 3 hours

Servings: 2

Ingredients:

1/8 cup grated Parmesan cheese

1/4 package cream cheese, softened

1/8 cup mayonnaise

6 oz crabmeat, drained and flaked

Directions:

In a slow cooker, combine the ingredients. Add sweetener to taste and a sliced clove of garlic.

Stir, cover, and cook on low for 2-3 hours.

Nutrition:

Calories: 190 Fat: 16g

Carbs: 3g

Protein: 8g

Cholesterol: 55mg

Sodium: 231mg

Cod and Zoodles Stew

Preparation time: 5 minutes

Cooking Time: 2 hours

Servings: 2

Ingredients:

1/8 cup low-sodium broth

1/2 bell pepper, diced

1/2 lb. sablefish or any whitefish

14 oz diced tomatoes

1 zucchini, made into zoodles

Directions:

Prepare seasonings: onion, garlic, pepper, and salt to taste.

Place all the ingredients in the crockpot and add the prepared seasonings—cook on high for 2 hours.

Nutrition:

Calories: 209 Fat: 20g

Net Carbs: 3g Protein: 15g

Cholesterol: 74mg

Sodium: 291mg

Slow-Cooked Tilapia

Preparation time: 10 minutes

Cooking Time: 4 hours

Servings: 2

Ingredients:

1 lb. tilapia, sliced

1/2 fresh lemon, juiced

1/2 cup mayonnaise

Directions:

Whisk mayo and lemon juice in a bowl. Add some chops of garlic.

Spread the mixture on all sides of the tilapia. Cook on low for 3-4 hours.

Nutrition:

Calories: 189 Fat: 18g Carbs: 4g Protein: 22g

Salmon Lemon and Dill

Preparation time: 10 minutes

Cooking Time: 2 hours

Servings: 2

Ingredients:

1 tsp extra-virgin olive oil

2 lb. salmon

1 lemon, sliced

A handful of fresh dill

Directions:

Rub salmon with the oil, salt, pepper, garlic, and fresh dill. Put the salmon in the crockpot and place lemon slices on top. Cook on high for 1 hour or low for 2.

Nutrition:

Calories: 159 Fat: 16g Carbs: 2g

Protein: 37g Cholesterol: 114mg

Sodium: 209mg

Creamy Crab Zucchini Casserole

Preparation time: 20 minutes

Cooking Time: 5 hours

Servings: 2

Ingredients:

1/4 cup heavy cream

1 medium zucchini squash

2 oz. cream cheese

4 oz. crab meat

1/3 tbsp butter

Directions:

Spiralize zucchini squash on wide ribbons and season with salt. Place the ribbons in a steamer basket and heat for 5 to 7 minutes.

Put all ingredients in a slow cooker, including seasonings such as garlic, onions, pepper, and salt to taste. Put the zucchini spirals on top—Cook within 5 hours on low.

Nutrition: Sodium: 209mg

Calories: 162.6 Fat: 11.9g Carbs: 2.8g

Protein: 7.2g Cholesterol: 114mg

Lobster Bisque

Preparation time: 20 minutes

Cooking Time: 6 hours

Servings: 2

Ingredients:

1 1/3 lobster tails, fan parts cut out

2/3 tsp Worcestershire sauce

2 tbsp tomato paste

2/3 cup lobster stock

2/3 cup heavy cream

Directions:

Enhance the broth: slowly add broth to an onion-garlic sauté. Put the broth plus all the other listed fixing except the heavy cream in the crockpot, including desired spices to taste (paprika, thyme, black pepper)—Cook within 6 hours on low.

Nutrition:

Calories: 400 Fat: 30g Carbs: 7g Protein: 23g

Cholesterol: 163mg Sodium: 1758mg

Spicy Shrimp Fra Diavolo

Preparation Time: 10 minutes

Cooking Time: 3 hours

Servings: 2

Ingredients:

1 teaspoon olive oil

1 onion, diced

5 cloves of garlic, minced

1 teaspoon red pepper flakes

1 can fire-roasted tomatoes

½ teaspoon black pepper

salt to taste

¼ pound shrimp, shelled and deveined

1 tablespoon Italian parsley

Directions:

Set the crockpot to high heat and heat the oil. Sauté the onion and garlic for 2 minutes.

Add the pepper flakes and tomatoes—season with black pepper and salt.

Add the shrimps. Adjust the heat setting to low and cook for 2 or 3 hours.

Garnish with parsley.

Nutrition:

Calories: 134

Carbohydrates: 3.41 g

Protein: 13.99g

Fat: 3.44 g

Sugar: 1.5g

Sodium: 609mg

Fiber: 0.4g

Shrimp Scampi with Spaghetti Squash

Preparation Time: 10 minutes

Cooking Time: 2 hours and 20 minutes

Servings: 4

Ingredients:

1 cup broth

2 teaspoon lemon-garlic seasoning

1 onion, chopped

1 tablespoon butter

3 pounds spaghetti squash, cut lengthwise and seeds removed

¾-pounds shrimp, shelled and deveined

Directions:

Pour broth in the slow cooker and add the lemon-garlic seasoning, onion, and butter. Place the spaghetti squash inside the slow cooker and cook on high for 2 hours until soft.

Add the shrimps and cook for 20 more minutes on high.

Nutrition:

Calories: 239

Carbohydrates: 16.79g

Protein: 21.19g

Fat: 6.28g

Sugar: 6.63g

Sodium: 1016mg

Fiber: 5.6g

Tuna and White Beans

Preparation Time: 10 minutes

Cooking Time: 5 hours and 15 minutes

Servings: 4

Ingredients:

4 tablespoon olive oil

1 clove of garlic, minced

6 cups of water

1-pound white beans, soaked overnight and drained

2 cups chopped tomatoes

3 cans white tuna, drained and flaked

2 sprigs of basil

salt and pepper to taste

Directions:

Set the crockpot to high heat and add oil. Sauté the garlic for 2 minutes and add water.

Stir in the beans—Cook within 5 hours on low.

Add in the tomatoes, tuna, and basil—season with salt and pepper to taste.

Continue cooking on high for 15 minutes.

Nutrition:

Calories: 764 Carbohydrates: 12.05g

Protein: 62.84g Fat: 25.43g

Sugar:4 g

Sodium: 559mg

Fiber: 6.03g

Crockpot Swordfish Steaks

Preparation Time: 10 minutes

Cooking Time: 2 hours

Servings: 6

Ingredients:

6 swordfish steaks

½ cup olive oil

¼ cup lemon juice

½ teaspoon Worcestershire sauce

¼ teaspoon black pepper

1 teaspoon cayenne pepper powder

¼ teaspoon paprika

Directions:

Place the swordfish steaks in the crockpot. Pour the other ingredients over the swordfish steaks.

Close the lid and cook on high for 2 hours. Serve.

Nutrition:

Calories: 659

Carbohydrates: 1.63g

Protein: 46.59g

Fat: 50.78g

Sugar: 0.7g

Sodium: 113mg

Fiber: 0.2g

Sweet and Sour Shrimp

Preparation Time: 10 minutes

Cooking Time: 5 hours

Servings: 3

Ingredients:

1 package Chinese pea pods, cleaned and trimmed

1 can pineapple tidbits

½ teaspoon ginger, ground

½ pounds shrimps, shelled and deveined

1 cup chicken broth

½ cup pineapple juice

2 tablespoon apple cider vinegar

salt to taste

Directions:

Put the peas in the bottom of the crockpot. Add the pineapple tidbits and ginger.

Place the shrimps on top. Add the chicken broth, pineapple juice, and apple cider vinegar.

Season with salt. Cook on low for 5 hours.

Nutrition:

Calories: 236

Carbohydrates: 3.5 g

Protein: 17.12 g

Fat: 1.33 g Sugar: 1.5g

Sodium: 970 mg

Fiber:0.6g

Lazy Man's Seafood Stew

Preparation Time: 10 minutes

Cooking Time: 3 hours

Servings: 6

Ingredients:

1-pound large shrimp

1-pound scallops

1 can crushed tomatoes

4 cloves of garlic, minced

1 tablespoon tomato paste

4 cups vegetable broth

1 teaspoon dried oregano

½ cup onion, chopped

½ teaspoon celery salt

1 teaspoon dried thyme

1/8 teaspoon cayenne pepper

¼ teaspoon red pepper flakes

2 teaspoons salt

2 teaspoons pepper

Directions:

Put all the listed items in the crockpot, then stir to combine.

Close the lid and cook on high for 3 hours or 30 minutes on high setting.

Nutrition:

Calories: 135 Carbohydrates: 9.26g

Protein: 20.37g Fat: 1.29g

Sugar: 3.76g Sodium: 1906mg Fiber:1.3g

Halibut Vinaigrette

Preparation Time: 15 minutes

Cooking Time: 3 hours

Servings: 6

Ingredients:

2 tablespoon fresh lime juice

1 tablespoon fresh thyme

½ teaspoon crushed red pepper

salt and pepper to taste

4 fillets of halibut fish

1 bunch kale, torn

1 cup of water

1 shallot, sliced

Directions:

Mix lime juice, thyme, red pepper, salt, and pepper. Sprinkle the spices on the halibut fillet.

Place the kale in the crockpot and place the halibut fillet at the bottom. Pour in water and sprinkle shallots on top—Cook within 2 to 3 hours, low.

Nutrition:

Calories: 81

Carbohydrates: 1.25g

Protein: 13.68 g

Fat: 2.12g

Sugar: 0.48g

Sodium: 323mg

Fiber:0.2 g

Crockpot Crab Legs

Preparation Time: 10 minutes

Cooking Time: 3 hours

Servings: 10

Ingredients:

5 pounds crab legs

1 tablespoon butter

1 teaspoon garlic powder

2 lemons, juiced

salt and pepper to taste

Directions:

Put all ingredients in the pot. Fill the crockpot with ¼ water.

Cook within 3 hours, low. Serve.

Nutrition:

Calories: 294 Carbohydrates: 1.31g

Protein: 49.27g Fat: 8.87g

Sugar: 0.48g Sodium: 175 mg Fiber: 0.1 g

Asian-Inspired Ginger Tuna Steaks

Preparation Time: 10 minutes

Cooking Time:4 hours

Servings: 2

Ingredients:

2 pounds tuna steak

2 tablespoon coconut aminos

2 tablespoon sherry wine

½ cup of water

6 sprigs of onion, chopped

3 cloves of garlic, minced

1 teaspoon ginger, grated

salt and pepper to taste

Directions:

Place the tuna steak at the bottom of the crockpot.

Add the rest of the ingredients, then marinate.

Cook within 3 to 4 hours, low.

Nutrition:

Calories: 387

Carbohydrates: 12.87g

Protein: 30.65g

Fat: 20.29g

Sugar: 12.9g

Sodium: 91mg

Fiber: 2.4g

Rustic Buttered Mussels

Preparation Time: 5 minutes

Cooking Time:

3 hours

Servings: 6

Ingredients:

2 pounds mussels, cleaned

½ cup white wine

2 cloves of garlic, minced

1 ¼ tablespoon salt

2 tablespoons butter

Directions:

Place all ingredients in the crockpot.

Cook within 3 hours, low or until the mussels have opened.

Nutrition:

Calories: 167

Carbohydrates: 6.13g

Protein: 18.19g

Fat: 7.23g

Sugar: 0.23g

Sodium: 1918 mg

Fiber:0g

Boiled Lobster Tails

Preparation Time: 15 minutes

Cooking Time:3 hours

Servings: 4

Ingredients:

4 lobster tails

1 cup of water

4 ounces of white cooking wine

½ stick of butter

½ tablespoon salt

2 tablespoon lemon juice

1 teaspoon rosemary

Directions:

Place all ingredients in the crockpot.

Cook within 3 hours, low or until the lobsters are red.

Nutrition:

Calories: 151

Carbohydrates: 0.56 g

Protein: 30.9g

Fat: 2g

Sugar: 0g

Sodium: 1522mg

Fiber: 0g

Creamy Shrimp Chowder

Preparation Time: 15 minutes

Cooking Time:

4 hours

Servings: 8

Ingredients:

½ cup butter

1 cup heavy whipping cream

32-ounce chicken broth

2 cups sliced mushroom

8-ounce cheddar cheese shredded

24-ounce small shrimp

Directions:

Place crockpot on high settings. Pour in chicken broth and mushrooms.

Cover and cook for two hours. Stir in butter and whipping cream mix well.

Cover and cook for 30 minutes. Stir in cheese.

Cover and cook for 30 minutes, and halfway through, stir to mix.

If needed, cook for another 30 minutes more until cheese is thoroughly melted and incorporated. Stir every 15 minutes. Add shrimp, stir and cook for 30 minutes.

Nutrition:

Calories: 451

Carbohydrates: 4g

Protein: 29g

Fat: 33g

Sugar: 0g

Sodium:

571mg

Fiber: 0g

CHAPTER 13:

Side Dishes

Chinese Broccoli

Preparation time: 15 minutes

Cooking time: 1 hour

Servings: 4

Ingredients:

1 tablespoon sesame seeds

1 tablespoon olive oil

10 oz broccoli

1 teaspoon chili flakes

1 tablespoon apple cider vinegar

3 tablespoons water

¼ teaspoon garlic powder

Directions:

Cut the broccoli into the florets and sprinkle with the olive oil, chili flakes, apple cider vinegar, and garlic powder.

Stir the broccoli and place it in the slow cooker.

Add water and sesame seeds.

Cook the broccoli for 1 hour on high.

Transfer the cooked broccoli to serving plates and enjoy!

Nutrition:

calories 69

fat 4.9g

fiber 2.1g

carbs 5.4g

protein 2.4g

Slow Cooker Spaghetti Squash

Preparation time: 15 minutes

Cooking time: 4 hours

Servings: 5

Ingredients:

1-pound spaghetti squash

1 tablespoon butter

¼ cup of water

1 teaspoon ground black pepper

¼ teaspoon ground nutmeg

Directions:

Peel the spaghetti squash and sprinkle it with the ground black pepper and ground nutmeg.

Pour water in the slow cooker.

Add butter and spaghetti squash.

Cook within 4 hours on low.

Chop the spaghetti squash into small pieces and serve!

Nutrition:

calories 50 fat 2.9g

fiber 6.6g carbs 0.1g

protein 0.7g

Mushroom Stew

Preparation time: 15 minutes

Cooking time: 6 hours

Servings: 8

Ingredients:

10 oz white mushrooms, sliced

2 eggplants, chopped

1 onion, diced

1 garlic clove, diced

2 bell peppers, chopped

1 cup of water

1 tablespoon butter

½ teaspoon salt

½ teaspoon ground black pepper

Directions:

Place the sliced mushrooms, chopped eggplant, and diced onion into the slow cooker.

Add the garlic clove and bell peppers.

Put salt and ground black pepper in the vegetables.

Add butter and water and stir it gently with a wooden spatula.

Cook the stew within 6 hours on low.

Stir the cooked stew one more time and serve!

Nutrition:

calories 71g

fat 1.9g

fiber 5.9g

carbs 13g

protein 3g

Cabbage Steaks

Preparation time: 15 minutes

Cooking time: 2 hours

Servings: 4

Ingredients:

10 oz white cabbage

1 tablespoon butter

½ teaspoon cayenne pepper

½ teaspoon chili flakes

4 tablespoons water

Directions:

Slice the cabbage into medium steaks and rub them with the cayenne pepper and chili flakes.

Rub the cabbage steaks with butter on each side.

Place them in the slow cooker and sprinkle with water.

Close the lid and cook the cabbage steaks for 2 hours on high.

When the cabbage steaks are cooked, they should be tender to the touch.

Serve the cabbage steak after 10 minutes of chilling.

Nutrition:

calories 44

fat 3g

fiber 1.8g

carbs 4.3g

protein 1g

Mashed Cauliflower

Preparation time: 20 minutes

Cooking time: 3 hours

Servings: 5

Ingredients:

3 tablespoons butter

1-pound cauliflower

1 tablespoon full-fat cream

1 teaspoon salt

1 teaspoon ground black pepper

1 oz dill, chopped

Directions:

Wash the cauliflower and chop it.

Place the chopped cauliflower in the slow cooker.

Add butter and full-fat cream.

Add salt and ground black pepper.

Stir the mixture and close the lid.

Cook the cauliflower for 3 hours on high.

When the cauliflower is cooked, transfer it to a blender and blend until smooth.

Place the smooth cauliflower in a bowl and mix it with the chopped dill.

Stir it well and serve!

Nutrition:

calories 101 fat 7.4g

fiber 3.2g carbs 8.3g protein 3.1g

Bacon-Wrapped Cauliflower

Preparation time: 15 minutes

Cooking time: 7 hours

Servings: 4

Ingredients:

11 oz cauliflower head

3 oz bacon, sliced

1 teaspoon salt

1 teaspoon cayenne pepper

1 oz butter, softened

¾ cup of water

Directions:

Sprinkle the cauliflower head with the salt and cayenne pepper then rub with butter.

Wrap the cauliflower head in the sliced bacon and secure with toothpicks.

Pour water in the slow cooker and add the wrapped cauliflower head.

Cook the cauliflower head for 7 hours on low.

Then let the cooked cauliflower head cool for 10 minutes.

Serve it!

Nutrition:

calories 187

fat 14.8g

fiber 2.1g

carbs 4.7g

protein 9.5g

Cauliflower Casserole

Preparation time: 15 minutes

Cooking time: 7 hours

Servings: 5

Ingredients:

2 tomatoes, chopped

11 oz cauliflower chopped

5 oz broccoli, chopped

1 cup of water

1 teaspoon salt

1 tablespoon butter

5 oz white mushrooms, chopped

1 teaspoon chili flakes

Directions:

Mix the water, salt, and chili flakes. Place the butter in the slow cooker.

Add a layer of the chopped cauliflower. Add the layer of broccoli and tomatoes.

Add the mushrooms and pat down the mix to flatten. Add the water and close the lid.

Cook the casserole for 7 hours on low. Cool the casserole to room temperature and serve!

Nutrition:

calories 61

fat 2.6g

fiber 3.2g

carbs 8.1g

protein 3.4g

Cauliflower Rice

Preparation time: 15 minutes

Cooking time: 2 hours

Servings: 5

Ingredients:

1-pound cauliflower

1 teaspoon salt

1 tablespoon turmeric

1 tablespoon butter

¾ cup of water

Directions:

Chop the cauliflower into tiny pieces to make cauliflower rice. You can also pulse in a food processor to get excellent grains of 'rice.'

Place the cauliflower rice in the slow cooker.

Add salt, turmeric, and water.

Stir gently and close the lid.

Cook the cauliflower rice for 2 hours on high.

Strain the cauliflower rice and transfer it to a bowl.

Add butter and stir gently. Serve it!

Nutrition:

calories 48

fat 2.5g

fiber 2.6g

carbs 5.7g

protein 1.9g

Curry Cauliflower

Preparation time: 15 minutes

Cooking time: 5 hours

Servings: 2

Ingredients:

10 oz cauliflower

1 teaspoon curry paste

1 teaspoon curry powder

½ teaspoon dried cilantro

1 oz butter

¾ cup of water

¼ cup chicken stock

Directions:

Chop the cauliflower roughly and sprinkle it with the curry powder and dried cilantro.

Place the chopped cauliflower in the slow cooker.

Mix the curry paste with the water.

Add chicken stock and transfer the liquid to the slow cooker.

Add butter and close the lid.

Cook the cauliflower for 5 hours on low.

Strain ½ of the liquid off and discard. Transfer the cauliflower to serving bowls. Serve it!

Nutrition:

calories 158 fat 13.3g

fiber 3.9g carbs 8.9g

protein 3.3g

Garlic Cauliflower Steaks

Preparation time: 15 minutes

Cooking time: 3 hours

Servings: 4

Ingredients:

14 oz cauliflower head

1 teaspoon minced garlic

4 tablespoons butter

4 tablespoons water

1 teaspoon paprika

Directions:

Wash the cauliflower head carefully and slice it into the medium steaks.

Mix up together the butter, minced garlic, and paprika.

Rub the cauliflower steaks with the butter mixture.

Pour the water in the slow cooker.

Add the cauliflower steaks and close the lid.

Cook the vegetables for 3 hours on high.

Transfer the cooked cauliflower steaks to a platter and serve them immediately!

Nutrition:

calories 129

fat 11.7g

fiber 2.7g

carbs 5.8g

protein 2.2g

Zucchini Gratin

Preparation time: 10 minutes

Cooking time: 5 hours

Servings: 3

Ingredients:

1 zucchini, sliced

3 oz Parmesan, grated

1 teaspoon ground black pepper

1 tablespoon butter

½ cup almond milk

Directions:

Sprinkle the sliced zucchini with the ground black pepper.

Chop the butter and place it in the slow cooker.

Transfer the sliced zucchini to the slow cooker to make the bottom layer.

Add the almond milk.

Sprinkle the zucchini with the grated cheese and close the lid.

Cook the gratin for 5 hours on low.

Then let the gratin cool until room temperature. Serve it!

Nutrition:

calories 229

fat 19.6g

fiber 1.8g

carbs 5.9g

protein 10.9g

Eggplant Gratin

Preparation time: 15 minutes

Cooking time: 5 hours

Servings: 7

Ingredients:

1 tablespoon butter

1 teaspoon minced garlic

2 eggplants, chopped

1 teaspoon salt

1 tablespoon dried parsley

4 oz Parmesan, grated

4 tablespoons water

1 teaspoon chili flakes

Directions:

Mix the dried parsley, chili flakes, and salt.

Sprinkle the chopped eggplants with the spice mixture and stir well.

Place the eggplants in the slow cooker.

Add the water and minced garlic.

Add the butter and sprinkle with the grated parmesan.

Close the lid and cook the gratin for 5 hours on low. Open the lid and cool the gratin for 10 minutes. Serve it.

Nutrition:

calories 107 fat 5.4g

fiber 5.6g carbs 10g

protein 6.8g

Moroccan Eggplant Mash

Preparation time: 15 minutes

Cooking time: 7 hours

Servings: 4

Ingredients:

1 eggplant, peeled

1 jalapeno pepper

1 teaspoon curry powder

½ teaspoon salt

1 teaspoon paprika

¾ teaspoon ground nutmeg

2 tablespoons butter

¾ cup almond milk

1 teaspoon dried dill

Directions:

Chop the eggplant into small pieces. Place the eggplant in the slow cooker. Chop the jalapeno pepper and combine it with the eggplant.

Then sprinkle the vegetables with the curry powder, salt, paprika, ground nutmeg, and dried dill. Add almond milk and butter.

Cook the vegetables within 7 hours on low.

Cool the vegetables and then blend them until smooth with a hand blender. Transfer the cooked eggplant mash into the bowls and serve!

Nutrition:

calories 190 fat 17g fiber 5.6g

carbs 10g protein 2.5g

Sautéed Bell Peppers

Preparation time: 15 minutes

Cooking time: 5 hours

Servings: 6

Ingredients:

8 oz bell peppers, chopped

7 oz cauliflower, chopped

2 oz bacon, chopped

1 teaspoon salt

1 teaspoon ground black pepper

¾ cup coconut milk, unsweetened

1 teaspoon butter

1 teaspoon thyme

1 onion, diced

1 teaspoon turmeric

Directions:

Place the bell peppers, cauliflower, and bacon in the slow cooker.

Add the salt, ground black pepper, coconut milk, butter, milk, and thyme.

Stir well, then add the diced onion.

Add the turmeric and stir the mixture.

Close the lid and cook 5 hours on low.

When the meal is cooked, let it chill for 10 minutes and serve it!

Nutrition:

calories 195 fat 12.2g fiber 4.2g

carbs 13.1g protein 6.7g

Fresh Green Beans

Preparation time: 15 minutes

Cooking time: 2 hours

Servings: 4

Ingredients:

Bacon, chopped – 6 Slices

Onions, minced - ½ Cups

Garlic, minced – 1 Teaspoon

Fresh green beans, 1 Pound

Water – 1 Cup

Black pepper, grounded – 1 Pinch

Salt to taste

Directions:

Put onions, garlic, and salt in a medium skillet and cook on medium heat until it becomes tender.

Now transfer all these to your crockpot and place the chopped fresh beans and bacon over it.

Add water. Add salt if required.

Close the crockpot and set on low cooking for about 2 hours.

Check intermittently and stir after cooking done, season with pepper.

Serve hot.

Nutrition:

Calories 97

Carbs 7g

Cholesterol 14mg

Protein 6.2g

Sodium 343mg

Crockpot Cauliflower Side Dish

Preparation time: 15 minutes

Cooking time: 2 hours

Servings: 12

Ingredients:

Fresh cauliflower – 16 Ounces

Sour cream – 8 Ounces

Chicken bouillon granules – 3 Teaspoon

Cheddar cheese - 1½ Cups

Butter, cubed - ¼ Cup

Stuffing mix – 1 Cup

Mustard, grounded – 1 Teaspoon

Walnuts, chopped - ¾ Cup

Salt to taste

Directions:

Clean the cauliflower, wash and dry and keep aside. In a large bowl, put bouillon, sour cream, mustard, and mix entirely.

Add cauliflower and mix the ingredients properly.

Transfer the mix to your Keto crockpot and set low cooking for about 2 hours. Stir occasionally.

Once cooking is over, transfer it to a serving dish. Take a large skillet and heat butter.

Add walnut and stuffing mix and toast it slightly and spread over the cooked food. Serve hot.

Nutrition:

Calories 276 Carb 9.7g

Fat 18g Cholesterol 57mg

Protein 10g Sugar 2g Fiber 3g

Slow Cook Crock Pot Zucchini Tomato Casserole

Preparation time: 15 minutes

Cooking time: 2 hours

Servings: 8

Ingredients:

Zucchini, medium size, diced – 6 Cups

Butter, melted – 4 Tablespoons

Tomatoes, medium size – 2 Nos.

Breadcrumbs, soft – 1 Cup

Egg, beaten – 1 Nos.

Onion, minced – 2 Tablespoons

Cheddar cheese – 1 Cup

Fresh parsley, minced – 3 Tablespoons

Fresh basil, minced – 1 Tablespoon

Cheese, processed – 1 Cup

Garlic powder - ½ Teaspoon

Salt to taste

Pepper to taste

Directions:

Sauté zucchini in a skillet by adding 2 tablespoons of butter until it becomes crisp.

Drain it and keep aside.

Mix all the rest of the fixing in a bowl.

Add the cooked zucchini and butter. Transfer the mix to a crockpot and set low cooking for about 1.30 – 2 hours.

Check occasionally and stir. Serve hot or after settling.

Nutrition:

Calories 224

Carb 8g

Fat 16g

Cholesterol 90mg

Sodium 527mg Fiber 2g

Protein 10g

Sugar 2g

Chicken Cauliflower – Side Dish

Preparation time: 15 minutes

Cooking time: 6 hours

Servings: 4

Ingredients:

Cooked chicken, diced – 2 Cups

Cauliflower rice – 2 Cups

Italian seasoning – 1 Tablespoon

Mushroom, chopped – 2 Cups

Parmesan and Garlic cheese - ½ Cups

Whipping cream - ¼ Cups

Egg white – 4

Mozzarella cheese (Optional)

Directions:

Combine the cauliflower rice, mushrooms, chicken, and Italian seasoning. Transfer the mix to a 4-quart crockpot.

Take another bowl and mix egg white, parmesan, and cheese. Pour the mix over the cauliflower mix in the crockpot.

Set the slow crockpot for 6 hours cooking. Check occasionally.

Serve cold and top with mozzarella, optional.

Nutrition:

Calories 72.5

Carb   7.1g

Fat 3.8g

Cholesterol 9.3g

Potassium 78.5mg

Sodium 180.5mg

Protein 3.5g

Sugar 0.4g

Slow Cook Crockpot Broccoli

Preparation time: 15 minutes

Cooking time: 4 hours

Servings: 10

Ingredients:

Broccoli, frozen, chopped – 6 Cups

Cheddar cheese, grated - 1½ Cups

Condensed cream of celery soup - 10¾ Ounces

Onion, chopped - ¼ Cup

Worcestershire sauce - ½ Teaspoon

Pepper to taste

Crackers, butter flavored – 1 Cup

Butter – 2 Tablespoon

Directions:

Combine broccoli, onion, 1 cup cheese, soup, Worcestershire sauce, and add pepper to taste in a large bowl.

Grease the bottom of crockpot. Transfer the mixture to the crockpot.

Spread the crackers on top and spread the butter—cover and cook for about 4 hours.

Once done, sprinkle the remaining cheese. Cook again within 10-15 minutes until the cheese starts to melt. Serve hot.

Nutrition:

Cal 159

Carbs 9g

Fat 11g

Fiber 1g

Sugar 1g

Cholesterol 25mg

Protein 0g

Sodium 431mg

Balsamic-Glazed Brussels Sprouts

Preparation time: 15 minutes

Cooking time: 6 hours

Servings: 6

Ingredients:

Brussels sprout - 2 pound

Chicken broth - 2 cups

Balsamic glaze - 2 tablespoons

Extra virgin olive oil - 2 tablespoon

Roasted pine nuts - ¼ cups

Parmesan cheese grated - ¼ cups

Salt to taste

Pepper as required

Directions:

Wash and trim out the head portion of Brussels. Cut the Brussels in half.

Put the Brussels into a slow cooker. Add ½ teaspoon salt.

Cook within 5-6 hours, low. Transfer the cooked Brussels to the serving dish.

Garnish with pepper and salt—spread balsamic glaze.

Sprinkle the remaining olive oil and spread roasted pine nuts. Dress with parmesan on top. Serve hot.

Nutrition:

Carbs 9.6 g

Fiber 3.5 g

Fat 0.3 g

Cholesterol 0.0 g

Protein 3.2 g

Potassium 359.0 mg

Sodium 179.1mg

Italian Mushrooms – Crockpot Side Dish

Preparation time: 15 minutes

Cooking time: 5 hours

Servings: 6

Ingredients:

Fresh mushrooms – 1 Pound

Onion, sliced – 1 Large

Butter, melted - ½ Cup

Italian salad dressing mix – 1 Packet

Directions:

Spread onion and mushrooms in a 4-quart crockpot cooker.

In a bowl, mix salad dress and butter and pour on top of the vegetable in the pot.

Cover and pot. Cook for about 5 hours. Check occasionally to confirm the tenderness of the vegetable. Serve hot.

Nutrition:

Cal 99

Carbs 6g

Cholesterol 20mg

Sugar 1g

Protein 3g

Fiber 1g

Sodium 281mg

Keto Slow Cooker Pepper Jack Cauliflower side dish

Preparation time: 15 minutes

Cooking time: 4 hours

Servings: 6

Ingredients:

Cauliflower heads, cut florets – 1 Head

Whipped cream - ¼ Cup

Cream cheese – 4 Ounces

Pepper Jack, shredded – 4 Ounces

Bacon cooked and crumbled – 6 slices

Butter – 2 Tablespoon

Pepper, grounded - ½ teaspoon

Sal to taste

Directions:

Grease a 4-quart crockpot slow cooker slightly.

Put cauliflower, whipped cream, cream cheese, pepper, salt, and butter into the crockpot.

Set to slow cook for 3 hours. After 3 hours, add pepper jack and stir properly to combine.

Continue cooking for about one hour, until the cauliflower becomes tender. Add crumbled bacon to it. Serve hot.

Nutrition:

Cal 272

Carbs 6.1g

Fat 21.29g

Protein 10.79

Fiber 2.01g

Greens Mix

Preparation Time: 10 minutes

Cooking Time: 8 hours

Servings: 6

Ingredients:

2 cups of spinach, chopped

2 cups of kale, chopped

1 lb. ham shanks, sliced

4 pickled jalapeno peppers, diced

1/2 teaspoon of baking soda

1 teaspoon of olive oil

black pepper to taste

garlic powder to taste

Directions:

Put all the items into the slow cooker. Cover its lid and cook for 8 hours on Low setting.

Mix well and garnish as desired. Serve warm.

Nutrition:

Calories 77.8

Fat 7.13 g

Cholesterol 15 mg

Carbs 0.8 g

Sugar 0.2 g

Fiber 0.3 g

Sodium 15 mg

Potassium 33 mg

Protein 2.3 g

Mayo Salad

Preparation Time: 10 minutes

Cooking Time: 5 hours

Servings: 8

Ingredients:

1 cup of water

3 media eggplant, peeled and cubed

3 large eggs, boiled, peeled, and cubed

1/8 cup of diced onion

½ cup of mayonnaise

1 tablespoon of finely fresh parsley, chopped

½ tablespoon of dill pickle juice

½ tablespoon of mustard

Salt and black pepper to taste

Directions:

Put the eggplant and water into the slow cooker. Cover its lid and cook for 5 hours on Low setting.

Toss the slow-cooked eggplant with the remaining fixings in a salad bowl.

Mix, then serve warm.

Nutrition:

Calories 114 Fat 9.6 g

Cholesterol 10 mg

Carbs 3.1 g Sugar 1.4 g

Fiber 1.5 g

Sodium 155 mg

Potassium 93 mg

Protein 3.5 g

Seasoned Carrots

Preparation Time: 10 minutes

Cooking Time: 4 hours

Servings: 8

Ingredients:

½ cup of avocado oil

3 lbs. carrots, sliced

1 teaspoon of onion powder

2 teaspoons of garlic powder

2 teaspoons of salt

½ teaspoon of paprika

½ teaspoon of black pepper

2 cups of chicken broth

Directions:

Put all the items into the slow cooker. Cover its lid and cook for 4 hours on low setting.

Mix, then serve warm.

Nutrition:

Calories 252 Fat 17.3 g

Cholesterol 141 mg

Carbs 7.2 g

Sugar 0.3 g Fiber 1.4 g

Sodium 153 mg

Potassium 73 mg

Protein 5.2 g

Quinoa Brussels Sprout Salad

Preparation Time: 10 minutes

Cooking Time: 6 hours

Servings: 4

Ingredients:

½ cup of cabbage, diced

½ cup of quinoa, rinsed

½ carrot, peeled and shredded

¾ cup of water

¼ teaspoon of salt

1 cup of Brussels sprout, diced

½ cup of red onions, sliced

1 tablespoon of brown swerve

2 tablespoons balsamic vinegar

1 tablespoon of vegetable oil

1 tablespoon of sunflower seeds

1 teaspoon of ginger, grated

1 garlic clove, minced

Black pepper, to taste

Directions:

Put the quinoa and water into the slow cooker. Cook for 6 hours on Low setting.

Strain the cooked quinoa and add to a salad bowl.

Toss in all other fixings and stir it. Mix well and garnish as desired. Serve warm.

Nutrition:

Calories 195

Fat 14.3 g

Cholesterol 175 mg

Carbs 4.5 g

Sugar 0.5 g

Fiber 0.3 g

Sodium 125 mg

Potassium 83 mg

Protein 3.2 g

Saucy Beans

Preparation Time: 10 minutes

Cooking Time: 2 hours

Servings: 4

Ingredients:

1 cup of green beans

½ cup of bacon, diced

¼ medium onion, diced

½ teaspoon of salt

½ teaspoon of pepper

½ teaspoon of dry mustard

½ tablespoon of Worcestershire sauce

½ tablespoon of balsamic vinegar

1 tablespoon of tomato paste

3 tablespoons of dark brown swerve

½ cup of chicken stock

½ cup of water

Directions:

Put all the items into the slow cooker, cook for 2 hours on low. Serve warm.

Nutrition:

Calories 151 Fat 14.7 g

Cholesterol 13 mg Carbs 1.5 g

Sugar 0.3 g Fiber 0.1 g

Sodium 53 mg

Potassium 131 mg

Protein 0.8 g

Cucumber Quinoa Salad

Preparation Time: 10 minutes

Cooking Time: 6 hours

Servings: 8

Ingredients:

½ cup of quinoa, rinsed

¾ cup of water

¼ teaspoon of salt

½ carrot, peeled and shredded

½ cucumber, diced

½ cup of frozen edamame, thawed

3 green onions, diced

1 cup of shredded red cabbage

½ tablespoon of soy sauce

1 tablespoon of lime juice

2 tablespoons of swerve

1 tablespoon of vegetable oil

1 tablespoon of freshly grated ginger

1 tablespoon of sesame oil

pinch of red pepper flakes

½ cup of peanuts, diced

Directions:

Put the quinoa and water inside the slow cooker. Cook for 6 hours on low.

Strain, then add to a salad bowl. Toss in all other fixings. Serve warm.

Nutrition:

Calories 261 Fat 27.1 g Cholesterol 0 mg

Carbs 6.1 g Sugar 2.1 g

Fiber 3.9 g Sodium 10 mg

Potassium 57 mg

Protein 1.8 g

Zucchini Spaghetti

Preparation time: 30 minutes

Cooking time: 2 hours

Servings: 16

Ingredients:

2 lbs. zucchini, spiralized

2 cups of water

Cilantro to serve

Directions:

Put all the items except cilantro into the slow cooker, and cook for 2 hours on low.

Garnish this spaghetti with cilantro and serve.

Nutrition:

Calories 139

Fat 4.6 g

Cholesterol 1.2 mg

Carbs 7.5 g

Sugar 6.3 g

Fiber 0.6 g

Sodium 83 mg

Potassium 113 mg

Protein 3.8 g

BBQ Smokies

Preparation Time: 10 minutes

Cooking Time: 2 hours

Servings: 6

Ingredients:

1 (18 oz.) bottle barbeque sauce

1 cup of sugar-free tomato sauce

1 tablespoon of Worcestershire sauce

1/3 cup of diced onion

2 (16 ounce) packages little wieners

Directions:

Put all the fixings inside the slow cooker, cook for 2 hours on low. Serve.

Nutrition:

Calories 251 Fat 24.5 g

Cholesterol 165 mg

Carbs 4.3 g Sugar 0.5 g

Fiber 1 g Sodium 142 mg

Potassium 80 mg Protein 51.9 g

Marinated Mushrooms

Preparation Time: 10 minutes

Cooking Time: 12 hours

Servings: 12

Ingredients:

4 cubes chicken bouillon

4 cubes beef bouillon

2 cups of boiling water

1 cup of dry red wine

1 teaspoon of dill weed

1 teaspoon of Worcestershire sauce

1 teaspoon of garlic powder

4 lbs. fresh mushrooms

1/2 cup of butter

Directions:

Put all the items inside the slow cooker, and cook for 12 hours on a low setting. Serve warm.

Nutrition:

Calories 159 Fat 34 g

Cholesterol 112 mg

Carbs 8.5 g Sugar 2 g

Fiber 1.3 g Sodium 92 mg

Protein 7.5 g

Cowboy Mexican Dip

Preparation Time: 10 minutes

Cooking Time: 2 hours

Servings: 24

Ingredients:

12 beef tamales, husked and mashed

1 (15 oz.) can chili

1 can tomatoes and green chilis

1 (1 lb.) loaf processed cheese, cubed

Directions:

Place all the fixings into the slow cooker, cook for 2 hours on low, and then serve.

Nutrition:

Calories 107

Fat 29 g

Cholesterol 111 mg

Carbs 7 g

Sugar 1 g

Fiber 3 g

Sodium 122 mg

Potassium 78 mg

Protein 6 g

Glazed Spiced Carrots

Preparation Time: 10 minutes

Cooking Time: 8 hours

Servings: 6

Ingredients:

2 lbs. small carrots

1/2 cup of peach preserves

1/2 cup of butter, melted

1/4 cup of packed brown swerve

1 teaspoon of vanilla extract

1/2 teaspoon of cinnamon, ground

1/4 teaspoon of salt

1/8 teaspoon of ground nutmeg

2 tablespoons of xanthan gum

2 tablespoons of water

Toasted diced pecans, optional

Directions:

Put all the items into the slow cooker and cook for 8 hours on a low setting. Serve.

Nutrition:

Calories 220

Fat 20.1 g

Cholesterol 132 mg

Carbs 63 g

Sugar 0.4 g

Fiber 2.4 g

Sodium 157 mg

Potassium 42 mg

Protein 6.1 g

Garlic Green Beans with Gorgonzola

Preparation Time: 10 minutes

Cooking Time: 4 hours

Servings: 6

Ingredients:

2 lbs. fresh green beans, halved

1 can (8 oz.) sliced chestnuts, drained

4 green onions, diced

5 bacon strips, cooked and crumbled, divided

1/3 cup of white wine

2 tablespoons of minced fresh thyme

4 garlic cloves, minced

1 1/2 teaspoons of seasoned salt

1 cup of (8 oz.) sour cream

3/4 cup of crumbled Gorgonzola cheese

Directions:

Put all the fixings into the slow cooker except cheese and bacon.

Cook within 4 hours on low. Garnish with bacon and cheese, then serve.

Nutrition:

Calories 331 Fat 32.9 g

Cholesterol 10 mg Carbs 9.1 g

Sugar 2.8 g Fiber 0.8 g

Sodium 18 mg Potassium 37 mg

Protein 4.4 g

Party Sausages

Preparation Time: 10 minutes

Cooking Time: 2 hours

Servings: 16

Ingredients:

2 lbs. smoked sausage links, sliced diagonally

1 bottle (8 oz.) Catalina salad dressing

1 bottle (8 oz.) Russian salad dressing

1/2 cup of packed brown swerve

1/2 cup of apple cider

Sliced green onions, optional

Directions:

Throw all the items into the slow cooker, then cook for 2 hours on low. Garnish and serve.

Nutrition:

Calories 190

Fat 17.25 g

Cholesterol 20 mg

Carbs 5.5 g Sugar 2.8 g

Fiber 3.8 g

Sodium 28 mg

Potassium 47 mg

Protein 23 g

Collard Greens

Preparation Time: 10 minutes

Cooking Time: 10 hours

Servings: 6

Ingredients:

4 bunches collard greens, trimmed and diced

1 lb. ham shanks

4 pickled jalapeno peppers, diced

1/2 teaspoon of baking soda

1 teaspoon of olive oil

black pepper to taste

garlic powder to taste

¼ cup of vegetable stock

Directions:

Put all the items into the slow cooker, cook for 10 hours on Low setting. Garnish and serve.

Nutrition:

Calories 121 Fat 12.9 g

Cholesterol 17 mg Carbs 8.1 g

Sugar 1.8 g Fiber 0.4 g Sodium 28 mg

Potassium 137 mg Protein 5.4 g

Garlic Chili Sprouts

Preparation Time: 10 minutes

Cooking Time: 4 hours

Servings: 4

Ingredients:

1 lb. brussels sprouts halved

1 tablespoon of olive oil

salt and black pepper, to taste

½ teaspoon of sesame oil

1 garlic clove, minced

¼ cup of coconut aminos

¼ cup of water

1 teaspoon of apple cider vinegar

½ tablespoon of stevia

1 teaspoon of garlic chili sauce

½ pinch red pepper flakes

Directions:

Put everything into the slow cooker, then cook within 4 hours on low and serve.

Nutrition:

Calories 236 Fat 21.5 g

Cholesterol 54 mg Carbs 7.6 g

Sugar 1.4 g Fiber 3.8 g Sodium 21 mg

Potassium 41 mg Protein 4.3 g

Crispy Sweet and Sour Brussels Sprouts

Preparation time: 15 minutes

Cooking time: 8 hours

Servings: 6

Ingredients:

2 tbsp coconut oil or ghee

1 tbsp maple syrup

½ tbsp fish sauce

½ tbsp lemon juice

2 lbs. fresh Brussels sprouts

Optional:

Salt

A bit of hot sauce

Directions:

Cut each of the Brussels sprouts in half and then place them in your crockpot.

Melt the coconut oil or ghee. Drizzle the melted oil or ghee over the Brussels sprouts and toss them using your hands to ensure they are completely coated. Sprinkle salt over the Brussels sprouts.

Cook on low heat for 8 hours.

While cooking, mix the fish sauce, maple syrup, lemon juice, and the hot sauce if you are using it.

After the Brussels sprouts are done cooking, add the sauce into the crockpot and toss before serving.

Nutrition:

Calories: 157 Carbs: 21g Fat: 5g Protein: 9g

Baked Vegetables in the Crock-Pot

Preparation time: 15 minutes

Cooking time: 4 hours

Servings: 4

Ingredients:

1 head of broccoli, cut into florets

½ lb. Brussels sprouts halved

3 tbsp coconut oil, melted

Garlic powder

Salt and pepper

Directions:

Put all of the listed vegetables in a bowl and pour the coconut oil over them. Toss to ensure all of the vegetables are coated.

Place the vegetables in the crockpot. Sprinkle with the garlic powder and the salt and pepper.

Cook it on low heat for 4 hours.

Nutrition:

Calories: 105

Carbs: 0g

Fat: 0g

Protein: 0g

Crispy Veggies

Preparation time: 15 minutes

Cooking time: 4 hours

Servings: 6

Ingredients:

3 cups of your favorite vegetables, cut into pieces that are about the same size.

1 tbsp olive oil

Salt and pepper

Garlic powder

Directions:

Place all of the vegetables in a gallon-sized Zip Lock bag. Pour the olive oil into the bag with the vegetables and close the bag.

Shake the bag until the vegetables are completely coated with the olive oil. Place the vegetables into the crockpot and then sprinkle the garlic powder, salt, and pepper over the vegetables.

Cook on low heat for 4 hours.

Nutrition:

Calories: 150

Carbs: 18g

Fat: 8g

Protein: 2g

Oven Roasted Brussels Sprouts in the Crock-Pot

Preparation time: 15 minutes

Cooking time: 6 hours

Servings: 5

Ingredients:

1 ½ pound of Brussels Sprouts, halved

3 tbsp EVOO (extra virgin olive oil)

¾ tsp salt

½ tsp pepper

Directions:

Place the Brussels sprouts, the salt, pepper, and the EVOO in a large bowl and toss until the sprouts are completely coated.

Place the sprouts in the crockpot—Cook within 6 hours, low. Season with salt and serve.

Nutrition:

Calories: 111

Carbs: 6g

Fat: 9g

Protein: 3g

Chili Lime Acorn Squash

Preparation time: 15 minutes

Cooking time: 6 hours

Servings: 8

Ingredients:

2 acorn squash

1 tbsp coconut oil or ghee

1 tbsp lime juice

1 tsp chili powder

Directions:

Melt the coconut oil or the ghee and then mix in the chili powder and the lime juice.

Cut the acorn squash into wedges and then place the wedges into the crockpot.

Drizzle the oil mixture over the acorn squash wedges. Cook on low heat for 6 hours.

Nutrition:

Calories: 56

Carbs: 15g

Fat: 0g

Protein: 1g

CHAPTER 14:

Broth, Stock & Sauces

Bacon Jam

Preparation time: 10 minutes

Cooking time: 3 hours

Servings: 3

Ingredients:

3 tablespoons bacon fat, melted and divided

1-pound cooked bacon, chopped into ½-inch pieces

1 sweet onion, diced

½ cup apple cider vinegar

¼ cup granulated erythritol

1 tablespoon minced garlic

1 cup brewed decaffeinated coffee

Directions:

Grease the slow cooker with 1 tablespoon of the bacon fat.

Add the remaining 2 tablespoons of the bacon fat, bacon, onion, apple cider vinegar, erythritol, garlic, and coffee to the insert. Stir to combine.

Cook uncovered for 3 to 4 hours on high, until the liquid has thickened and reduced.

Cool completely.

Nutrition:

Calories: 52

Fat: 5g

Protein: 1g

Carbs: 1g

Fiber: 0g

Cholesterol: 5mg

Roasted Garlic

Preparation time: 10 minutes

Cooking time: 8 hours

Servings: 2

Ingredients:

6 heads garlic

¼ cup extra-virgin olive oil

salt, for seasoning

Directions:

Arrange a large sheet of aluminum foil on your counter.

Cut the top off the heads of garlic, exposing the cloves. Put the garlic, cut side up, on the foil and drizzle them with the olive oil. Lightly season the garlic with salt.

Loosely fold the foil around the garlic to form a packet. Place the packet in the insert of the slow cooker.

Cook within 8 hours on low. Cool the garlic for 10 minutes and then squeeze the cloves out of the papery skins.

Store the garlic in a sealed container in the refrigerator for up to 1 week.

Nutrition:

Calories: 25

Fat: 2g

Protein: 0g

Carbs: 2g

Fiber: 0g

Cholesterol: 0mg

Golden Caramelized Onions

Preparation time: 10 minutes

Cooking time: 9 hours

Servings: 3

Ingredients:

6 sweet onions, sliced

¼ cup extra-virgin olive oil

½ teaspoon salt

Directions:

Toss the onions, oil, and salt in a large bowl. Transfer the mixture to the insert of the slow cooker.

Cook within 9 to 10 hours on low. Serve, or store after cooling in a sealed container in the refrigerator for up to 5 days.

Nutrition:

Calories: 64 Fat: 5g Protein: 1g

Carbs: 5g Fiber: 2g Cholesterol: 0mg

Ghee

Preparation time: 2 minutes

Cooking time: 6 hours

Servings: 2

Ingredients:

1-pound unsalted butter, diced

Directions:

Place the butter in the insert of the slow cooker.

Cook on low with the lid set slightly open for 6 hours.

Pour the melted butter through a fine-mesh cheesecloth into a bowl.

Cool the ghee for 30 minutes and pour it into a jar.

Store the ghee in the refrigerator for up to 2 weeks.

Nutrition:

Calories: 100

Fat: 11g

Protein: 0g

Carbs: 0g

Fiber: 0g

Cholesterol: 30mg

Spinach-Cheese Spread

Preparation time: 10 minutes

Cooking time: 5 hours

Servings: 4

Ingredients:

1 tablespoon extra-virgin olive oil

8 ounces cream cheese

1 cup sour cream

½ cup shredded cheddar cheese

½ cup shredded mozzarella cheese

½ cup parmesan cheese

½ sweet onion, finely chopped

2 teaspoons minced garlic

12 ounces chopped spinach

Directions:

Grease an 8-by-4-inch loaf pan with olive oil.

Mix the cream cheese, sour cream, Cheddar, mozzarella, Parmesan, onion, garlic, and spinach in a large bowl until well mixed.

Move it to the loaf pan, and place the pan in the insert of the slow cooker.

Cook within 5 to 6 hours on low. Serve warm.

Nutrition:

Calories: 245

Fat: 21g

Protein: 9g

Carbs: 5g

Fiber: 1g

Cholesterol: 57mg

Hot Crab Sauce

Preparation time: 10 minutes

Cooking time: 5 hours

Servings: 4

Ingredients:

8 ounces cream cheese

8 ounces goat cheese

1 cup sour cream

½ cup grated asiago cheese

1 sweet onion, finely chopped

1 tablespoon granulated erythritol

2 teaspoons minced garlic

12 ounces crabmeat, flaked

1 scallion, white and green parts, chopped

Directions:

Mix the cream cheese, goat cheese, sour cream, Asiago cheese, onion, erythritol, garlic, crabmeat, and scallion in a large bowl until well mixed.

Move it to an 8-by-4-inch loaf pan and place the pan in the slow cooker's insert.

Cook within 5 to 6 hours on low. Serve warm.

Nutrition:

Calories: 361 Fat: 28g

Protein: 17g Carbs: 10g Fiber: 2g

Cholesterol: 88mg

Enchilada Sauce

Preparation time: 10 minutes

Cooking time: 7 hours

Servings: 4

Ingredients:

¼ cup extra-virgin olive oil, divided

2 cups puréed tomatoes

1 cup of water

1 sweet onion, chopped

2 jalapeño peppers, chopped

2 teaspoons minced garlic

2 tablespoons chili powder

1 teaspoon ground coriander

Directions:

Grease inside the slow cooker using a 1 tablespoon of the olive oil.

Place the remaining 3 tablespoons of the olive oil, tomatoes, water, onion, jalapeño peppers, garlic, chili powder, and coriander in the insert.

Cook within 7 to 8 hours on low. Serve over poultry or meat.

Nutrition:

Calories: 92

Fat: 8g

Protein: 2g

Carbs: 4g

Fiber: 2g

Cholesterol: 0mg

Creamy Alfredo Sauce

Preparation time: 5 minutes

Cooking time: 6 hours

Servings: 6

Ingredients:

1 tablespoon extra-virgin olive oil

4 cups chicken broth

2 cups heavy (whipping) cream

3 teaspoons minced garlic

½ cup butter

1 cup grated parmesan cheese

2 tablespoons chopped fresh parsley

freshly ground black pepper, for seasoning

Directions:

Grease the slow cooker with olive oil.

Stir in the broth, heavy cream, and garlic until combined—Cook within 6 hours, low.

Whisk in the butter, Parmesan cheese, and parsley. Season with pepper and serve.

Nutrition:

Calories: 280 Fat: 27g

Protein: 7g

Carbs: 4g

Fiber: 0g

Cholesterol: 84mg

Queso Sauce

Preparation time: 10 minutes

Cooking time: 3 hours

Servings: 4

Ingredients:

1 tablespoon extra-virgin olive oil

12 ounces cream cheese

1 cup sour cream

2 cups salsa Verde

1 cup Monterey jack cheese, shredded

Directions:

Grease the slow cooker with olive oil.

Mix the cream cheese, sour cream, salsa Verde, and Monterey Jack cheese in a large bowl until blended.

Transfer the mixture to the insert—Cook within 3 to 4 hours, low. Serve warm.

Nutrition:

Calories: 278

Fat: 25g

Protein: 9g

Carbs: 4g

Fiber: 0g

Cholesterol: 72mg

Classic Bolognese Sauce

Preparation time: 15 minutes

Cooking time: 7 hours

Servings: 10

Ingredients:

3 tablespoons extra-virgin olive oil, divided

1-pound ground pork

½ pound ground beef

½ pound bacon, chopped

1 sweet onion, chopped

1 tablespoon minced garlic

2 celery stalks, chopped

1 carrot, chopped

2 (28-ounce) cans diced tomatoes

½ cup of coconut milk

¼ cup apple cider vinegar

Directions:

Grease the slow cooker with a 1 tablespoon of the olive oil.

In a large skillet over medium-high heat, heat the remaining 2 tablespoons of the olive oil. Add the pork, beef, and bacon, and sauté until cooked through about 7 minutes.

Mix in the onion plus garlic and sauté for an additional 2 minutes.

Transfer the meat mixture to the insert and add the celery, carrot, tomatoes, coconut milk, and apple cider vinegar.

Cook within 7 to 8 hours on low. Serve.

Nutrition:

Calories: 333 Fat: 23g

Protein: 25g Carbs: 9g Fiber: 3g

Cholesterol: 98mg

Simple Marinara Sauce

Preparation time: 10 minutes

Cooking time: 7 hours

Servings: 12

Ingredients:

3 tablespoons extra-virgin olive oil, divided

2 (28-ounce) cans crushed tomatoes

½ sweet onion, finely chopped

2 teaspoons minced garlic

½ teaspoon salt

1 tablespoon chopped fresh basil

1 tablespoon chopped fresh oregano

Directions:

Glaze the slow cooker with 1 tablespoon of the olive oil.

Add the remaining 2 tablespoons of the olive oil, tomatoes, onion, garlic, and salt to the insert, stirring to combine.

Cook within 7 to 8 hours on low.

Garnish with the basil and oregano, serve or store.

Nutrition:

Calories: 66 Fat: 5g Protein: 1g arbs: 7g

Fiber: 2g Cholesterol: 0mg

Chicken Bone Broth

Preparation time: 15 minutes

Cooking time: 24 hours

Servings: 8

Ingredients:

1 tablespoon extra-virgin olive oil

2 chicken carcasses, separated into pieces

2 garlic cloves, crushed

1 celery stalk, chopped

1 carrot, chopped

½ sweet onion, cut into eighths

2 tablespoons apple cider vinegar

2 bay leaves

½ teaspoon black peppercorns

water

Directions:

Grease the slow cooker inside with the olive oil.

Place the chicken bones, garlic, celery, carrot, onion, apple cider vinegar, bay leaves, and peppercorns inside the slow cooker. Put water for about 1½ inches from the top of the slow cooker.

Cover and cook on low for about 24 hours. Strain then serves.

Nutrition:

Calories: 99 Fat: 6g

Protein: 6g Carbs: 5g

Fiber: 0g Cholesterol: 7mg

Herbed Vegetable Broth

Preparation time: 15 minutes

Cooking time: 8 hours

Servings: 8

Ingredients:

1 tablespoon extra-virgin olive oil

4 garlic cloves, crushed

2 celery stalks with greens, roughly chopped

1 sweet onion, quartered

1 carrot, roughly chopped

½ cup chopped parsley

4 thyme sprigs

2 bay leaves

½ teaspoon black peppercorns

½ teaspoon salt

8 cups of water

Directions:

Grease the slow cooker with olive oil.

Place the garlic, celery, onion, carrot, parsley, thyme, bay leaves, peppercorns, and salt in the insert. Add the water.

Cook within 8 hours, low. Strain, then serve or store.

Nutrition:

Calories: 27 Fat: 2g

Protein: 0g Carbs: 2g

Fiber: 0g Cholesterol: 0mg

Beef Bone Broth

Preparation time: 15 minutes

Cooking time: 24 hours

Servings: 8

Ingredients:

1 tablespoon extra-virgin olive oil

2 pounds beef bones with marrow

2 celery stalks with greens, chopped

1 carrot, roughly chopped

1 sweet onion, quartered

4 garlic cloves, crushed

2 tablespoons apple cider vinegar

½ teaspoon whole black peppercorns

½ teaspoon salt

2 bay leaves

5 parsley sprigs

4 thyme sprigs

water

Directions:

Grease the slow cooker with olive oil.

Place the beef bones, celery, carrot, onion, garlic, apple cider vinegar, peppercorns, salt, bay leaves, parsley, and thyme in the insert. Add water until the liquid reaches about 1½ inches from the top.

Cover and cook on low for about 24 hours.

Strain the broth, and serve or store.

Nutrition:

Calories: 59

Fat: 3g

Protein: 5g

Carbs: 3g

Fiber: 0g

Cholesterol: 0mg

Carolina Barbecue Sauce

Preparation time: 10 minutes

Cooking time: 3 hours

Servings: 2

Ingredients:

3 tablespoons extra-virgin olive oil, divided

2 (6-ounce) cans tomato paste

½ cup apple cider vinegar

½ cup of water

¼ cup granulated erythritol

1 tablespoon smoked paprika

1 teaspoon garlic powder

1 teaspoon onion powder

½ teaspoon chili powder

¼ teaspoon salt

Directions:

Grease the slow cooker with 1 tablespoon olive oil.

In a large bowl, whisk together the tomato paste, remaining olive oil, vinegar, water, erythritol, paprika, garlic powder, onion powder, chili powder, then salt until blended.

Pour the mixture into a slow cooker insert.

Cook within 3 hours, low.

After cooling, store the sauce in a container in the refrigerator for up to 2 weeks.

Nutrition:

Calories: 21

Fat: 1g

Protein: 0g

Carbs: 2g

Fiber: 1g

Conclusion

When you shift to the ketogenic diet, it is essential to take into consideration your overall health; just like any eating plan, you need to maintain a healthy lifestyle to go with the diet. A healthy lifestyle is a choice. Just because we have thrown around the word "diet" does not mean that you should think of the ketogenic diet as something that only comes and goes. If you choose to use this dietary plan, you need to remember that it is something you have to use not necessarily for the rest of your life, but you will have to incorporate many of the healthier aspects for the rest of your life if you want to stay healthy. It takes diligence to do this, but it is well worth it. When you start living a healthier life, you may want to start small by changing your regular meal plan to one of the slow cooker ketogenic recipes each day. Slow changes like this can help you too, within one or two weeks, switch over without as much pressure. Eventually, you can turn all of your meals into those that are approved, and if you miss a day or two, don't knock yourself up. Like anything you choose to do, this takes time before your body fully adjusts.

If your objective is losing weight and get healthy by using the ketogenic diet, remember that weight loss has to include exercise. Even if you cut carbs out almost entirely and follow every facet of the ketogenic diet, you still need to exercise. Make exercise a daily habit of your new lifestyle just the same as you make the food you regularly take a daily part of your lifestyle. Doing so will maximize all of your weight loss results.

What you need to know is that your body will respond to the demand that you put on it, and it will respond to the Keto food changes and exercise with time. If you ask your muscles to lift something heavy, it will get stronger and lift something heavy. If you ask your muscles to stay stagnant and sit on the couch, they will shrivel up and do exactly that.

Exercise damages your muscle, which then allows your body to remodel the muscle to prevent further injury. Each time you train the small fibers, you injure them and force them to get bigger and stronger. It means that intense exercise is essential.

Your muscles respond to calories. Research shows that people who restrict their calories end up losing muscle mass with slower digestion or metabolism. Essential calorie restriction is not enough. It is necessary that you eat and that you eat well and exercise simultaneously.

The proteins and the fluid in your muscle fibers are broken down and rebuilt approximately every 7 to 15 days. Training can change this by impacting the type of proteins and the amount of protein your body produces.

Energy from your fat stores can be released and stored inside your muscle tissue, but you need ample nutrients and patience as this process takes place. Eating right is always the best way to go, and so is eating enough. Weight loss without proper calorie consumption is not something you should aim for.

The way your hormones respond to exercise and how they impact your weight loss depends heavily on your nutritional status, the number of calories you are consuming. Eating 2800 calories of pizza is not the same as 2800 calories of lean salmon and broccoli.

Your muscles (the ones that will help you to burn fat or stay healthy) respond to calories. Research shows that people who restrict their calories to try and lose weight end up losing muscle mass with a slower metabolism. Simple calorie restriction is not enough. Some people who use stricter calories and field exercise ended up fatter than where they started. It is essential that you eat and that you eat well. It cannot be stress enough that with the keto diet, you do need to enjoy lots of fats and lots of proteins. You cannot hope to generate the same amount of energy your body derives typically from simple carbohydrates if you do not make sure you are getting enough fat. Remember, fat is now your primary energy source, so it should constitute a large part of your diet.

That said, you can reduce your carbohydrates quickly and make the change fast, or you can do it slowly and make the change gradually. As an athlete wanting to build muscle mass or better tone your body, you need to work hard enough for your body to burn off all the items included in the meal but also make sure that you have high energy adequate to complete your workouts. You don't want to starve your body. Remember, the key to this particular diet is to get as many fats as you can.

Naturally, the time you spent eating out versus cooking at home is bound to change. Most people, when they switch to healthier diets, find that it is simply easier to have complete control over what you eat. You can never really trust a strange company to offer things how you like it, nor can you be sure that they will have healthier choices. Eating out doesn't have to go away altogether, but the more you learn about the ketogenic diet, the more you can make wise choices when you have to attend things like company dinners or birthday events. Look up restaurants ahead of time and find out which ones serve the ketogenic friendly dish or at least have something that you can convert into a ketogenic friendly item.

Printed in Great Britain
by Amazon